# UNIVERSITY OF NORTH CAROLINA AT CHAPEL HILL
DEPARTMENT OF ROMANCE LANGUAGES

## NORTH CAROLINA STUDIES
## IN THE ROMANCE LANGUAGES AND LITERATURES

*Founder:* URBAN TIGNER HOLMES

*Distributed by:*

UNIVERSITY OF NORTH CAROLINA PRESS
CHAPEL HILL
North Carolina 27514
U.S.A.

NORTH CAROLINA STUDIES IN THE
ROMANCE LANGUAGES AND LITERATURES

Number 212

MEDIEVAL MAN

# MEDIEVAL MAN
## HIS UNDERSTANDING OF HIMSELF, HIS SOCIETY, AND THE WORLD
### ILLUSTRATED FROM HIS OWN LITERATURE

BY

URBAN T. HOLMES, Jr.

*Edited, with an Introduction, by*

URBAN T. HOLMES, III

CHAPEL HILL

NORTH CAROLINA STUDIES IN THE ROMANCE
LANGUAGES AND LITERATURES
U.N.C. DEPARTMENT OF ROMANCE LANGUAGES
1980

**Library of Congress Cataloging in Publication Data**

Holmes, Urban Tigner, 1900-1972
  Medieval man, his understanding of himself, his society, and the world.

  (North Carolina studies in the Romance languages and literatures; no. 212)
  Bibliography: p.
  1. Civilization, Medieval. 2. Literature, Medieval — History and criticism. I Holmes, Urban Tigner, 1930-    II. Title. III. Series.

CB351.H56      940.1      80-13223
ISBN 0-8078-9212-2 (University of N. C. Press)










I. S. B. N.  0-8078-9212-2










Depósito legal: v. 1.447 - 1980      I. S. B. N. 84-499-3837-6
Artes Gráficas Soler, S. A. - Olivereta, 28 - Valencia (18) - 1980

*To my dear wife
whom I married fifty years ago*

## PREFACE

This book is not a compilation composed laboriously from a carefully laid out set of notes. It has flowed in free style from the typewriter of the author, and the notes have been added later as a guide to available sources. There is much quotation, at length, in translation, from writings of the times. Where there is a good English translation of the literature already published, such as James Bruce Ross and Mary Martin McLaughlin's *The Portable Mediaeval Reader*, I have used this without hesitation, giving suitable recognition.

In most of this quoted material the translation is my own. I give references to printed editions of the original text; but in a number of cases the only printed original is an unreliable text and at other times no printed edition is available anywhere.

Some of these unpublished works have been edited by students who have not published them. For instance, the wonderful *Sydrac*, a popular scientific encyclopedia of the later thirteenth century, has not been accessible in print except in a rare sixteenth-century publication. I have been using an edition recently established in two dissertations by Sapelo Treanor and William Holler which are in the Library of the University of North Carolina. I have often felt that if this text were easily available in English there would be little excuse for our publishing this present book. The curious reader could then turn to the thirteenth-century original, in translation.

I have algo used the *Enfances Garin de Monglane*, now edited by Jack Brown, and Huon de Meri's *Tournoiement d'Antecrist*, edited by Margot Bender. These and many other unpublished editions are now in the Library of the University of North Carolina.

The many published editions of Old French texts to which we refer are best found listed in the *Critical Bibliography of French Literature, The Medieval Period*, edited by D. C. Cabeen. In that bibliography the best published texts are listed first.

# CONTENTS

|  | Page |
|---|---|
| PREFACE | 9 |
| INTRODUCTION, by Urban T. Holmes, III | 13 |
| I. AN OVERVIEW | 19 |
| II. MAN AND NATURE | 33 |
| III. THE INTELLECTUALS AND THE CHURCH | 51 |
| IV. THE PEASANTS | 78 |
| V. THE TOWN DWELLERS | 98 |
| VI. THE BARONS AND KNIGHTS | 133 |
| VII. THE MINSTRELS | 164 |
| VIII. WRITING AND THE MEN OF LETTERS | 182 |
| POSTSCRIPT "GOD AND MAN" | 195 |
| APPENDIX: "THE 'ELIDUC' OF MARIE DE FRANCE" | 215 |
| BIBLIOGRAPHY | 231 |

# INTRODUCTION

## Urban T. Holmes, Jr.: A Son's Recollection

Urban T. Holmes, Jr., died early Friday morning, May 13, 1972, in Memphis, Tennessee, where he was lecturing at a three-week short term at Memphis State University. On May 5 he had phoned me from Memphis, and in the course of the conversation commented on the fact that he had finally mailed to a publisher the day before a manuscript of a book on medieval man, which he had promised for four or five years. There is little doubt that the strain of completing this work, amid all the other responsibilities of a very active retirement, contributed to a fatal heart attack just short of his fiftieth wedding anniversary and seventy-second birthday. This is the book of which he spoke, and it is a testimony in a strange, almost literal sense, to that for which my father gave his life.

The narrative within these pages is not that of a closely reasoned development of a given thesis. This book is "vintage Holmes." As is true of all his writings, but perhaps most particularly this one, the reader meets not only medieval man and his self-understanding, but he comes to know the author himself. The twelfth century afforded my father an opportunity for self-expression and definition, and provided him a means for stating certain themes in life which were of particular importance to him.

To read this book is to sit with Dr. Holmes and listen to his fascinating and sometimes seemingly endless monologue upon the lives of such as Gerald the Welshman, Alexander Neckham, Chrétien de Troyes, and many others who were for him familiar friends and for his children household words. There have been few scholars whose conversation could so delightfully reflect a lifetime of wandering through western Europe with those men and women, now so long dead, who left their records in stone, metal, wood, wattle, cloth, clay and paper of their daily routines, fondest hopes, and deepest fears. At the same time, it was not simply reporting that my father did, but through these characters he spoke of his own aspirations and values.

Dr. Holmes was a humanist in the best sense of the word. He believed in man not as the measure of all things, but as the final and supreme act of God's creation. I doubt that he would put it this way, since he was not a theologian and never claimed to be, but he had a very Greek notion of the relation of God and man. Man was for him God's partner in creation, and as he fulfilled the vocation God had given him, he became more like God. He deplored any suggestion that humanism was necessarily opposed to his Christian faith. I remember well his great indignation when our parish priest chose in a Sunday sermon to deride humanism as the enemy of the Christian religion.

In this regard he also believed that scholarship had an immediate and lasting relevance to life. Despite what some may have thought, he was never the remote scholar or absent-minded professor. His work had for him an obvious application, and he resented the not infrequent implication that as a medievalist he was "impractical" or "out of touch." Since he was the son of a naval officer, a candidate for the diplomatic service, and an employee of the OSS during World War II, politics were discussed as much in our home as scholarship. Ideas for him always had consequences in human action, and those who were unwilling to learn or simply ignorant of the ideas of the past were destined to live in the present and face the future with impoverished thoughts and, consequently, irresponsible actions. He knew the world in which he lived and he had an uncanny insight into people — an insight which he was often hesitant to express out of fear of hurting someone.

This relates to Dr. Holmes' belief that medieval man was in many ways quite childlike. His feelings lay on the surface, and while he was no less complex than contemporary man, he was a great deal less repressed. Consequently, the paradox of the human personality lay exposed for study. In this book my father speaks of both the generosity and the cruelty of medieval man, his sublime thoughts and vulgar manner, and regards the contradiction not so much as something to be condemned from the vantage point of eight hundred years, but something from which to learn. Man was always for my father a strange contradiction, and he believed himself to be one more example. I think he would have liked to have been as childlike as medieval man, and at moments he was; but generally he hid those feelings in the fear that he might be ridiculed or misunderstood.

Anyone who reads this book or who has listened to Dr. Holmes recount the life of medieval man knows that it was very hard living in those days. The sheer pain — emotional, as well as physical — of life in the twelfth century cannot be hidden in our more romantic notions of chivalry and knights of old. My father was quick to disabuse us of such notions. A trip to the local movie theater with him to see Hollywood's version of Robin Hood was an education for us, his children, because he demolished the scenario with a detailed running commentary. Medieval life was close to the earth, without much to separate man's existence from that of the animals that cluttered the yard and wandered through the most elegant living quarters. My father was quite ready to remind us all that modern plumbing, screens on windows, and deodorants are all very recent. Dr. Holmes himself was only two generations removed from the "medieval life" of the backwoods farms of Arkansas and Georgia — a fact probably not widely known by many of his colleagues and students. It was his mother and mine that brought into the family culture urban living as an alternative to the rural South.

It took great courage to live and achieve in the medieval world, and Dr. Holmes exemplified that in his own life. Without recounting the details, I think it can be said that in his studies my father found the support to overcome the hardships of his own life, which were often of a very unmanageable kind, to arrive at a sense of great fulfillment in the last ten or fifteen years. Before my mother was stricken by the illness that troubled her last years she spoke to me in her own quiet way of the incredible courage of her "gentle knight." With all his scholarly brilliance, which no one could question, and amid all the eccentricities which those who love him enjoy recounting, there is no doubt that my mother would join myself and my sisters in wanting him to be remembered above all as a man who never shrank from life in all its dimensions, and yet who faced it with a courage born of the same faith and expectation, hope and love, that characterized medieval man at his best.

My father was a man of immense curiosity, filled with wonder. Like our Norse ancestors of a thousand years ago, he loved to seek new things and risk innovative ideas. Sometimes his speculations bordered on the fantastic, but he was never dull. There was nothing pedantic in his scholarship, and he enjoyed every minute of his research and teaching. I doubt that he would appreciate the suggestion that he was more a Dionysyian than Apollonian man — he drank little and while I'm told he was a capable dancer, he never did dance to my memory — but that was where his spirit lay. He was a man of imagination and humor, and this enabled him to live effectively in the twelfth century as well as the twentieth with understanding and respect for the citizens of both eras, and to excite the lives of those who read, heard, and lived with him.

He enjoyed the spirit, if not always the humor of the oft-repeated suggestion that on his gravestone should be carved the words:

>  Born — 1900
>  Died — 1172

But then he would add with that sudden seriousness to which he was given: "You know, Terry, it really isn't true."

\* \* \*

A further word is in order to explain what I have done in editing this book. Dr. Holmes wrote the original manuscript under considerable pressure, personal and professional, and in haste over a period of several years. The text followed a kind of associative thought, with frequent breaks and obscure transitions. The footnotes were never completed. There were gaps in the discussion, particularly in the eighth chapter.

What I have done is to attempt some kind of systematic progression of thought, filling in what seems to have been omitted and making the transitions explicit. Where this has been a matter of completing a sentence, changing the wording, or rearranging a sequence, I have done so without any notation. Where, however, I have added substantive material, it will be found within brackets ([]), in order that the reader might know when he is dealing with the *ipsissima verba* of the master or when it is only the commentary of his son. The title of the book itself and most of the chapter titles have been changed to reflect a little more accurately their contents.

I am grateful to those who have assisted me in this task. Robert M. Cooper of the faculty at Nashotah House, Nashotah, Wisconsin, checked the ninth chapter for any errors in the philosophical analysis. Kenneth R. Jones, a former student of my father's and a colleague of mine at the University of the South, read the entire manuscript after I had worked on it and noted certain items that needed checking or re-working. Sarah Shaber of The University of North Carolina Press in Chapel Hill edited the entire manuscript and identified all the references, which was perhaps the most difficult chore of all. I am also most appreciative of Frances Evans who typed the final manuscript.

I feel fortunate that we have been able to bring to the reading public Dr. Holmes' last work. It is regrettable that he never saw it to completion and was unable to share its contents personally with those for whom he wrote it. Those who knew my father will remember the enthusiasm with which he spoke of his beloved Middle Ages, and I am sure they will find this book a charming reminiscence. For those who never knew him, I hope these pages will provide some small introduction to a great medievalist and a delightful man.

I wish to thank Professor Lawrence Sharpe and Professor Alfred Engstrom for the many hours they spent making corrections and completing references.

URBAN T. HOLMES
University of the South
Sewanee, Tennessee

# I
## AN OVERVIEW

Because the plan of this book is to permit the reader to judge medieval man's concept of human nature from the way in which he organized his life, in all classes of society, I will begin with some general observations on this subject. It is quite possible that the reader may disagree with some of my conclusions. It does seem odd to begin a book with a list of conclusions; but to do so will make it easier to reflect throughout these pages, and to follow a straight path of argument.

The philosophy of western Europe was Augustinian. [For example, the great St. Bernard of Clairvaux (1090-1153), perhaps the most powerful churchman of his day, was a kind of *Augustinus redevivus*. St. Thomas Aquinas (c. 1225-1274), the outstanding intellect of this period, saw himself as only continuing in the tradition of the Bishop of Hippo.] People believed that every creature, every thing, had been created by God within His general plan. He created the angels, the demons, and man. Within His overall purpose, He intended man to have a certain freedom of choice between good and evil. In this way the good men, worthy of blessedness in the hereafter, could be separated from those who were not worthy. God gave to the demons certain power in the tempting of man. To make this differentiation more possible, God endowed each man with a soul which brought him the power of reason. Also, God's special agent in the ordering of man is nature.

### Being "Natural"

Since nature is God's agent, it follows that most of nature could not be evil. That which is natural is close to God. This belief sometimes brought out seeming contradictions. The Divine Mind praises celibacy and approves no sexual intercourse except in wedlock; yet natural love makes for immortality of the race, according to God's plan. These positions were hard to reconcile. The natural functions of the body produced filth; but this filth was tolerated to an extent beyond what seems proper to us moderns. I even ask myself whether the extreme cleanliness of today might not have seemed a little ungodly to the medieval man.

Earthly rulers, kings, and lesser folk, were appointed by God in most cases, and they were respected accordingly. Those who fought in God's cause, against any infidel, gained Heaven thereby. To kill perjurors and to slay in self-defense were not mortal sins. Women should be honored, but at the same time Christians did not forget that all women were the sisters of Eve, who led Adam into mortal sin. Punishment for murder and vengeance for sexual abuse lay largely in the hands of the family of the victim, while at the same time amends had to be made to God. Lying, graft, nepotism, and, to a large degree, simony were wrong, but they were not unnatural and were generally tolerated a little.

The great ethical precept of the Middle Ages was *mesure*, defined as "moderation" in almost everything. To fit moderately into the pattern of life around you was considered most praiseworthy. Some great souls suffered martyrdom, and they were canonized for their saintly witness. But a gadfly social reformer, such as Gerald the Welshman, was generally speaking not much appreciated. Great personal asceticism was much revered and respected, but not always for what we might now consider the right reasons.

There were virtually no painkillers, physical, psychic, or spiritual, that could be used by medieval people. Pain from heartaches and from the most exquisite bodily torture had to be borne stoically, and such pains occurred frequently. As a result people very often showed a cruel streak. They were capable of making fun of the handicapped, and played extreme practical jokes. Victims were burned with hot irons, and thrown into stinking privy heaps (*que vous fussiez en une longaigne*). Ordinary people were capable of inflicting the most frightful tortures. I am sure that in all this behavior they had great faith in the justice of God, and a firm belief that in Heaven all wrongs would be righted. Because they had no concept whatsoever of the nature of diseases and because their daily routine was constantly dangerous, they lived always under a sword of Damocles. Their hope was in God alone.

The spread of learning among medieval men was on a level which had remained almost constant since the beginning of mankind. Reading, calculating, and reflection were confined to a few specialists, the clerks. In the Middle Ages there was a considerable body of women who had seized the opportunity to acquire a certain amount of learning: in fact some moralists felt it necessary to warn prospective husbands against such learned wives. Those men and women who could not read and who had only a rudimentary grasp of general ideas were so much in the majority that most daily concerns were geared to them. Most folk did not travel far from their homes, but, strange to relate, they were often multilingual. A kind of pidgin Latin was much spoken by the clerks alongside the vernacular. Many dialects were prevalent, and minor languages, like Judaeo-language, Breton, and Gaelic, abounded. One medieval authority said that there were seventy-two languages. Because of this wide facility in language, when one did travel, there was hospitality everywhere on a scale which is quite lacking in our modern world.

One final matter must be noted. Family blood ties were usually not very close. [That is to say, in terms of our contemporary notion of the nuclear family, consisting of mother and father, the children, and perhaps the grandparents, family ties were fairly loose. The concept of a tightly-knit family came out of the modern Puritan culture. The medieval notion of the basic social unit was rooted in the tribal customs of the Indo-European culture, whose kinship groups were often identified with the members of a household or of a settlement. Within this unit there was a deep sense of loyalty.]

The observations made in this present book are based on material from the twelfth and thirteenth centuries, an era often called the twelfth-century renaissance. I have purposely not made regular use of Dante, who wrote well into the fourteenth century. The scholarship of the Divine Comedy is so vast and so varied that it dwarfs observations made on other periods of the Middle Ages. I can note here, however, how little change in outlook there is between the twelfth and fourteenth centuries. What we are describing from the material in this book can be paralleled fully in Dante. For instance, in *The Inferno* the so-called "sins against nature" are placed low in Hell, and sodomy is much more of a sin than incontinence between the sexes. Similarly, Dante's estimation of women is inconsistent: he honors the noble, yet describes the lesser sort, the successor to Eve.

Ives de Chartres, in his *Decretum* of 1094, uses the important medieval expression *naturam humanam* to explain the difference between those things which are "natural" to man, and those which are unnatural. For example, persons who are hilarious at a funeral are behaving contrary to this "human nature." Unlike modern philosophies, the Christian doctors of western Europe did little disputing over what was meant by "human nature," and Ives apparently spoke with little fear of contradiction. God alone creates. Furthermore, He has created man in His own image, and endowed every man with a human soul. The soul is the source of "the nature of man." God alone could alter the physical nature of a human being when it suited His divine purpose.

How did medieval man, who believed in his nature, live in the world? This book has been written to protray this "Augustinian" man at work and at play. I want to know the norms of reaction and behavior which lay before each class of society in its pilgrimage to salvation, the ultimate goal of human destiny.

No creature who was not "baptizable" shared any portion of man's "nature." However, medieval man did believe that the world was full of baptizable souls belonging to creatures who today would be considered unreal or unhuman, and he believed that they lived in close proximity to himself. Fairies, beings known as "shape-shifters," dwarfs, and giants all inhabited the earth. I might also add that angels and demons were not considered as potential participants in human nature. They originated in a heavenly rather than an earthly sphere, though they could move from one to the other.

In this parade of the past, showing mankind as it appeared normally and abnormally in the Middle Ages, I may seem to be analyzing once again the customs and daily life of the twelfth and thirteenth centuries.[1] This is true to some extent, but my purpose here is different. I cite in translation more complete passages and, more

---

[1] See Urban T. Holmes, *Daily Living in the Twelfth Century* (Madison: University of Wisconsin Press, 1970).

important, I seek to catch the thought that is behind it all. It is the living man of the Middle Ages rather than the strangeness of his customs and practice, when viewed by a modern, which is my focal point.

*The Human Ecology*

At the beginning of this study of the medieval man's concept of human nature I must explain how man was limited in actually being a human being. He did not know the real truth about this limitation, and many of our modern historians are no better informed. For brevity's sake we will utilize the findings of an excellent demographer, J. C. Russell,[2] who has brought together and digested in good proportion the writings of many experts in this field.

The population within the Roman Empire, which included Britain and France, started to decrease around A. D. 100.[3] In the fifth and sixth centuries the entrance of Germanic tribes into British and French areas increased the population numbers, but not for long. In A.D. 543 the Black Death spread westward from upper Egypt and over a period of nearly seventy years considerably lowered the population. This catastrophe, perhaps more than any other, caused the desertion of most Roman towns in the western European area and precipitated speculation about the ruins that remain. The ruins remained standing for many centuries in Britain and, I am convinced, they were thought of by writers of the mid-medieval period as the remains of a great glory in the days of King Arthur and his "Old Bretons." These medieval observers had no idea of the history of Roman Britain or of the Romanized Celts. Remember, tradition tells us that Arthur "lived" in the fifth century.

The population was definitely on the rise again by 950, and by the twelfth century it once more had reached the Roman levels. It then became necessary to enlarge the old Roman walls of most of the cities. By the year 1200 there were some 25,000 people within the Paris walls. When the Taille list of 1292 was made, there were at least 53,200 commoners in Paris, to which must be added an estimate of 60,000 clerics, those students, priests, and others who

---

[2] J. C. Russell, "Late Ancient and Medieval Population," *Transactions American Philosophical Society*, N.S., 48, part 3 (1958).
[3] *Ibid.*, pp. 71ff.

did not pay the taille, or hearth tax. The population of all of France, including the Low Countries, can be estimated at 10,000,000 in 1200.[4] By 1400 the population of France was reduced again by 40 per cent, due principally, of course, to the Great Plague of 1348-50.

In those centuries of the Middle Ages which now interest us most, malaria and tuberculosis were the great killers. Tuberculosis, particularly, hit young people between the ages of fifteen and thirty-five years. Malaria, known as quartan and tertian fevers, was most common in those areas near stagnant ground water where mosquitoes could breed, and this, unfortunately included the moats of nearly all towns. If people escaped open wounds and did not drink too much water away from their own home districts, the chances for a long healthy life, into one's sixties and seventies, were not bad. Queen Eleanor of England died at the age of eighty-two, and she certainly led an active life. Gerald the Welshman was about seventy-six when he died in 1222, and in his history of Louis IX Joinville mentions a very old knight as attending the Queen. Professor Russell brings together some interesting observations on the longevity of the monks of the eastern Mediterranean area, who spent most of their lives on the tops of high columns. St. Simeon was one of the earliest of these. In their isolated existence these monks were not subject to bites from rats, fleas, nor to infections by contact with other people; their diet was extremely simple, and I might add that the water they drank came from a local source to which they must have soon become immunized. Some of these people even lived to be about a hundred years old, considered to be about the upper limit today.

Historians cannot fully comprehend the question of infant mortality in the Middle Ages. Professor Russell, however, from data that have been carefully analyzed, lists life expectancy at birth at 35.28 years, and at the age of five, after the infant hazards were over, the expectancy was 39.87 years.[5]

Venereal diseases did not plague the people in the Middle Ages as far as we know, but there is reason to believe that coronary disease was more common then than it is today. People ate a considerable amount of animal fats, and there are frequent allusions

---

[4] *Ibid.*, p. 108.
[5] See tabulated data, *ibid.*, p. 31.

to death from acute indigestion, as in the case of Henry I of England, which may well have indicated a coronary condition. We judge that strokes were also more common at an early age, as in the case of Louis VII of France.

We will summarize these facts with a statement that the average man did not expect to live much beyond fifty years. That was the end of youth, according to the classification of Isidore of Seville: *Infantia* (till 7), *Pueritia* (7-14), *Adolescentia* (14-28), *Iuventus* (28-50). Life ended with *Gravitas* (50-70) and *Senectus* (over 70).

The older one became, the more confined was his world. After age fifty eyesight tends to be poor, even with the aid of lenses, which were not available until 1317. An ear trumpet and a cupped hand were the only aids to deafness. The pain and crippling of arthritis went completely unchecked. Travel was severely limited, especially for the infirm, as the only means of transportation were the horse, the litter, and, occasionally, the boat.

*The Extraordinary Man*

In the pages that follow man is considered in two aspects. The cleric was concerned with human beings in their relation to God and the universe. The ordinary citizen in the Middle Ages thought of man as one of his own species, disposed to react and behave according to a generally recognized code. These views give two basic divisions to this present book: man and God as observed by the clerical philosophers, and man in his normal behavior as described by his contemporary. The first of these belongs to the history of philosophy; the second demands close observation of the social structure.

There is a third aspect of humanity which was constantly present in medieval minds: the varieties of abnormal men, who were considered to be either demons or portents from the Divinity sent to warn man that great events or changes were about to come. This third aspect may be said to have "inhabited" the interstices of the two divisions or "cities" of the world. Giants, dwarfs, persons with abnormal limbs and features, and men who could transform themselves into animals and birds were a few of these beings. However, humans as they saw themselves in the Middle Ages will make up much of this present book.

The definition of man was that of a being possessed of a soul, having therefore the elements of reason, created in the image of God, but with possible variations desired by God's will for a specific purpose. Outside this category came ordinary animals and demons. Thus in Chrétien de Troyes' *Yvain* when Calogrenanz, wandering in the Forest of Broceliande, comes upon the Giant Herdsman, he asks: "Please tell me, are you a good thing, or a bad?" The strange creature replies, "I am a man." Then Calogrenanz asks, "What kind of man are you?" "Such as you see. I have never been anything else."[6] This meant that the wild creature was not a demon and that he had not been temporarily transformed from another type of being.

The *Elioxe*, and certain other materials from the twelfth century, informs us that the more educated people of that time could be troubled by the concept of a good fairy, who was neither angel nor demon but a portent. In the *Elioxe* we read:

> Often you have heard many a tale about King Arthur and his Court, Gawain his nephew and his other barons on whom the tale is constructed. This is about Arthur and about fairies, but don't you make the mistake of believing that that is true. But about these five Swan knights and their group we are told all this in books that have antiquity.[7]

Wace, the author of the *Brut* and the *Rou*, two famous chronicles, also was a bit hard-headed concerning such matters:

> ...Broceliant is a forest very long and wide in Brittany about which the Bretons tell fables... they are used to seeing fairies there, if the Bretons are being truthful, and many other strange things.... I went there to find marvels. I saw the forest and I saw the land. I looked for wonderful things and I did not find them. I was a fool to go there and I came away like a fool. I looked for foolishness and I considered myself silly.[8]

---

[6] Chrétien de Troyes, *Yvain*, in *Christian von Troyes sämtliche erhaltene Werke*..., ed. Wendelin Foerster (Halle: Niemeyer, 1884-1932), II, vv. 328ff.

[7] *Elioxe* is the name given H. A. Todd's edition of "La Naissance du Chevalier au Cygne," *PMLA*, 4, nos. 3-4 (1888-89), vv. 3292ff.

[8] Wace, *Le Roman de Brut de Wace*, ed. Ivor Arnold (Paris: SATF, 1938-40), vv. 6395-6420.

Such portents as dwarfs, hunchbacks, even giants and animals who gave the appearance of being hybrids, were quite possible to see in real life. However, there were men in the twelfth century who had their doubts about the existence of fairies. Some did believe in them. The author of the *Elioxe* is obliged to speak of the fairy by the same name in order to pursue his story. It is interesting how he describes her habitat:

> Here is a maiden courteous and charming. From the great mountain she came descending. I do not know that I should continue describing her beauty. She was fair, well built, and of high rank. Her dwelling was there in the mountain; maidens she had there within to do her bidding. They too dwelt in the caverns of the mountain. She had come down into the open country [*pré*] for her enjoyment. [9]

Elioxe by her special powers was able to prophesy the birth of the seven children which she will bear when she marries King Lothaire, and of her death, which will follow. She says of her dwelling, "My land is well guarded and there is great care there."

In the *Enfances Garin de Monglane*, fairies are of a more imaginative kind: "Exactly at midnight three fairies came, Morgue la Fée, sister of Arthur, and Ydain whom she loved, and there came also Gloriande whom Jesus loved so well...." [10]

These fairy women had special powers, and they were as old as the hills. You will note that they seemed associated with belief in the existence of King Arthur. In the *Lai Lanval* of Marie de France, Lanval encounters in a meadow outside the town a fairy, who wishes to be his invisible mistress. She finally appears in public to take him with her to the land of Avalon as he is being tried in the court of King Arthur. In view of this and of the statement made by the author of *Elioxe*, we are tempted to believe that King Arthur and fairy women often went together in the minds of twelfth- and thirteenth-century doubters. The existence of neither was fully believed by the more intelligent people.

We have reason to hold, then, that medievals were troubled about the exact position of a *fée* in the hierarchy of human life.

---

[9] *Elioxe*, v. 199.
[10] Jack David Brown, "Les Enfances Garin: A Critical Edition," diss. University of North Carolina, 1971, vv. 495ff.

The Celts associated fairies with humans who had already died, or passed into the *sidh* on fairy mound. They thought that one could sometimes, in any group of fairies, recognize faces of the dead. In quasi-modern Celtic tradition the fairies were confused with witches, a strange development, because the witch was associated with the Devil. In Robert Burns' "Tam o' Shanter" Tam saw a dead little girl:

> There was ae winsome wench....
> Her cutty sark...
> That while a lassie she had worn
> ... ... ... ... ... ... ... ...
> Ah! little kend thy reverend grannie
> That sark....
> Wad ever grac'd a dance of witches! [11]

In the *Bard of Sleep (Bard Cwsg)* of Ellis Wynn, a Welsh moralist of the eighteenth century, the protagonist is carried up into the air by mischievous fairies. He looks into their faces and sees many that he had known while they were alive.

We may say in sum that medieval man conceived of three kinds of beings who resembled man: the average human, the evil demons, and the "monstrous" humans who had soul and reason along with their strangeness, who were portents created deliberately by God.

### The Three Divisions of the Middle Ages

It is customary to use the term Middle Ages very freely. This period lasted about a thousand years, from A.D. 500 to 1500. Granted that circumstances were continuously changing, one can say that there were three disjunctive divisions during this time.

The years from 500 to 1000 have often been referred to as the Dark Ages, when communication was extremely poor and when there were few effective political units west of Constantinople. Even in warfare, which was at that time both a joy and a dreadful sorrow to these early people, discipline and organization were practically nonexistent. Theirs was an age of super warriors. One gigantic man of great strength could dominate a battle or a campaign.

---

[11] "Tam O'Shanter" in Robert Burns, *Poems and Songs*, ed. James Kinsley (London: Oxford University Press, 1969), vv. 164-78.

At the same time it was an age of somewhat blind faith. The direct intervention of God into all the vicissitudes of His faithful, in the form of miracles, was expected continually, and by the same token, the hostility of demons was anticipated on every side. There was almost no experimental medicine and miraculous cures were sought by everyone.

In this time of disorganization, the great monasteries were beacons of order and light. The most effective forms of learning, the organization of travel, and the operation of agriculture were all controlled by them, although Byzantium continued to exercise a slight degree of control over western Europe. The Byzantines gave small subsidies, or disguised bribes, to many of the small kings and lords, such as the *fainéant* kings at Pavia in the early tenth century, and as a consequence could ask to be kept informed of their movements. The account written by Liutprand of Cremona is most fascinating in this regard. He had been well received when he went as an envoy to Byzantium from Pavia, but when he represented Otto the First of Germany, who was becoming important, the Greek emperor was distinctly hostile to him.

Diplomatic relations were carried on at a very personal level, and one's social and ethnic origins were very important to affairs of states. For example, the position taken by the Jews in this period is not entirely clear. There were many who were travelling merchants, carrying goods from the East. This is evident in Gregory of Tours' *History of the Franks*, composed during the sixth century. Venality was attributed to the Jews and they were generally handled accordingly. In truth venality was a trait shared by everyone, whatever their race or class. These men were often judged by standards of justice or mercy that contemporary man would find strange. Gregory of Tours writes about a cleric Riculfus who had been caught in the deepest intrigue and suffered for it when discovered.

> Riculfus the clerk was condemned to death. I could save his life with the greatest difficulty, but I could not excuse him from torture. Nothing, no metal, could endure the torture which this miserable fellow took. From the third hour of the day, stretched on the rack with his hands bound behind his back, he was beaten with cudgels, rods, double whips, not by only one or two individuals but by all those who could approach his limbs. All were tormen-

tors. When he was just about to die, he confessed the whole plot.[12]

The second division of the Middle Ages (1000 to 1300) saw the rise of the great schools, the *studia generalia*, later called universities. Many wealthy farmers' sons destined to become feudal heirs and to participate in a life of combat were often made clerks in their youth so that they might acquire education and background. When the proper time arrived, they were removed from the clerical milieu and returned to their fathers' status. As we might expect as a consequence their public behavior was guided less by personal feelings and more by reason.

The lower orders of the clergy could marry and had no permanent ecclesiastical obligation, which allowed a certain free movement between the clerical and lay classes. This can be observed in the description of Guilhem de Nevers, the lover of Flamenca in the Provençal romance of that name. He was an active young knight unusually well experienced in the affairs of worldly love. When it suited him in relation to his amorous adventures, he reverted to being a clerk in the parish church of Bourbon, where Flamenca was living. He had only to replace his tonsure. He knew the liturgy and the music and was a trained singer. It is clear that he had been at least an acolyte, in lower orders. When he had succeeded in his amours he once more returned to position of a civil baron.

During this second period the schools were very important in the lives of most people. Philosophy, canon law and civil law were studied extensively, and there was a great growth of discipline and of scholastic participation. Some national feeling began to show itself. Learning was far from general, but it was pursued by many and most of the public had respect for it. This interest marks the beginning of our modern literature and of schools and scholarly institutions as we know them.

In the last division of the Middle Ages (1300-1500) there was much social change. Revolts were more and more successful. [For example, a civil war left France in constant turmoil in the early fifteenth century. The "Hundred Years War" in England thwarted any kind of leadership there throughout the fifteenth century, ending

---

[12] Gregory of Tours, *The History of the Franks*, trans. O. M. Dalton (Oxford: The Clarendon Press, 1927), v. 48.

only when Henry Tudor seized the throne. In Germany, after the death of Charles IV, king of Bohemia, in 1378, parochial particularism reigned.]

Certain new inventions made life different from the earlier periods of the Middle Ages. The first of these was the introduction of gunpowder in about 1337, a radical change which demanded the introduction of more plate armor. Strongholds also were built in a new fashion: they had lower walls with rounded corners. This change in defense building can be observed very aptly at Ragusa, or Dubrovnik, as it is now called, in Yugoslavia. The town has two sets of walls. The higher ones, towers with squared walls, were built in the twelfth century. Outside this early rampart is a fifteenth-century defense which is lower, with rounded edges. This newer kind of rampart warded off cannon balls more easily.

Another invention, of vast significance, was the introduction of printing with movable type. The process of stamping with seals goes back to Sumerian days, and perhaps earlier, but around 1435, Gutenberg devised the process of making an individual stamp for each letter of the alphabet. These stamps could be built into complete words, and the type could be taken down again and made into other words. This process revolutionized the book industry. What is perhaps not as well known is that careful examination of the Bible printed by Gutenberg in 1450-55 shows that the printer at first did not have enough type to print more than a single page at a time. The labor involved was incredible!

This later period also saw improved perspective in drawing and painting, additional use of hydraulic power, and so on. Much better relationships were cultivated with the Moslem peoples. Trade greatly increased, and with it developed the use of gold as money, the silk industry, and a revolution in ship building. All this produced wealth. The prime force behind this advancement was the Italian state, a hundred years in advance of the other Christian nations. It also came from the Portugal of John I and from the marriage of his daughter Isabella to the Duke of Burgundy in 1430. This new kind of society began to change the Middle Ages as we know them and produced what I call the "waning of the Middle Ages," leading up to the Italian Renaissance which flourished in western Europe from 1515 on. Purely medieval institutions were scarcely alive at this point. Feudalism, knighthood, tourneys, currency based on the silver penny (or denier), and the predominance of ecclesiastical influence in law and letters declined.

This last period of the Middle Ages is more familiar to moderns than are the earlier periods because it is possible to see it visually. As I have noted, the improved drawing and painting and the spread of printed books project this period vividly to us today. Fifteenth-century ladies with high-pointed headdress, men with short jerkins and peaked caps, and mendicant friars, such as the Friar Tuck, are what most people in the modern world see when the Middle Ages are mentioned. But in these pages attention will be focused mostly, though not entirely, on the less familiar middle period, the twelfth-century Renaisance, a time that was feudal and ecclesiastical in accent, heightened by the Crusades; a time when many of the types of literature that we favor today, romances, lyrics, *novelle*, true history as opposed to chronicle, and biographies, began to be launched in the vernacular languages. The years 1000-1300 will be our Middle Ages.

[The aim of this initial chapter has been to give the reader something of an introduction to our approach to the period and the method of this study. It is important that the particular orientation of the author be understood, as one would want to know the attitude and qualifications of a guide leading a tour through an art museum or an archeological site. We hope that the reader now has some feel for the period under consideration and the nature of the exploration we project. It is now appropriate that we move in more closely to look at medieval man as he understood himself, revealed in the pattern of his life and his unselfconscious reflections upon himself.]

II

MAN AND NATURE

The chief medical book of the twelfth and thirteenth centuries was the *Aphorismes* of Hippocrates, a source which was commentaried frequently throughout the Middle Ages. There were, as well, the works of Galen (ca. 130-ca. 200) and various encyclopedias, such as the "Fountain of all Science" by the so-called philosopher Sydrac, which dates from the last years of the thirteenth century.[1] I am not concerned here with the scientific value of such a work; I want to know the scientific opinion of the average man who could be considered informed in his time.

*Man's Body*

The *Sydrac* is a compilation of medieval knowledge far more sophisticated than might be expected. It combines a science of astronomy which rejects the flat earth theory with a biology confused with botany. For example, it states that the world is round and that therefore there are men living at the Antipodes.

> There are men there such as we are, and they see clearly the light of day and night — the sun, the moon, and the stars, even though they are below us and our earth. They

---

[1] This is best preserved in the shortest extant form, which is to be found in MS. fr. 1160 of the Bibliothèque Nationale in Paris. I have used in this book the excellent unpublished editions established by Sapelo Treanor and William McFall Holler: Treanor's "Le Roman de Sydrac, fontaines de toutes sciences," Diss. University of North Carolina, 1939; and Holler's "Le livre de Sydrac: Fontaine de toutes sciences, Folios 57-112," Diss. University of North Carolina, 1972.

farm and labor as we do, and this is because of the roundness of the earth.[2]

This will be a surprise to those who thought that Columbus discovered the roundness of the earth! The *Sydrac* goes on to say, however, that "Man is mostly part of his father, because the *esclate* (ejaculation) descends into the womb and there is formed into the fetus." The *Sydrac* adds that the closest relative of a man who has no child is the child of his brother.

> Man should love both his sister's son and his brother's son; but according to *umanité*, human nature, his brother's children are closer to him than those of his sister, for the child belongs more to the man than to the woman.... the ejaculation *(esclate)* descends from the man into the belly of the woman by the will of God — it is formed there... but it holds more to the man from which it came out just as a shoot from a tree. The tree is its father; the earth is its mother, who keeps it and feeds it. It could not exist without the two, but it belongs more to the tree whence it has come than to the earth where it was planted....[3]

[This common understanding of conception, in which the potential individual or soul lay to all intents and purposes within the male semen or "seed" and the woman had only a passive role of supporting the growth of the "seed," was part of the medieval androcentricity. It lies behind the medieval belief, found in Augustine, but developed in Thomas Aquinas, that prostitution and other forms of extra-marital heterosexual intercourse were wrong, but not nearly as bad as *vitium contra naturam*, venereal behavior contrary to nature. Such action was, in the order of its greater seriousness, masturbation, fellatio or anal intercourse with a woman, sodomy or homosexuality, and bestiality. In essence, such behavior constituted a form of murder, since the living soul was ejaculated where it could not find the support system for life (i.e., outside the womb of a woman).]

Health in man depends upon the proper equilibrium of the four humors: blood, phlegm, white or yellow bile, and black bile. If

---

[2] Treanor, "Sydrac," pp. 159-60.
[3] Holler, "Sydrac," pp. 4-5.

these are out of order throughout the body, this is *cachesis;* if there is an overabundance of humors, this is termed *discrasia*. When humors are only partially in disequilibrium, the condition is called disease, and there are many manifestations: gout, sciatica, and swollen joints because of excessive phlegm. Too much bile causes a tertian or a continuous fever, and excess of blood engenders a purulent fever. Superabundance of humor is a repletion. Such an excess occurs mostly in head, lungs, stomach (most folk were thought to die of stomach trouble, under which they mistakenly included coronary thrombosis), bowels, spleen, liver, womb, kidney, and bladder.

The indications of repletion can easily be seen in the urine. In the case of repletion of phlegm, the urine is white and thick. When black bile is the culprit, the urine is scanty, darkish, and thick, and somewhat foamy. In the case of yellow bile, the urine is also scanty with a yellowish foam, and the urine is thickish, as with jaundice. When blood is the culprit, the urine is very red and thick, of a dark substance. All the humors are plentiful in the liver.

[This brings to mind an illustration of the analogy of proportionality in the history of philosophical metaphysics, based on the medieval understanding of the humors, which, because of the importance of this issue, has been repeated in theological discussions over the past seven hundred years. Those using the illustration are often, I am sure, quite unaware of its origin in the medical theories of the Middle Ages. The original illustration appears in the *Summa Theologica* of Aquinas, where he is discussing the "names of God" (i.e., what may be predicated of God).

> In names predicated of many in an analogical sense, all are predicated because they have reference to some one thing; and this one thing must be placed in the definition of them all.... Thus, for instance, *healthy* applied to animals comes into the definition of *healthy* applied to medicine, which is called healthy, as being the cause of the health of the animal; and also into the definition of *healthy* which is applied to urine, which is called healthy in so far as it is the sign of the animal's health.[4]

---

[4] Thomas Aquinas, *Summa Theologica*, I, 13, 6.

We can see readily that the Angelic Doctor, like any good teacher (and the *Summa Theologica* constitutes his lecture notes), is explaining a difficult point of theology to his pupils by using an illustration they all immediately understand.]

These humors possessed certain qualities first recognized by Aristotle: blood is hot and moist, phlegm is cold and moist, black bile is cold and dry, and yellow bile is hot and dry. Medicines that cause the superfluity to egress through the proper exits must be administered. This is called purging; vomiting, stools, urinating, hemorrhoids, menstruation, sponging of skin, sweating, scarifying, cupping, eruptions on the skin, spitting, sneezing, retching, and above all, bleeding from a vein are all methods of the egress of bad humors. In administering purgatives, the predominating complexion of the individual must be taken into account; and in all cases summer is not a good time for these purgings (see Galen). There are four ages to a man's life which are related to the predominance of the humors: youth (warm and moist); the second stage, 25 to 40 (hot and dry); the third stage, 35 to 55 or 60 (cold and dry); above age 55 man is cold and moist.

The next step in the speculation on man as a physical being was to wonder how the body operated. Adelard of Bath (early twelfth century) had studied among the Moslems, and his queries did not follow the usual pattern of a medieval cleric. He was one of the tutors of Henry II of England, and I wonder whether the King's approach to the problems of man may in part have been greatly influenced by Adelard. In his *Perdifficiles Quaestiones Naturales* Adelard imagined many strange questions in an imaginary discussion with his nephew.

17. Why are those who have good intelligence lacking in memory, and *vice versa?*
18. Why are the seats of imagination, reason, and memory found in the brain?
19. Why is the nose located above the mouth?
20. Why do men get bald in front?
21. How, as the voice comes to the ear, can it penetrate any obstacle?
22. Why, since one can see from the darkness into the light, can one not see similarly from the light into the darkness?
31. Why can we smell, taste, and touch?

32. Why is joy the cause of weeping?
33. Why do we breathe out of the same mouth now hot and now cold air?
36. Why were the fingers made unequal?
37. Why is the palm of the hand made concave?
38. Why can infants not walk immediately after they are born, as animals do?
39. Why are men nourished more by milk?
42. Why, since women are more frigid than men, are they more wanton in desire?
43. Why do all men die?
46. Why are living people always afraid of dead bodies? [5]

Adelard makes the statement that most men do not use their powers of reason. They put their faith simply in the mention of an old book title. What else can authority be called, he asks, except a halter? Reason has been given to individuals so that as the first judge they may distinguish between the true and the false. [This attitude is quite contrary to popular contemporary ideas that medieval man lived on the hash of blind faith in ancient books of dubious scholarship.]

Seventy-five years later a considerable amount of speculation about man and his powers and his weaknesses went on in the first part of the thirteenth century among the Oxford school of Franciscans. The chief scholar amongst them was Roger Bacon, who wrote:

> But experience is of two kinds: one is gained through our external senses, and in this way we gain our experience of those things that are in the heavens by instruments made for this purpose, and of those things here below by means attested by our vision. Things that do not belong in our part of the world we know through other scientists who have had experience of them. As, for example, Aristotle on the authority of Alexander sent two thousand men through different parts of the world to gain experimental knowledge of all things that are on the surface of the earth, as Pliny bears witness in his *Natural History*. This experience is both human and philosophical, as far as man can act in

---

[5] Adelard of Bath, *Perdifficiles Quaestiones Naturales*, in *The Portable Medieval Reader*, eds. James Bruce Ross and Mary Martin McLaughlin (New York: Viking Press, 1949), pp. 622-23. (Slightly adapted.)

accordance with the grace given him; but this experience does not suffice him, because it does not give full attestation in regard to things corporeal owing to its difficulty, and does not touch at all on things spiritual. It is necessary, therefore, that the intellect of man should be otherwise aided, and for this reason the holy patriarchs and prophets, who first gave sciences to the world, received illumination within, and were not dependent on sense alone. [6]

This last sentence summarizes the Franciscan's reply to Adelard. [However, the Dominicans, and in particular Aquinas, were more in accord with Adelard. Descartes followed in the traditions of the Franciscans, but Kant brought the Thomistic empiricism once more into the ascendency.]

*The Inductive Method*

Gerald the Welshman (1146-1222) was much concerned with the observation of physical man. [7] The powers of observation of Gerald, who spent much of his mature life in the vicinity of Oxford near Bicester, were remarkable. In his writings about the Irish and the Welsh he deliberately turned to the scientific approach, much earlier than is supposed in the common assumption that science was born during the Renaissance. Gerald's works were written in the period 1184-1196. He phrased the first phonological law: that initial Irish *s-* corresponds to Welsh *h-*: *sen* versus *hen*. He observed the special musical talents of the Welsh, and gave the best descriptions yet of the birds of those regions. Gerald was also inspired by Seneca's *Questiones,* and Seneca and Aristotle must share much of this credit for the continued science of the observation of man in the twelfth century.

I will quote certain passages in which Gerald narrates his reasons for observing physical man.

> I performed for some time publicly in the schools, and then, for three years and more, on the more mature advice

---

[6] Roger Bacon, *Opus Maius, Portable Medieval Reader,* p. 628.

[7] These statements are, for the most part, reproduced from my article "The *Kambriae Descriptio* of Gerald the Welshman," *Mediaevalia and Humanistica,* NS., I (1970), 217-31.

of masters, I undertook with devout and avid enthusiasm to polish the threshold of theology. Through the grace of God I established foundations of arts and letters, and Canon Law, as well as Thelogical disciplines. Arter leaving the school and gymnasium, I returned home, and in order not to become torpid through sloth — for I recognized that the mind if it is idle is lost — I began my treatise of the *Topography of Ireland* with its secrets and mysteries, and of other kingdoms throughout the world, very diverse and still more strange — a task not attempted by anyone else. [8]

Gerald says elsewhere: "Driven by a thirst for knowledge, I have carried my investigations into the mysteries of Nature further than most of my contemporaries." He did not comprehend at all the centuries of past time. In explanation of his studies on Ireland and Wales, he remarked: that "fine histories of other lands have already been written: I have thought it therefore more worthy to apply myself with industry to the arrangement of the history of my native land, which has been until now almost completely overlooked...." [9] Gerald was referring to the fact that the Eastern lands had already been discussed in ancient tales of Alexander the Great and others. He was going to study the Western world from his own observation. Gerald's investigations are really the first conscious history of his contemporaries.

Gerald, with his desire to observe his contemporaries, wandered quite far afield. Here is a fine description of King Henry II of England:

It were not amiss in this place to draw the portrait of the king, so that his person as well as his character may be familiar to posterity; and those who in future ages shall hear and read of his great achievements may be able to picture him to themselves as he was. For the history on which I am employed of Ireland must not suffer so noble an ornament of our times to pass away with only a slight notice.... No man indeed is born without faults, but he is best who has the least; and the wise will think that nothing which concerns mankind is devoid of interest.... Henry of England had a reddish complexion, rather dark,

---

[8] Gerald the Welshman, *Giraldus Cambrensis Opera*, ed. J. S. Brewer, Rolls Series no. 21, 8 vols. (London: Longman & Co., 1861-91), I, 410.
[9] *Ibid.*, VI, 8.

and a large round head. His eyes were grey, bloodshot, and flashed in anger. He had a fiery countenance, his voice was tremulous, and his neck a little bent forward. His body was fleshy, and he had an enormous paunch, rather by the fault of Nature than through gross feeding.... In order to reduce and cure as far as possible this natural tendency and defect, he waged a continual war, so to speak, with his own belly by taking immoderate exercise. For in time of war, in which he was almost always engaged, he took little rest, even during the intervals of business and action. Times of peace were not seasons of repose and indulgence to him, for he was immoderately fond of hunting, and he devoted himself to it with excessive ardor. At the first dawn of day he would mount a fleet horse, and tirelessly spend the day in riding through the woods penetrating the depths of forests and crossing the ridges of hills. On his return home in the evening he was seldom seen to sit down, either before he took his supper or after, for notwithstanding his own great fatigue, he would weary all his court by being constantly on his legs. But it is one of the most useful rules of life, not to have too much of any one thing [*mesure*], and even medicine is not in itself perfect nor always to be used; even so it befell this king. For he had frequent swellings in his legs and feet, increased much by his violent exercise on horseback, which added to his other complaints; and if they did not bring on serious disorders, at least they hastened that which is the source of all — old age. In stature he may be reckoned among men of moderate height, which was not the case of his sons, the two eldest being somewhat beyond middle height, and the two youngest somewhat below.

When his mind was undisturbed and he was not in an angry mood, he spoke with great eloquence, and — what was remarkable in those days — he was well learned.... He was inordinately fond of hawking and hunting whether his falcons stooped on their prey or his sagacious hounds, quick of scent and swift of foot, pursued the chase. Would to God he had been as zealous in his devotions as he was in his sports.... He could scarcely spend an hour to hear Mass, and then he was more occupied in counsels and conversations about affairs of state than in his devotions.... I had almost forgotten to say that his memory was so good that, notwithstanding the multitudes who continually surrounded him, he never failed to recognize anyone he had ever seen before, nor did he forget important matters which he had ever heard.... If this king had been finally chosen of God and turned himself to obey God's commands, such were his natural endowments that he would have been ... the noblest of all princes of the earth in his times.[10]

In Gerald's description of the Irish people of his day we have another masterpiece:

> They are a rude people, subsisting on the produce of their cattle only, and living themselves like beasts — a people that are not yet departed from the primitive habits of pastoral life.... These people are not only rude in their dress, but they suffer their hair and beards to grow enormously in an uncouth manner, just like the modern fashion recently introduced; indeed, all their habits are barbarian. But habits are formed by mutual intercourse; and as these people inhabit a country so remote from the rest of the world, and lying at its farthest extremity, forming, as it were, another world, and are secluded from civilized nations, they learn nothing, and they practise nothing but the barbarism in which they are born and bred, and which sticks to them like a second nature.... Their clothes are also made after a barbarous fashion. Their customs is to wear small, close-fitting hoods hanging below the shoulders a cubit's length, and generally made of parti-coloured strips sewn together. Under them they use woollen rugs instead of cloaks, with breeches and hose of one piece, or hose and breeches joined together, which are usually dyed of some colour [*trews*]. Likewise in riding they use neither saddles, nor boots, nor spurs, but only carry a rod in the hand, having a crook at the upper end, with which they both guide and urge their horses. They use reins which serve the purpose both of a bridle and a bit, and which do not prevent the horses from feeding, as they always live on grass. Moreover, they go to battle without armour, considering it a burthen and esteeming it brave and honourable to fight without it....[11]

We are not unknowingly confusing what men like Gerald had to say about customs with their speculations on the inadequacy of the human body and the puniness of man's existence. These thoughts were coexistent in Gerald's mind and in the mind of

---

[10] *Portable Medieval Reader*, pp. 356-61. (Adapted.)
[11] *Ibid.*, pp. 411-15.

medieval man in general, who looked at nature always with one eye on supernature.

A concept of physical man in his relation to nature which has that "double vision," is expressed rather beautifully in verse by Alain de Lille. In his poem he is inspired, of course, by Isaiah 40:6, but the thoughts expressed were acceptable to the Middle Ages:

> Every creature in this world, in book or in representation, is a mirror of ourselves — a faithful sign of our life, of our death, of our condition, of our fate.
>
> The rose represents our condition, a fine explanation of our being, a reading of our life. When it flourishes in the early morning it has no bloom and then it blossoms; at eventide it decays.
>
> Therefore the flower expires while breathing; while it raves in its wanness, dying while rising, old and new at the same time, simultaneously an old woman and a maid, the rose withers as it comes up.
>
> Just so, the springtide of human life blooms a little bit in the first morn of youth, but soon the evening closes off this morn of life, and the twilight of life brings it to an end. When someone orates upon its charm, its charm even then disappears.
>
> As time blows on the flower, it becomes as grass, the gem is made mud, man becomes ash while he offers tribute to his death.[12]

To quote Gerald the Welshman once again, from a long poem on the creation of the world:

> Ingenious man sees the secrets of nature, and he cogitates on the causes and the course of things: the movement of the stars, the eclipses of sun and moon, and whence come the phases of the moon. What produces lightning, what cause generates thunder, whence comes its force and whence its noise? Why the ocean tides, whence in varying colors Iris marks the rains in this orb? Why the earth trembles, what creates the movement of the winds in the air, and whence the variations of the weather? So does

---

[12] Alan de Lille, "Omnis caro fenum," in *The Oxford Book of Medieval Latin Verse*, ed. F. J. E. Raby (Oxford: The Clarendon Press, 1959), pp. 369-70.

man dwell on earth, so does he exalt heaven in his breast, an inhabitant of the earth in his body, of the pole in his mind. What comes from earth corruption terminates, but what he collects from the heavens remains for ever. That which is of earth returns to earth; the spirit aspires to the stars and seeks to know what is his own in both places.[13]

*The Ambiguity in Behavior*

We must turn now to another aspect of human nature on which, so far, we have touched but lightly: proper human behavior.

Numerous shades of good behavior and of ill behavior abounded in the Middle Ages which are hard to reconcile with even our permissive twentieth century. Man could kill quite freely, and yet murder is a mortal sin of great seriousness. As I read in medieval literature, I find that chastity is abused at every turn, but everyone rails against the sinfulnes of woman and her company. This same double standard also seems to apply to lying, stealing, and gluttony. Unquestionably there was a duality of behavior which we cannot possibly condone today. Basically this dualism can be traced to man's recognition that what God has made cannot be completely sinful. God will test us as He wills. It is the ultimate decision which we make in the use of our free will which damns us or saves us.

It would not be difficult to compile from many sources the best manners which the medieval man hoped to see in his contemporaries, but we think it would be more representative to make a list from the advice to the lover in the great *Roman de la Rose*. The god of love is informing the lover about the pleasing qualities that will make him acceptable. This could apply, of course, to a man or woman at any stage.

> First one must show no *vilanie*, which means having nothing to do with people who are *vilain*, those who are unkind, unhelpful, and without friends. Proceeding on further, one should not repeat slander or say anything about an individual which might well be kept silent. Be friendly, greet people, important or unimportant, in the streets as you pass along. Do not tell vulgar stories or use

---

[13] Gerald the Welshman, "What a Piece of Work is a Man!," *ibid.*, p. 374.

filthy words. Serve all women, and correct someone else who speaks ill of them. Do not display vain pride. Above all, be attractive, show *cointerie!* Dress well and buy good footwear, as your pocketbook permits. You should have a good tailor who knows how to sew fine stitches and make your sleeves well fitting. Wear fresh, new shoes quite frequently, so closely fitting that lower-class people will wonder how you got into them and how you will take them off. When you go out, carry gloves, a silk purse, and wear an attractive belt. If you cannot afford this, do the best you can. At Pentecost, a young man can wear a chaplet of roses around his head, which is cheap enough. Do not allow any dirt to be on you. Wash your hands, polish your teeth, and have no sign of dirt in your fingernails. Sew on your sleeves, comb your hair, but do not make use of any face make-up which is for women only, or for sodomites.

Continue to be light-hearted... if you have a talent with which you can please others, use this. Everyone should practise in all places. If you can sing, or dance, or excel in tourneys, practise these things whenever you can. You should be generous in your gifts to others.[14]

People then were not so restrained as we are in the display of body fluids. After all, they had no concept of the presence of germs and viruses. In the *Flamenca*, the protagonist Guillem longs to have a view of Flamenca's face, but she is in church with her watchful husband, and her face is covered by a wimple, which was standard feminine attire in those days, now known only in religious habits. Fortunately for him she lifts the lower corner of this veil in order to spit on the church floor.[15]

The presence of blood in bowls, on rags, or on the ground did not provoke much concern. These fluids were just normal body humors. Human feces did have a most disagreeable odor, and one seldom succeeded in eradicating it very effectively. In his Liberate Rolls, King Henry III of England had the position of the privy moved in his great hall at London because the smell was very unpleasant. Note that we say "moved," not "removed." The odor

---

[14] See Guillaume de Lorris and Jean de Meun, *Le Roman de la Rose...*, ed. Ernest Langlois, SATF (Paris: Firmin-Didot, 1920), II, ll. 2077ff.

[15] *Le Roman de Flamenca*, ed. Paul Meyer, BFMA 8 (Paris: Bouillon, 1901), vv. 3130-34.

of decayed flesh also was most unpleasant, but it could be tolerated when necessary. After a conflict, dead bodies could be left *in situ* for an indefinite time. After the slaughter of the Frenchmen who had been brought to England to oppose the hated King John, their bodies were left in the field, where they were chewed by dogs and by other carrion-eating beasts and birds.[16]

Practical joking of a somewhat extreme kind was tolerated in the Middle Ages. That is why the verbs *compissier* and *conchier* were often used, and many times diluted slightly in meaning. For example, *conchier* was regularly employed with the meaning "deceive."[17]

Despite what may appear to us as a rather indelicate or "backwoods" life style, medieval man did have a sense of order. The ultimate source of order was God, and those who held authority under God's will were responsible to Him for what they represented. The office of a king is a religious one. Control was in the personal pleasure of the divinely appointed king; but in using the goods of his subjects, the king is responsible to the higher law of God. A good prince obeys the law while a "tyrant" oppresses the people by his force. God may inflict a tyrant upon a sinful people, but when the people cease to be sinful, then God will free them from their oppressor. A tyrant must be borne in patience until he meets his just end by God's judgment. But when the Christian subject is asked to perform an act that is contrary to divine law, he may display passive resistance. He may pray to God that the scourge be removed. John of Salisbury went so far as to suggest that a private individual might lawfully enforce God's law against a legitimate ruler; but by the late twelfth century it was felt that the whole membership of a community and the *baronagium* (community of barons) acting through the King's court could oppose tyranny. As is true in so much of medieval thought, there is obviously a duality here. There is not always a clear line between a concept and its opposite.[18] There is apt to be always the spirit

---

[16] The Liberate Rolls in an English version are printed in Thomas Hudson Turner, *Some Account of Domestic Architecture in England, from Richard II to Henry VII...* (Oxford: J. Henry and J. Parker, 1859).

[17] The reader will understand that these verbs mean to "soil with urine" and "with feces" respectively.

[18] See John Dickinson "The Medieval Conception of Kingship as Developed in the *Policraticus* of John of Salisbury," *Speculum*, 1 (1926), 303-37.

of *Sic et Non* — "Yes and No." In Peter Abelard's philosophy, both sides of a case are often in suspense. In the *De Arte Honeste Amandi* of Andreas Capellanus there is expressed a possible duality of decision. Gerald the Welshman, in his *Descriptio Kambriae* extols the virtues of his Welsh people, and yet he shows how they can be punished for their faults.

This duality of decision can be illustrated best by the problem of chastity as it presented itself in the Middle Ages. It was recognized fully from the writings of St. Paul and others that adultery and fornication were mortal sins. At the same it was believed that immortality in all its forms was God's will. Immortality of the soul was dominant in the Christian faith; but what of immortality of the body, which, it was believed, can be achieved only by sexual intercourse? [This was an idea for which there was ample precedent in the Old Testament.] Even high ecclesiasts were often in a haze over this duality.

There was a joking story which may have had some truth in it. A group of bishops were stopping at a hostel. They asked the proprietor to give as much attention to their horses as he would be willing to give to them. In the morning they were astounded to find that their mounts had been shown all attention, to the extent of having a mate provided in each of the stalls. When questioned, the proprietor said that he was trying to give the horses the same care that he afforded the masters.

We may sum this up by saying that our medieval man often vacillated in keeping some commandments. He seemed to feel that some sins were not so grave under varying circumstances, and when the coordinating factors were different. But when the end of life was drawing near, there was little indecision to be tolerated. The ascetic way of life was chosen. We observe from the epics that knights could be much troubled at that time by the number of men they had killed — even though these killings were done in legitimate tourneys and battles, with proper defiance under conditions of self-defense. They went on difficult pilgrimages to the Holy Land for atonement. This happens in *Amis et Amiles* and in *Raoul de Cambrai*. Just so, sinful laxness in chastity and gluttony were recognized as just that.

The difficulties of life were great in the Middle Ages, so great that most people found it expedient to defend themselves with weapons at some point in their lives. Sexual intercourse was one of the best ways in which relief from tension could be achieved. Lovemaking was thought to have some medicinal value. Louis VII of France, in his later years, was rigorous in his personal morality. On one occasion he was told by his doctors that sexual relations would be good for him. The ecclesiasts in his suite told him that they would absolve him in advance. But he was very strict. He told them to send for the Queen. As they could not, he refrained from medication of this kind.

*Physical Appearance and Notions of Beauty*

This brings us to still another aspect. What did the medieval man think of man's physical appearance? One formula was followed to describe masculine beauty and another for feminine beauty. The first of these is made fun of a little in *Aucassin et Nicolette* (1210):

> Aucassin... was attractive and large and well cut in legs, feet, body and arms. He had blond hair, finely curled, and his eyes were gray-blue *(vairs)* and laughing, and his face was bright, and shapely, and his nose was high and well placed. [19]

Here is a typical example for the beautiful maiden:

> She was clothed in a white linen garment and shirt in such a way that both her sides were visible [had slashed *bliaut*]. She had a lovely body, low hips, her neck more white than snow on a branch. Her eyes were blue-gray and her face was white, the mouth fair, the nose well placed, her eyebrows brown, the forehead fair, the hair curly and somewhat blond. Gold thread never cast such a gleam as her hair against the daylight. Her mantle was of dark purple [royal purple], and she had it wrapped around her. [20]

Very frequently medieval writers emphasized that the eyes were far apart.

---

[19] *Aucassin et Nicolette, chantfable du XIII<sup>e</sup> siècle*, ed. Mario Roques, 2nd. ed. rev., CFMA no. 41 (Paris: Champion, 1929), sect. 2.

[20] Marie de France, *Lanval*, in *Les Lais*, ed. Ernest Hoepffner (Strasbourg: Heitz, 1921), ll. 119ff.

Again, in *Aucassin et Nicolette* there is a similar description, somewhat parodied:

> She had blond hair finely curled. The eyes were gay and laughing, the face shapely, the nose high and well placed. The lips were more red than a cherry or a rose in the summer season, and her teeth were white and fine. She had breasts, hard, which lifted up her gown just as if they were nuts; she was slender about the waist so that one could enclose it in two hands. The daisies lying under the instep of her feet, which she crushed with her toes, were outright black compared to her feet and legs, so very white was the little girl. [21]

Descriptions of this kind are frequent everywhere, and they agree in esentials. The ideal male was a curly blond, heavy in shoulders, slim in waist, full again in the hips, with muscular limbs. These details are not purely imaginary — a desirable dream. Here Anna Comnena, who had seen and admired him, describes the handsome Bohemond of Antioch:

> He was so tall in stature that he outtopped the tallest by nearly one cubit. He was narrow in the waist and sides, with broad shoulders and deep chest, powerful arms.... The build of his body was neither too slender nor overweighted with flesh... he had powerful hands and stood firmly on his feet... his neck and back were well compacted... he stooped slightly, but that was probably since birth. His skin all over was very white, but in his face the whiteness was tempered with red. His hair was yellowish, but it did not hang down to his waist like that of the other barbarians... he had it cut short to the ears. Whether his beard was reddish... I cannot say, for the razor had passed over it very closely and left a surface smoother than chalk.... His blue eyes indicated both a high spirit and dignity.... A certain charm hung about this man.... His wit was manifold and crafty... in conversation he was well informed, and the answers he gave were quite irrefutable. [22]

---

[21] *Aucassin et Nicolette*, sect. 12.
[22] *Portable Medieval Reader*, pp. 325-26. (Adapted.)

Bohemond was of Norman blood and it is probable that this Germanic type was the ideal of that age. Man were normally from 5 feet, 2 inches to 5 feet, 10 inches in height, but some of them are somewhat taller, and are remarked upon as giants.

I have examined many of the large personal seals of the twelfth century, and many of the reproductions of paintings and bas relief. Evidence is wanting, but I should say that although there was so little change in these figures from one district to another, in many areas there were local physical types, caused by inbreeding. In the *Roman de la Rose* there is a reference to an Orleans nose.[23] Some of the figures in the little pamphlet *Romanesque Art* (Victoria and Albert Museum, 1950) are distinctive. Among them, the Jewish elders whom Saint Paul is addressing (1160) show interesting types, and the Morgan Library David Leaf shows upper-class people. The description of "high and well seated" noses is well illustrated in some of these. The well known dwarf "Turoldus" appears in the Bayeux tapestry. The fiddler and the dancing girl on the Limoges casket are also very clear as types. The faces, for the most part, seem full, and the eyebrows prominent. In Oakeshott, Plates IV and V, there is an evident attempt to portray the strange face of an Egyptian. In Dr. Randall's marginal illuminations there is a rather large proportion of grotesque types.

*Summary*

In this chapter we have been dealing with the medieval man's ideas concerning physical man — and by this we mean *man*, not monsters such as those displayed on the margins of the *Mappae mundi*. In speaking of man's concept of beauty at the end, we will now stretch a point and say a few words about his understanding of the Pythagorean notion that abstract ethical concepts can be expressed numerically. Historians of architecture long ago proved

---

[23] I have examined in detail the figures on the Bayeux tapestry, Walter Oakeshott's *The Artist of the Winchester Bible* (London: Faber and Faber, Ltd., 1945), Jean Taralon's *Les Trésors des églises de France* (Paris: Hachette, 1966), Lilian M. C. Randall's *Images in the Margins of Gothic Manuscripts* (Berkeley: University of California Press, 1966), and many other illustrated books of the twelfth and thirteenth centuries showing faces, hoping to find some generalities of types. The results have not been significant.

their point that canons of beauty understood in this way are found in the fine medieval structures. Many students of literature are now seeking to prove this same point for some of the important works of literature in the medieval period. [The point is that medieval man, believing as he did in the neo-Platonic God who is ultimate reason *(logos)* or mind *(nous)*, and at the same time imbued with the Germanic sense of the numinous in all nature, found a harmony and coherence within the natural world that would follow from its being a prolongation of the divine. Beauty was simply the perception of the world as God conceived it, and this vision was a goal that underlay his most sincere aspirations. For the heirs of the sixteenth century, where beauty was divorced from goodness, it is hard to grasp the assumption of twelfth- and thirteenth-century man that the aesthetic sense is prior to any ethical concern. It is perhaps even more difficult to identify with his belief that since God is best known in the harmony of things, numerology becomes the key to the discernment of the One in the many.

Perhaps it would be saying too much, but it would certainly not be out of the spirit of this chapter, to conclude with the comment that medieval man knew himself to be only a journeyman mathematician, judged by the Master Mathematician, and therefore he could at the same time share in the mystical order of creation revealed in numbers and live comfortably with his own errors, trusting in a merciful Savior.]

## III

## THE INTELLECTUALS AND THE CHURCH

The class of society in the Middle Ages which speculated on the World and the relations of God with Man was the clergy, or schoolmen. In that part of the Middle Ages with which we are mostly concerned, the twelfth-century Renaissance, these men were in church orders, the majority in the lower orders. A sufficient definition of the clergy is those who were subject to canon law, as contrasted with the laity, who were controlled by civil law. The clergy spoke Latin habitually among themselves. That section of Paris where they lived was known as the Latin Quarter, a name which still exists for the Paris university section. These men were the scholars, the teachers, and the educated professional men of the time.

There were some learned persons who were not Christian clerks, some educated women who even practiced medicine, and many Jews, who were in a group by themselves and had their own schools. The Jews can be recognized in the sculptures and paintings of the time by the pointed caps which they wore. For example, the earliest picture of an autopsy that we have from the Middle Ages is one of a series of pictures in a thirteenth century ms. of Constantine's "On Stomach Disorders."[1] In this autopsy scene, the lady's corpse is lying on a table in a dissected state, while the doctors in their masters' gowns are talking. The little man who is doing the cutting wears a pointed cap. I can assume from this that a Christian was not permitted to cut into a dead body of another

---

[1] Oxford MS Ashmole 399, fols. 33-34.

Christian, for the dissecting surgeon was a Jew. [This fact also shows, incidentally, both medieval man's ability to live successfully within the ambiguity of his ethic and the practical expedients of life; and the untruth of suggesting that he has no empirical or scientific interests.]

## The Schools

It may seem puzzling to us that Western Europe was a reasonably literate society when only clerics were educated. We must keep in mind the nature of the clergy. There were two kinds, the secular and the monks. When in lower orders, the secular sort could marry. For example, the distress of that romantic couple of the early twelfth century was not caused because Abelard could not marry Heloise. He was free to do so, but Heloise knew this would jeopardize his future in holy orders. [In the medieval Church it was generally agreed that there were four lower or minor orders and three major or higher orders, which Abelard sought. Within that general agreement, however, there was some disagreement. Some taught that the major orders were bishop, priest, and deacon; and others believed that they were priest, deacon, and subdeacon, with the role of bishop considered an office within priesthood. The Western and Eastern Churches disagree as to the nomenclature of the minor orders, which included such titles as lector, porter, acolyte, and exorcist.]

The lowest grade in the lower orders was "simple tonsure." A boy of about seven years would be taken to the bishop by a guardian or a parent, and after receiving a slight snipping on the crown of the head, he was admitted to the rights and privileges of grammar schools and ecclesiastical discipline. The other four lower orders were: doorman, acolyte, reader, and exorcist; the major orders then, subdeacon, deacon, and priest. One had to be at least a deacon before he was granted permission to preach. (This is why St. Francis took deacon's orders.) The priest's duty was the cure of souls.

We know from the mentions of dark or purple clothing in literature, and from representations on such places as the Bayeux tapestry, that the clergy were expected to wear sober clothing — preferably black.[2]

The first schools that children attended were usually termed Psalter schools. They were semiprivate, and a few girls were admitted. Anyone could organize such a group to learn elementary reading. When Garin the Lotharingian had such training, he "could recognize the letters; he was set to learning them when he was small. He learned to read both Latin and Romance. He read the letters and understood the writing."[3] It will be noted that he was taught to read French as well as Latin. We doubt that this could have happened in a grammar school. In *Huon de Bordeaux* Garin de Saint-Omer, who has control of the harbor at Brindisi, takes a letter and breaks the seal: "... he read the letter, for he knew enough to do so."[4] In Marie's *Yonec*, the old woman, sister of the lady's husband, "went into another room; in her hand she carried her psalter where she wished to read her psalms."[5]

Simple reading, therefore, could be acquired in semiprivate groups. It is interesting to see the method of teaching reading. In her fable about the lion who could not get farther than the letter *B*, Marie de France lets us know that the phonic method was used in this instruction. Its use is evident also from the *Abécédé* of Huon le Roi.

In the vicinity of a monastic community it is quite probable that clerical reading schools were held in the town under some direction by the abbot. In Bury Saint Edmunds, Abbot Samson bought stone buildings for use as schools so that students could study in a rent-free house.

---

[2] [This dates back at least as far as the age of Charlemagne. Apparently this dress code was observed in the breach, because the Fourth Lateran Council (1215) forbade clerics to wear red or green stockings. Monastic garb was a sombre version of the dress of the day. It has not changed, as other dress has, over the centuries.]

[3] When Flora argues for the worth of her clerk as a lover she says: "Mine is in purple, yours in a hauberc *(lorica),*" in "Altercatio Phyllidis et Florae," *Oxford Book of Medieval Latin Verse*, ed. F. J. E. Raby (Oxford: Clarendon Press, 1959), no. 209b.

[4] *Huon de Bordeaux, chanson de geste*, eds. François Guessard and Charles Grandmaison, APF 5 (Paris: F. Vieweg, 1890), p. 81.

[5] Marie de France, *Yonec*, vv. 62-64, in *Les Lais*, ed. Ernest Hoepffner (Strasbourg: Heitz, 1921).

Certainly such schools were not conducted in the monastery proper, and the abbot was considered charitable for providing those premises. Undoubtedly he expected to increase vocations thereby, but the venture seems to have been independent of monastic discipline.

When a boy knew how to read, it was up to his family, surely, to determine whether in simple tonsure he would seek to pursue a clerical career. Admision would be sought for him to a grammar school, where he would then be under church discipline. A monastic grammar school could serve as a kind of boarding school for many young clerks. We know that St. Bernard went off to the school of Notre Dame du Château (today Châtillon-sur-Seine). Gerald the Welshman was sent to the school at St. Peter's abbey in Gloucester. Neither of these two was destined ultimately for a monastic career.

There must have been thousands of others in a similar situation. There were three such schools in London city.[6] I can only guess that they were at St. Paul's cathedral church, at St. Martin le Grand, and at Trinity (Oldgate). Westminster was then outside London.

Apparently life in such schools was very much like what we know today. FitzStephen says that each of these schools had its own ball-playing group, which would go on holy days after dinner to the common known as Smoothfield (Smithfield) outside the walls, where all young people, and the people as a whole, amused themselves. Cock-fighting was allowed in the classrooms of the schools once a year — on Shrove Tuesday, in the forenoon. On festival days the masters brought students together at the churches named after the saints whose days were being celebrated, and engaged in disputation and in recitations. They even disputed in Latin verse and discussed grammatical constructions, and participated in personal satire also.

FitzStephen adds that occasionally other schools had been started when special permission was granted. I take this to mean that outstanding masters could be allowed to set up school in their own houses for a limited clientele. I assume that such a teacher would use his undercroft, an area open to the street, for readings (*lectures*)

---

[6] For a description of London in the Middle Ages by FitzStephen see John Stow, *Survey of London*, introduction by H. B. Wheatley, rev. ed., Everyman's Library, 589 (New York: E. P. Dutton, 1960).

and discussion sessions. Some students might be lodged in the *soler*, top floor room, of the house; or they could be lodged similarly in other nearby houses. Student letters show that the master was usually made responsible for the young men's welfare. Their money was usually turned over to him for safe-keeping.

We may assume that the *grammar* schools maintained in Paris, mostly on the Rue de Fouarre, were similar to those grammar schools. In addition large cities, of which Paris is the notable example, housed *studia generalia*. The masters in such schools were distinguished, and they drew students who wanted further study in grammar, dialectic, and rhetoric from all over Europe. They also experimented with the quadrivium — geometry, arithmetic, astronomy, and *musica*. Music was not instruction in performance on an instrument nor in singing, as we have already hinted, but Pythagorean number theory, or the law of proportions, as taught from a monochord instrument. These theories of proportion were carried over into all the arts, notably architecture. It is now believed that literary composition was also frequently based on these proportions. In addition, certain of the more distinguished masters spoke on physics, that is, "natural science," and there were those also who taught the higher learning: canon law and theology.

Gerald the Welshman claimed that he spent twenty years in the schools, which would mean that he spent some ten years in the Benedictine school at Gloucester, about five years in the *Studia* at Paris (part of this time at Sainte Genèvieve on the hill there), and then returned to Paris for three more years in canon law. He finished with two years in theology at Lincoln Cathedral.

At Paris in the grammar schools on the Rue de Fouarre, the classes were directly under the *magister* of the cathedral. Also in Paris, the school at Ste. Geneviève and the school at Saint Victor were conducted by Augustinian canons who later were allowed to have certain monastic rules of their own, and were then known as Victorines. The *Universitas* at Paris refers to the entire group of masters and students who taught under the jurisdiction of the chancellor of the cathedral, which at that time (1200) included Saint Victor and Mont-Sainte-Geneviève. This group became further organized in the thirteenth century, and the College of the Sorbonne, which specialized in theology, was founded about 1252. Some medicine was taught in Paris, although Montpellier was the most distinguished place for this subject. Civil law was not approved of, although I suspect that some sporadic instruction was given in it. For this subject matter the leading *studium* was at Bologna.

Classrooms were the same in all important *studia generalia*. There would be a fairly large ground-floor room, the floor perhaps covered with straw on which the students could sit, as they did at the Rue de Fouarre, or there may have been low benches. The students wrote on their knees. The *clerc lisant*, or teacher, had a chair with arms, and he sat facing the class. It is possible that he sometimes had a reading stand, of appropriate height, set before him.

In passing I would note that all kinds of floors in medieval buildings were usually covered with straw.

The *collegium*, or college, is a school with one master or more, set up with endowments, to serve students of a special type; they might be students from one area, such as Beauvais, Wales, or Brittany. Nominally their masters were approved by the chancellor of the cathedral. Colleges of this sort began gradually — starting with the Dix-huit Clercs in Paris at the close of the twelfth century. A minimum of lodging, which usually consisted of straw on the floor of a large room, and food, often soup or stew, were offered free to the members of the college.

Conditions improved in the thirteenth century, and then notably in the fourteenth when such colleges began to multiply. They were usually set up in a *studium generale* town, such as Paris, and later Oxford. In London such colleges, as FitzStephen hints, could be of a fly-by-night nature — presumably without endowment. As organization increased within the *studia*, the term and the concept of a university as an institution comprising all schools was first used. Do not forget that all these students and masters were of the clergy, under canon law, until the mid-fifteenth century. As a group they were difficult to deal with. The civil guards, the *serjants* of the King's provost, were forbidden to touch them. Only the *serjants* of the Bishop's court or *officialité* had any jurisdiction over them. In the 1230s there was a great suspension of classes in the schools at Paris, which influenced the growth of similar schools in England, Spain, and elsewhere, as the students then matriculated at other institutions.

## The Discipline of Learning

Between 1256 and 1265 the *Siete Partidas* was compiled under orders from King Alfonso of Castile. The laws listed there give remarkable information on life and institutions in the thirteenth century. What is said about the universities is most interesting: for a *studium generale* to be complete, each subject matter had to have at least one master. If one for each was not possible, those subject matters that had to be so staffed were grammar, logic, rhetoric, laws, and the decretals (canon law). The salaries of the masters must be paid in three installments: at the very beginning of the session, at Easter, and at the feast of St. John. Most important was the role of the librarian, who in the Spanish *Siete Partidas* is referred to as the *Estacionario*.

From just such a librarian Gerald the Welshman ordered a copy of the Civil Code in Paris, and he was greatly incensed when the volume was sold to someone else.

In the *Siete Partidas* there is a most enlightening section which prohibits clerics from taking part in or attending "juegos de escarnio" (performances with mocking intent). It is proper for them, however, to play in Christmas and Epiphany dramas and in the Easter plays.

The head of the school at Saint Victor after 1133 was Hugh of Saint Victor. His *Didascalicon* is famous as a great exposition of medieval learning. I must summarize a goodly portion of this, although I remind readers that much of it was undoubtedly over the heads of medieval students. Some of us may find that it is equally over our heads today.

Hugh of Saint Victor was a Fleming by origin. He had a clear, analytical mind which enabled him to define admirably in the *Didascalicon* the theory of study and teaching which was considered best in his time. [He was also a theologian of no mean ability, who rescued the dialectical method from the attack of Abelard, and paved the way for 13th century scholasticism.] He remarked that there are hosts of students, but very few learned men. The real arts, he said, are grammar and dialectic. Certain appendages of the arts: tragedies, comedies, satires, lyric, heroic, and satiric poetry, histories and stories, are confusing and overwordy. They demand much labor and bear very little fruit. The serious arts should be mastered first, but the appendages are pleasant, and the truth can often be remembered more easily if it is buried in a tale. The student must have both intelligence and memory. Natural intelligence discovers and memory preserves wisdom. Natural capacity is furthered by reading and meditation. Learning begins with reading, and its consummation is meditation. The goal of one who reads must be to retain what has been read, and here memory is essential. So, in reading, one should begin with better known things and proceed to the less familiar.

Hugh says that Bernard of Chartres was asked what was necessary for learning. He replied:

> Humility, zeal, quiet life with opportunity for inquiry — then poverty, and a foreign land. Discipline too should not be neglected, because knowledge is not able to develop in the shameless person.
> 
> Discipline begins with humility. The careful scholar listens to everyone freely, reads all, rejects no books, no teaching, and no person. He tries to learn from every one and every thing. It is a Platonic saying: I wish to learn modestly from someone else rather than exalt my own knowledge.
> 
> No knowledge should be considered cheap. No writing should be scorned, because every book teaches something worth while if it is treated in proper place and order. Since you cannot read everything, choose that which is more useful. Spend the most labor on this, but other books should not be unknown. When you begin to know something, do not look down upon others. Above all, do not accuse your ancestors and predecessors of simplicity. Such boasters do not wish to hear sermons because the material there is so simple that one can acquire such things by one's own intelligence. These people scorn the lecturers in divinity and thus do God an injury. A good student reflects on something for a long time before making judgments. When he finds wisdom he wishes to keep this always before his eyes. When he cannot penetrate at once to the deeper things, he does not revile it and say it is worthless if he cannot understand it.
> 
> Zeal for learning needs encouragement. The ancients succeeded because they loved wisdom and they have left monuments for posterity. Some of them gave up honors, abandoned human society, and went to live in desert places to get leisure for meditation. Thus they were not disturbed by desires which hurt the virtuous path. Parmenides sat

for fifteen years on a rock in Egypt. Prometheus meditated greatly while torn by the vultures on Mt. Caucasus. In old age the young scholar becomes more learned. Themistocles lived 107 years and complained that he was obliged to die just as he had begun to be wise. Plato died at eighty-one, and Socrates was ninety-nine. The old philosopher Pythagoras, Democritus, and others lived to be very old in their enjoyment of wisdom.

Homer, Hesiod, Simonides, and Tersilochus wrote their best poetry at the time of their death. Sophocles, who was berated when very old because he neglected his family affairs, was thought to be mad. He recited from *Oedipus* and convinced the judges. Cato the Censor did not hesitate to begin the study of Greek. According to Homer, Nestor was more eloquent when he was decrepit. This shows that extreme old age could not take away their learning from these worthy men. Quiet demands that the mind be not diverted by unlawful desires. Leisure and opportunity should suffice for honorable study.

Frugality should be practised by students, for a fat stomach does not make a keen mind. But students today boast of what they have spent, not of what they have learned. I cannot say anything worthy about their masters.

When we mention a foreign land, we must remember Ovid's saying in his *ex Pontine* letters that the sweetness of one's native land is still sweet for him. The strong man holds every country for his fatherland, and the virtuous man finds everywhere an exile. Since boyhood I [Hugh] have lived away from my native land, and I know how hard it is for the spirit sometimes to leave the poor man's hut, and how one can feel free when he despises palace halls and fine ceilings.[7]

Hugh of Saint Victor demands intelligence, memory, and frugality, humility (including discipline), zeal (lasting to very old age), quiet, poverty, and such detachment as one can best acquire in a foreign land. These are qualities which have been demanded of the best students at all times in all ages. It is interesting for us to realize, in our examination of what the medieval man wished of mankind, that the medieval man of the most developed kind had this same concept of the good student.

---

[7] Hugh of St. Victor cited in James Bruce Ross and Mary Martin McLaughlin, eds., *The Portable Medieval Reader* (New York: Viking Press, 1949), pp. 583-90. (Adapted.)

The Rules of the University of Paris, as drawn up in 1215, supplement our picture of the newly organized university commune. A lecturer in Arts must be twenty-one years old, must have heard other lecturers for a minimum of six years, and must himself agree to continue lecturing for two years. In assemblies there shall be no drinking. The masters will wear a black cope, the master's gown. A *pallium*, or short mantle, is allowed over this round black cope. Shoes must be simple, not ornamented or with long toes. A master has authority over his scholar, and he cannot teach in any room without the consent of the owner. A licentiate, or the privilege to teach, must not be acquired by bribery. The masters are allowed to arrange with third parties a sort of insurance for their students and themselves. The masters of theology must be thirty-five years old, with previous study for eight years, and must themselves have attended lectures for five previous years. Lectures may begin at tierce (around 9 o'clock). Anyone violating these rules will be excommunicated, revealing the very natural relationship medieval man saw between the concern of the spirit and the concerns of the mind, unlike the emphasis of American spirituality.

A master usually taught for two periods a day. In the morning he usually read and dictated, as not everyone had books. In the afternoon sessions there were exercises by the students which consisted of discussions and reading of essays. Classes were not held on special holy days, which varied according to the veneration paid locally to the various saints. The same custom applied in the shops. The life of St. Edward, by a nun of Barking, tells us that a shop of needlewomen did not close down on one occasion for the holy day of Saint Edward. The women did not intend disrespect; they had much work to finish in haste. The result was a malady from which they all suffered. [Reason did not overcome the fear of a capricious deity, who takes offense at failure to fulfill the letter of the law.] It might be said conservatively that from one to two days were missed on an average of once a week, in addition to Sundays.

The students then loved holidays, just as they do now:

> The very young must not study all the time and be continually depressed in school — rather they will try to enjoy a spell of rest — it is a senseless life to be always miserable. So the students, in the rain of studies, knowing that the end of term is coming now, begin to applaud, saying to each

THE INTELLECTUALS AND THE CHURCH        61

> other, "Up and away! Let's not stay here! Our heads have
> ached quite long enough; the joys which existed long ago
> are restored; they have long been hidden from us. Now
> they lie before us, through the merits of the saints. So let
> us shout, all is holiday. Now indeed it does not waste
> away! We are ready to be off. Not a word about teachers!
> But be ready, lover, to delight in the delicate love of your
> lass." [8]

Discipline among all the clerks was very weak. Students' behavior and activities were supervised only by the masters. Their ultimate future depended upon their patrons at home; these patrons were mostly their bishops, who demanded their return home when they were needed. Of course, in the case of younger students, parents often retained authority. Those students who were monks owed obedience to their abbots. As the Middle Ages developed into the Italian Renaissance, the authority of the university's chancellor became more evident; but in the twelfth and early thirteenth centuries we may assume that the student clerk consulted with his master concerning his prayers. "Graduation" was a public defense of one or more theses in one of the churches, usually of an afternoon, which was followed by a dinner. The new master might now teach a few classes, then he would go home to hold a job. In sketching this procedure, bear in mind the steps taken by Gerald the Welshman in 1179.

*Employment Practices*

Vast numbers of students did not "graduate" formally from the universities, but wound up exercising other talents. Bishop Jacques de Vitry, early in the thirteenth century, tells of three students who were on their way to Paris:

> I remember when I was at Paris that three young men from
> Flanders came there to study. Along the road they inquired
> of one another what each intended to do. One of them
> replied: "I want to work hard and study to be a master
> in Paris." Another said: "I want to be steeped in letters
> so that afterwards I can become a monk in the Cistercian
> Order." But the third one said: "I want to become an

---

[8] Bibliothèque Nationale MS. lat. 17509.

impresario (*organizator*), and actor." Now it turned out for each one just as he had intended in his heart. With my own eyes I saw the first student as one of the great teachers of Paris in the Arts; the second one heard theology for some time and became not only a monk but one of the great spiritual abbots of the Cistercians — the wish of each of them having been gratified by the Lord. The third one, with the Devil's help, became a wandering buffoon, a minstrel and organizer, shamelessly intruding at other peoples' tables and refusing to work. To each it was given according to his wish and his deserts. [9]

[In passing we might raise the question as to whether de Vitry understood or appreciated the role of the jester or buffoon in medieval society. He identified this student's ambition with the "help of the Devil," but actually the task of the jester was to make evident the incongruity and ambiguity that lies behind all life and to call the members of society to task amidst their presumption of rank and material wealth. The jester used humor to foil human pride, and while this could be in terms of the obscene or frightening dimensions of existence, it also could convey a sharp sense of the sacred. The jester played a role of almost institutionalized "risk," turning the society and its players upside down, in order that its members might not become captured in the univocal structures of their neat little worlds.]

Even those young who studied diligently were often unhappy in securing positions. There were no contracts, and no appeal beyond patronage. Deception could come from surprising quarters. Here is another tale told by Jacques de Vitry:

I have heard of a certain English prelate who, when he returned from Rome exhausted and without funds, reached a certain Lombard town where he was lodged in the house of a very rich man whose son was a clerk. A great dinner was prepared, although the bishop did not have the money to pay for it. The bishop invited his host to sit beside him at the table, and at the end of a month, according to his directions, a messenger came to him feigning to be arrived from England with a letter. This message related that the treasurer of the church had died. The bishop read this

---

[9] *Ibid.*

letter aloud before everyone, and he seemed quite sad. A little later he called the son of his host, whom he commended for liberality. He stated that this post was worth more than 200 sterling marks. He said he would award him this prebend. The father rejoiced exceedingly over this. When the table was cleared away, he kissed the feet of the prelate and said: "Lord, I have heard that you need money; I do not wish my son whom you are about to take with you to be a burden." He gave him 500 marks, at the same time accommodating him with a thousand pounds *tournois*. But when the clerk came to England and found the treasurer still living, he was in great confusion over loss of the prebend and his father's money, and he returned home grieving. [10]

A clerk, when he had studied satisfactorily for a proper length of time, usually twelve years, might become a monk, a teacher, a practising canon lawyer, or a chancellor for some important man, possibly even the King. Such clerks as this could "know too much." When Richard I succeeded his father, Henry II, he dispensed with the royal clerks who had been around his father: Peter of Blois, Gerald the Welshman, Walter Mapes, and a number of others. I suspect that Chrétien de Troyes was a chancellor, or secretary, to Marie, Countess of Champagne. These chancellors' posts demanded much strenuous travelling at the will of the overlord, in return for the privilege of being privy to power. The best of all posts was a living, in which the clerk became a parish priest, responsible for the cure of souls.

There were also other opportunities. As we have seen, an unstudious clerk might become a minstrel. If he had the wherewithal, he could acquire a parish with an income from tithes and from this money pay someone else to perform the active duties of a priest. This assistant, still another option, would be his vicar. One could also attach oneself as a physician to some patron, if one's talent ran to medicine. I suspect that young clerks who had not progressed very far with their books often were employed by prosperous burghers, as secretaries, to read, write, and cipher. In the Conversation Book of one Coyfurelly (ca. 1300) the guest, when departing from a night's lodging, calls out: "Call me the clerk," ("Huchiez

---

[10] *Ibid.*

moi le clerc"). He needed a clerk to count his money and reckon what he owed.

There must have been considerable crossing over from the clerical status to that of knight or serjant, and from cleric to burgher. Saint Bernard was one of a great number who fulminated against this.

> A man that puts the army before his clerical status, secular business before the Church, certainly proves that he prefers human things to divine, and earthly to heavenly things. Is it more dignified to be called seneschal than deacon or archdeacon? It is — but for a layman, not for a deacon.[11]

In these remarks St. Bernard is thinking of Stephen of Garlande, who followed his brother as seneschal of the court of Louis VI. While he was seneschal, he was also Archdeacon of Notre Dame and Dean of Orleans. Peter of Blois had much the same thing to say about clerks going into business. In each instance these delinquents must have been fairly advanced in their ecclesiastical status. We doubt that many people noticed when thousands of small clerics, not well advanced, crossed over to civil status. As has always been the case since the beginning of mankind, a certain amount of "pull" from friends at court was required in order to make swift advancement. Those who were impatient found it more agreeable to try something else. Academic excellence then, as now, was no assurance of rapid advance. Perhaps some form of "civil service" could have been the answer, as it was in Imperial China, where officials attained their status as a result of successful standing in the great imperial examinations. This system was the nearest approach to virtue in a situation of this kind. A boy could become a governor because he knew and could write to perfection from the Four Books and the Five Classics.

When a clerk served a master, he was dependent upon pay, board, and keep as it suited his overlord. When he labored actively in a parish or other purely ecclesiastical office he received tithes as granted to him by his bishop or, conceivably, by a lay patron. Every

---

[11] From a letter to Suger, Abbot of St. Denis, in Samuel J. Eales and Dom John Mabillon, *Life and Works of St. Bernard, Abbot of Clairvaux* (London: John Hodges, 1889), I, 285-86.

Christian in good standing was obliged by ecclesiastical law to give one tenth of all the produce of his land and other property. These tithes went, technically, to the priest of the parish where the lay patron was supposed to receive his sacraments. There, by virtue of order from the bishop, church council, and others, the tithes were divided into equal parts: one to the parish priest, one to the bishop, and another for alms, or charity. Sometimes the tithe was split four ways. The bishop, and sometimes a lay patron, had the right to assign these tithes to an individual. The priest's share would go as a living to the rector of the parish. The bishop's share might be paid to an outside individual or to various groups. As we have already said, a cleric could be the tithe recipient when he himself did no pastoral work. In this case he would pay a vicar for this service from a share of his tithe, keeping for himself the remainder.

This practice could bring on many abuses, but it also made it possible for some men of genius to devote themselves to great works elsewhere while receiving a living from their tithes. [Our reaction to this is probably conditioned in part by the Puritan work ethic: "an honest day's pay for an honest day's labor." What we forget is that behind this lies a radical individualism, which was not characteristic of the medieval man. Although his doctrine of the self was that of the monadic soul (see Chapter Nine), his pattern of life was influenced by a strong sense of community membership and loyalty. One participated in the goodness of this life, which was our common heritage, without too much concern about "keeping books" or who earned what. Bookkeeping was the obsession of the sixteenth century, not the twelfth or thirteenth.]

*Religious Communities*

Until this moment I have had little to say about the clergy regular: the monks, canons regular, and the nuns. The clergy regular are characterized by the fact that when they are fully admitted they take the oath of poverty, another of absolute obedience to their superiors, and almost always an oath of chastity. These vows meant strict discipline, which was almost entirely lacking in other medieval organizations. This discipline was the main reason for their superior efficiency [although to say this might be a judgment from the perspective of the Puritan ethic].

Hermits, or anchorites, had existed in the early Eastern church: some were individuals who lived alone in a desert or forest, commonly sealed up in a cell with only one window. They continued to exist in small numbers in the West down into the Middle Ages. Saint Benedict (sixth century) was, of course, the great authority who established monasticism in the better Western form that bespoke the practical Roman spirit. He taught moderation rather than extreme asceticism when he founded his order at Monte Cassino in Italy. He made their life coenobitic rather than hermitic. The inmates of a house were to live as a devout family of men with the abbot as their father. The waking hours were given up to worship and to labor, mostly manual. Pope Gregory I was a Benedictine, a fact which did much to promote the early growth of the order, along with the spirit of accomodation to the natural man that always characterized Western medieval Christianity.

The early dress of the monks was that of the humble peasants in the fields: a long gown of undyed wool, with a hood that came over the head, boots for heavy outdoor work, and a belt that went around the waist. [Contrary to pre-Vatican II, modern monasticism, medieval religious communities did not affect peculiar garb for its own sake. Their dress was practical and ascetical.]

Since their beginning they were devoted to preserving books, liturgy, and education, although this was far from easy. Reforms were periodically necessary. Early in the tenth century the best known reformers were organized; the Cluniacs. The separated monasteries of their order remained priories, and they all acknowledged the one abbot, the Abbot of Cluny. They had special appreciation for the finer types of learning, and a renaissance of letters spread abroad after their influence. They were known as the Black Monks. In turn another reform, a reaction against them, resulted in the formation of the Cistercian order, a still more ascetic type that began in 1098. [The spiritual life of medieval man was, as in all men, an ebb and flow of enthusiasm and institutionalization. The utility of the medieval society perhaps reveals itself in its ability to maintain this dynamic without fragmentation as occurred later.]

After the eleventh century, a less cloistered rule came into being, called the Rule of St. Augustine. Those who followed it lived in communities, but their restrictions were lighter, enabling them to practice the great professions: management of farms, maintenance of hospitals, and teaching of students. Again, the pragmatic nature of medieval spirituality revealed itself. The Augustinians were referred to as Canons Regular, or Augustinian Canons. They did not include women, so that where, let us say, a hospital cared for the sick of both sexes, the women who were associated with the Augustinian Canons were most often under the Rule of St. Benedict. Other canons regular were organized following the Augustinian Rule, chief among these was the Order of Premontré, or the Premonstratensian Canons, who, living mostly in the Champagne forests, sought to convert the Jews.

Groups of mendicant friars began to form in the twelfth century, culminating in the founding (in 1209 and 1215) and later development of the Franciscan and Dominican orders. At their origin, these religious folk did not have religious houses. They intentionally moved among the people, conforming to the ways of the poor, begging, and relaxed in fasts and liturgical observances. Many of the friars were not in order as high as the diaconate; hence they could not preach. They made up for their lack of cloister organization by a tightly centralized organization of their own. Most of these orders arose in the thirteenth century: the Franciscans, the Dominicans, the Carmelites, and the Augustinian friars (to be distinguished from the monks, discussed above).

The Carthusians, founded in 1084 by St. Bruno, are the only true monks (attached to a monastery) who do not descend from the Benedictines. Each Carthusian monk lives a semi-hermitic life and rarely meets with the others, as they are devoted to contemplation. Their monastery is known in English as a Charterhouse.

Orders of cloistered nuns corresponded to almost every one of the cloistered orders of monks. They are called second orders, the monks themselves being primary. The tertiary orders are groups of laymen, beginning with the tertiaries of St. Francis, who practice certain religious rules without the binding ones of celibacy and strict obedience.

These monastic orders, except for the tertiaries, were all of the clergy, but they had differing grades of rank, just as do members of the nonclerical society. These were lay brothers, clerics in lower orders, deacons and priests. Some were closely cloistered, some less so; but they had, in addition, taken the vows of poverty, chastity, and strict obedience, which set them apart by virtue of their discipline. Many practicing seamen were monks, as were many teachers, many farmers who were in charge of abbey farms, and many distinguished men of science and letters. However, they were despised somewhat as being "scab labor." Some of the communities, which were most productive in manufacture and agriculture, paid no tithes. They had their own parish churches and did not need to support the administration of the sacraments given by the secular clergy.

[The interlocking taxonomies of religious communities and their various orders, which in turn related to the secular world and its various degrees, were a visible reminder to medieval man that God's world was arranged in a marvelous hierarchy. In the non-corporeal sphere this was also embodied for him by the nine orders of angelic being, as described by Dionysius the pseudo-Areopagite. Medieval man was a popular Platonist. Earth and society mirrored the divine order of things.]

Alas, sin also entered in. There were legions of "naughty monks" who were absent from their monasteries without leave and who were leading very irregular lives. Irregular young monks flocked to university towns. They often sought shelter in brother houses and there was no police gazette to keep track of their gross misbehavior or of their previous excommunication. An obnoxious local highwayman could be a "monk" in ill repute. Eustaches, or Huistasces li Moines, was an "admiral" who served both John and Philip Augustus. He was considered a practitioner of the black arts by many, but he was mostly very clever. His departure from the monastery was due to some slight, imaginary or real.

We appreciate solemnly the piety and the fervor for God's work in such monks as St. Bernard, St. Hugh of Lincoln, Samson of Bury Saint Edmunds, and many thousands of souls similarly devoted; but there were, to be sure, some *bons vivants* who did no particular honor to their cloisters. They could be very amusing. Such a character undoubtedly was the Monge (Monk) of Montaudon. He was a humorous, mocking poet writing in Provençal. From an allusion in one of his poems, *car se dinz Acre's coillis*, we may assume that he flourished at the time of the Third Crusade (1187-92). He wrote an *enueg*, listing things he did not like:

> I am much annoyed by a talkative person when he is not much of a lover, and by a man who is always wanting to

## THE INTELLECTUALS AND THE CHURCH 69

kill somebody else, and by a horse that pulls on his rein. And I am still more disturbed by a young fellow who sports a shield that has received no blow — also by a bearded chaplain or monk, and by a flatterer with a good sharp tongue. I consider a lady annoying when she is very proud while poor, and also a husband who is too fond of his wife, even if she be the countess of Toulouse. I am bothered particularly by a knight who puts on airs while away from home — when in his own town he has no job except to pound up pepper in a mortar or to stand by the hearth. And I am disturbed beyond words by a foxlike man who carries a banner [meaning he has a following of other knights], and I don't like a poor hawk on the river bank and too little meat in a large pot. I don't care, either, for too much water in a few drops of wine. When first thing in the morning, I see a one-armed man or a blind one, it does not please me to travel along with him. I am annoyed by a long piece of music, and by meat that is tough. And I don't like to see a bad man in too great comfort, nor do I wish to run along a road when there is ice, or to flee away on a horse which is armoured.

It distresses me, by my eternal life, to eat without a fire when it is wintry everywhere — and to lie abed with an elderly female in a cold wind. It bores me and disturbs me when a pot-washer asks too many questions. I do not care for an ill-humoured husband when I note that he has a pretty wife and that he does not give me a chance at her. I surely do not like a very bad fiddler in a fine court, and a stingy fellow with a little land, or a poor lender in a game of dice. I do not like either a double fur lining in a mantle, or divided ownership in a castle, or a rich man with too little merriment, and when one uses a dart or a javelin in a simple tourney.

I am most offended, so help me God, by a long table with a short towel, and a man who cuts before you with scabies on his hands, and a coat of armor with heavy links. It bothers me to be in a port when it rains and the weather is very bad. Quarrel between friends is annoying when I know they are arguing over nothing.

And I will tell what troubles me particularly: an old slut who adorns herself too much... and a young fellow who keeps gazing at his own legs. I do not care for a fat woman whose private parts are too flat, or an overlord who thunders about and cannot sleep when he is sleepy. There is nothing worse than this in the world.

It troubles me, too, to ride a horse in the rain without a cloak, and to find in my horse's stall a pig which has emptied the horse's feeding trough. I do not care for a saddle when the pommel moves all around, or a brooch without a tongue, or a bad man in his own house who says and does nothing but evil.[12]

This poor fellow was bothered mostly by cold, perhaps he had thyroid trouble. [Otherwise, he revealed typical medieval viewpoints concerning table manners, sexuality and marriage (love has nothing to do with the latter, and perhaps not even the former), clothing, and persons of rank. It is a delightful passage, more honestly earthy than equivalent contemporary prose, yet revealing human foibles well known to us all.]

Before further discussing life in a monastery, we must describe the lay-out of the buildings. These establishments differ greatly in size. There were the vast foundations, such as Bury St. Edmunds, Cluny, Fountains Abbey, and small priories in which we may include such an establishment as Lianthony in Wales. For convenience we will remark in some detail on the Abbey of Cluny as reconstructed by Kenneth Conant for the last quarter of the twelfth century.[13]

The principal enclosure lay within a great battlemented wall. The main gate of St. Hugh led into the forecourt. The hospice for travellers was above the stable of St. Hugh. Another long stable structure parallel to it had lay brothers' quarters in the upper story. The Abott's palace was against the inner wall of this rear court. West of this cluster of buildings stood the great portal leading into the vast Abbey church. In this church, from the west entrance to the high altar, extended a succession of sixteen rows of columns, four columns to a row. The principal cloister of the Abbey, called the Cloister of Abbot Pontius, was against the south side of this church. One entered it from the Porta Galilea, which led out from the very center of the nave. Around the cloister, beginning at the north side, were chapter house, parlour, then, down the side, calefactory (warming room) and refectory (dining hall), with lavabo for

---

[12] A printed version of this verse may be found in R. T. Hill and T. G. Bergin, *Anthology of the Provençal Troubadors*, 2nd. ed. rev. (New Haven: Yale University Press, 1973), I, 140-42.

[13] See Kenneth J. Conant, *Cluny: Les églises et la maison du Chef d'ordre* (Mâcon: Impr. Protat Frêres, 1968).

hand-washing and a fountain in front of it; then along the south side were the storage cellar and atrium, which were behind the Abbot's palace. Adjacent to the cellar were the kitchens, the pantries, and the bakery. Along the south side of the huge refectory was the cloister of the novices; their novitiate was along the west side of this small cloister. A third cloister, of considerable size, was that of Notre Dame, on which faced the dormitories of the monks. The great infirmary hall was beyond, on a slant, with a gallery above the hall proper. The monks' cemetery was on the west side of the Chapel of Notre Dame.

It might be summarized, in brief, that there were six building clusters within the Abbey. In the forecourt and yard were the structures most often visited by people from the outside: then Abbot's quarters, the guest hospices, and the stables. West of this group stood the vast Abbey church, extending far back. The monks' living and working areas — assembly rooms, refectory, work rooms — were in the courts to the right of the church. The novices lived in a cloister area to the right of this principal cloister. Within the closure behind, to the east of the principal cloister were the dormitories and the cemetery; and behind all of this, at the east end, stood the infirmary, which housed not only the sick active inmates but also many elderly patrons of the abbey. It was a vast building, as large as the Abbey church, but also on a slant line. The cursory reader will wish to be reminded that the altar of a church was at the east end, which will make it easier to verify directions. Latrines for each structure were plentiful.

[When one thinks of the clear, ordered planning; the time it took to build such a place; and the relative permanence of such an establishment, we become readily aware of why medieval man thought of his world as a divinely ordered cosmos.]

A small priory, in turn, had its principal church, and then on its long south side a single cloister, along the east side of which were vestiary, treasury, perhaps library room, and the chapter-room. The refectory was on the entire south side. There were, of course, some variations, but there was enough convention here to give a general idea of all.

Medieval eyes were not as strained as ours are apt to be, but I doubt that there could have been much copying, and even reading, in the dim light that existed in most monastery rooms. I postulate, therefore, that much of the copying and reading which went on in a medieval monastery was actually performed under the open skies in the cloister, not far from the small room which was designated as the library. After visiting many famous medieval monastery libraries, that is the impression that I have been obliged to acknowledge.

The government of a large monastery is quite clear to one who reads Jocelyn's *Life of Abbot Samson of Bury Saint Edmunds*. The Abbot has full authority over everyone and everything, as allowed by law. The sacrist was the treasurer of the Abbey while the subsacrist controlled expenditures. The cellarer, who had charge of the housekeeping and of the entertainment of nonclerical guests was on equal footing with the sacrist, and often they were in dispute with each other. He usually had a law court of his own where he tried those guilty of economic offenses. The prior was the abbot's representative. When necessary he had a subprior and the third prior under him. The precenter directed the music and the schools. There were a number of masters. Under the cellarer was the guestmaster, who had charge of the guest house. The pittancer and almoner had charity duties. There was a physician and an *infirmarius*, who managed the infirmary. In the library was a master of the ambry and a custodian of books. There was a novice master who had direction of the professed novices in training.

We assume that young boys whose relatives sought to place them in the monastery were accepted by the abbot and then assigned to the novice master, who directed their schooling until they were permitted to profess or take their monastic vows. They were then assigned positions in the choir, that is, the places in the choir procession which were assigned them on the right or left side, corresponding to their dates of profession; in all processions they maintained this order. The abbot's choir seat was on the right-hand side facing and farthest from the altar. The prior's place was directly across from the abbot's.

Various clerks who were not monks were employed as auditors and the like. In the eyes of the community these men were inferior to the monks. More menial duties were handled by lay brothers who had no position in the choir. The abbot and the cellarer in their justice courts often had to deal with true laymen, peasants, knights, and burghers. These people came under civil law and were not clerical. Their cases would be handled by a lay official, an *avoez*. In Marie de France's lay, *Guigemar*, the somewhat elderly husband of Guigemar's lady-love, is an *avoez*.

The position assumed by a religious house in a community varied with the amount of land it owned and the kind of commerce in which it was involved. Abbeys and priories operated grist mills, they maintained large farms, and had markets for the sale of goods. But above all, they managed the distribution of charity among the poor and needy. The task of laying out the dead, to judge from such authors of the time as Chrétien de Troyes and Marie de France, was assumed by these orders. The convents, of course, were administered along much the same lines of guidance, although the abbess [normatively] had no right in the administration of sacraments [although there are clear instances where she had spiritual jurisdiction over priests]. For these matters each convent had its chaplains.

*The Libraries*

Because the monasteries, particularly the large ones, had books and libraries, it is only reasonable to assume that they furnished much of the material and the opportunity for literary and philosophical speculations. An historian of medieval thought should examine thoroughly all the catalogues of these early libraries. There were great cathedral libraries also. The catalogue of the books in the library of Lincoln Cathedral prepared by Hamo at the close of the twelfth century, is particularly helpful. The *studium generale* at Paris in the twelfth century included the abbeys of Saint Victor and Mont Sainte-Geneviève. Saint Victor was particularly rich in books. This library was described in a mocking way by Rabelais in his *Pantagruel*. The Franciscans and the Dominicans conducted important schools, notably at Paris in the thirteenth century, and must therefore have collected notable libraries.

We have already referred to the various colleges which began to be organized among the secular clergy beginning in the thirteenth century. Probably all of them had libraries. In present-day England these survive at Oxford and Cambridge. In France, the college and monastic libraries were plundered during the French Revolution; but there were many concerned people at the time who gathered up these manuscripts and saw that they were preserved in State collections such as the Arsenal. Some of the holdings of smaller churches were put into cathedral libraries at that time, for example, the books of the Count's Chapel of Saint Estienne, at Troyes, some of which are now in the library of the Troyes Cathedral.

## *The Secular Clergy*

When we write about the clergy and the state of the Church in the Middle Ages, the sources that we necessarily use are, for the most part, brisk stories, complaints about abuses, and descriptions of inadequacy. This kind of material is most common, to the point, and often it is all that we have to illustrate our discussions of the Middle Ages. We are reminded, however, of the words of one of the great news commentators of today, who said that many listeners complain that they hear nothing but bad news. He went on to add that bad news is always "news." News of success is not cogent, and often it is not very interesting. This sort of thing is equally true for those of us who comment graphically on the history and the life of early times. In reporting the operations of the Church and of the monasteries, our histories have too little good to say about them. I must remind readers that for the many clerks who did not do their work properly there were many, many others who performed their functions and deserve much praise. This was undoubtedly true of the vast body of parish priests who served as the sacramental instrument in the multitude of individual churches in the twelfth and thirteenth centuries. (We are using here a term which has expressive meaning among pastoral theologians.) These priests doubtless shared in most of the common foibles of their time, but they endeavored sincerely to bring the sacraments to their people.

One can catch a glimpse of the parish priest in his good work in some unexpected places. In the *Flamenca*, largely a flippant tale, we see the local priest in his church. He has one young clerk who assists him, who rings the bells, serves as acolyte, sweeps and cleans, and does all the lesser duties. This boy lives in an upper room near the bells. Guilhem, who has less praiseworthy intentions, takes his place. The mass in this small church is described in the proper order. Pax is given by the young clerk, who carries a copy of the

*Evangeli* through the congregation with the words, "The Lord be with you." He puts away the vestments after the people leave.

Certain fabliaux also describe the priest in his milieu. One is that of the Priest and the mulberries. A parish priest is riding his horse towards a rural church where he will be saying the evening hours — vespers and compline. His mount goes forward when he unwittingly says "Get up" as he reaches for some mulberries, and the beast is captured by Tibert the Cat and Renart the Fox. They go to church and recite the hours for him. In the fable of the priest who says the Passion, the priest has lost his bookmarks, and when he goes to say the Good Friday service for his peasant parishioners, he mixes up the order of prayers and versicles. Jacques de Vitry narrates many amusing mistakes about the parish priest Maugrinus in Paris, who does not know his Latin very well. The bishop often imposes fines upon him for this.

Gerald the Welshman leveled many criticisms against his superiors, notably the Archbishop of Canterbury. Archbishop Hubert Fitz Walter (d. 1305) was, however, a very effective man in his office. [He was a close confident of Richard I, becoming archbishop in 1293 and administering the kingdom as his justiciar from 1294, when the latter was off for four years in the French wars. He resigned as justiciar at one time (1298), only to be recalled because he was the only official capable of curbing the enthusiams and excesses of King John. There is no doubt that he, like many medieval prelates, was more a political success than a pastoral expert; but then he was not expected to be this kind of "shepherd."]

We can be reasonably certain that those myriads of small churches, of which one of the loveliest is that of Iffley, just outside of Oxford, functioned in a more or less faithful manner. Mass was early on days of obligation, and a little later on Sundays, just as the *Flamenca* describes for the little parish church in Bourbon. Because there was a scattered rural population, many of the churches were small and deep in the woods. [Congregations were natural communities *(Gemeinschaften)*, unlike the bureaucratic, large parishes *(Gesellschaften)* that developed in the West with the industrial revolution.] There is an amusing illustration of these small rural churches in *Vair Palefroi* (Piebald Palfrey), which is the most genteel of the fabliaux. The wedding of the old man and his young bride is to be held in a church that is deep in the forest. The bride is placed upon the horse, the palfrey in question, and is conducted by two mounted escorts to the church. The route was long and the hour was early. The escorts fell asleep, and the palfrey wandered on his own.

*Summary*

In conclusion I feel obliged to stress quite often that business and administration in the Middle Ages were not organized with efficiency in our modern sense except in the larger and better monastic orders and among certain banking interests mostly operated by Jewish families. The Jews had wider connections, largely through actual family unity, in the important centers. We can include under this last heading certain non-Jewish Italian families in the Mediterranean area.

A sure result of the lack of efficiency was a kind of easy-going balance between celestial aspiration and a practical *modus vivendi*. For example, a considerable amount of graft was tolerated. Graft exists today, of course, everywhere; but in our computer age it is a very ugly word, and any sign of such a thing must be stamped out with vigor. [The modern Puritan ethic, especially since the advent of business machines and sophisticated bookkeeping, has been applied with a vengeance.] We deplore that much of it still goes on in Oriental and African nations, with little understanding of the kind of personal ethic that exists there now as it did in the Middle Ages in Europe.

Little people have had to live in every period of mankind, and where the prevailing wages are insufficient, we must expect some profit-seeking on the side and in the dark. The full account of dealings of this kind cannot be well filled in from information coming to us from the Middle Ages; but a later detailed narrative, such as the *Diary* of Samuel Pepys is most revealing, and it is very clear that this much and more must have been prevalent at the time of the twelfth-century Renaissance.

[This undoubtedly brings us a long way from the intellectuals — the schoolmen, the monastics and friars, and even the secular clergy — whom we have discussed in these pages. It prepares the way for the next chapter on the peasants. It would be wrong, however, to conclude that any great "gulf" of worldview separated them. People lived together in a very intimate relationship in those days, and what went on in the monastery cloister or lecture hall was not that different in the final analysis from what transpired in the huts below the hill. What was different was the level of understanding of the common life they all shared.]

## IV

## THE PEASANTS

We will turn now from the contemplation of the class of man who best understood man's relations with God and the World Soul and consider the class which understood these things least of all — the peasants. Interesting to relate, peasants were constantly cited in terms of praise for their practical wisdom. Of the 2,000 extant proverbs in the Old French language the *Proverbes au vilain (Peasant Sayings),* preserved in six different manuscripts, have contributed proverbs to almost all the other collections. We are not concerned with whether these sayings were actually taken down from the peasants. It is the reputation of that class which concerns us. I am citing examples mostly from the *Proverbes au vilain* collection.[1]

The peasant says to his ploughboy: "The affection of a master is not permanent."[2] Fine singing is a bore (Mor. 239). Wine can do what water cannot (Mor. 1090). A poor man makes a poor argument (Mor. 1711). Everyone who has a tongue goes to Rome (Mor. 2964). If one has both bread and health he is rich if he does not know it (Mor. 2060). The temperature depends upon the season (Mor. 2250). A widow woman has no friend (Mor. 2470). An empty chamber makes a silly woman (Mor. 2500). A goat

---

[1] For the definitive edition of Old French proverbs, see Joseph de Morawski, ed., *Proverbes français anterieurs au XV<sup>e</sup> siècle* (Paris: E. Champion, 1925). Henceforth cited in the text of this chapter as Mor., followed by the number of the proverb cited.

[2] Marie de France, *Eliduc,* vv. 60-63, in *Les Lais,* ed. Ernest Hoepffner, CFMA (Strasbourg: Heitz, 1921).

scratches so much that he gets a bad lie (Mor. 2297). The penance should fit the sin (Mor. 2248). Rome was not made in a day (Mor. 2223). An intimate master makes a poor vassal (Mor. 1722). One who helps is not completely bad (Mor. 1385). He is no friend who leaves nothing (Mor. 1362). A tired ox walks softly (Mor. 1034). You will never see any one so generous as one who has nothing (Mor. 967). Two men full of pride cannot very well ride a single ass (Mor. 267). You cannot strip a naked man (Mor. 843).

Medieval peasants were poor, and had to rebuild from the beginning after every hostile force had passed by, burning their wooden houses and destroying fruit trees. They needed a wry wisdom.

## Types of Peasants

Peasants included the free peasant tenant and those who were serfs on the land of their overlord. The free peasant held a small fief for which he was obligated to give a rent to the master to whom he owed fealty. This rent could be paid by service in the master's fields, but often it was a semi-humorous duty which had to be rendered on rent day. For example, rent could be described as the steam from a roast chicken, dutifully delivered to the lord's Court. Most often payment was some sort of produce.

The Chronicler Geoffroi de Vigeois describes a certain peasant who delivered on rent day a requisite cartload of wax to the Viscount Ebles de Ventadorn. The peasant was drunk at the time. When he drove up to the castle he found the Count of Poitou, William IX of Aquitaine, the troubadour, paying a visit to Ebles. He whacked the wax barrel with his hatchet and cried: "Sire Conte, see how the great Ebles receives rent from *his* peasants!" The wax tumbled about. The Count was impressed, and so was Ebles. The peasant received a great reward for his nonchalance.

At times a free peasant did so well with his lands and his cattle that he became wealthy. He then had no onerous duties to perform, and he could enjoy some ease. This kind of rich peasant is even a type in medieval literature, for he is the kind of peasant who is able to marry a daughter of an impecunious knight. [3]

---

[3] An example of this sort of convoluted duties and payments systems: in the sixteenth century the land of Bartas in Gascony owed a knight's fee,

The offspring of such a union of convenience were not admired by the minstrels. In the *Romance Fergus,* the son of such a union is described as having base qualities from his father while being a not too proper baron from his mother's family. In the fabliau *Li Vilaine Mire* this situation is part of the basic plot. A peasant has taken to wife a poor knight's daughter, although he knows that he is a bit old and lacks charm. Thus he decides he will beat his young wife every morning and leave her weeping in order to keep the young pages away. In the evening, when he returns from the plough, he plans to make up, thinking all will be well. This procedure he repeats day after day, but the wife gets even. Some messengers from the king pass by looking for a celebrated doctor. The peasant's wife says that her husband is the doctor, but that he will not admit it. She emphasizes that he must be well beaten before he will admit his medical skill. The messengers, of course, cudgel the peasant most effectively. Molière found a version of this *fabliau* somewhere, and it forms the basis of his *Médecin malgré lui.*

The serfs were different from the free peasants. They were descended from families who lost their personal liberty during the ninth century, when every man in the fields sought protection from a powerful lord in return for the relinquishing of freedom of movement. Finally, the serfs were freed in France — at the close of the thirteenth century.

Our own observations of the serf's condition are drawn from the literature of the twelfth century and from the earlier part of the thirteenth. All serfs were obliged to remain on their lord's land. They were required to pay fees for almost any privilege: when they wished to marry off of the land, to move away, or indulge in trade on their own. The so-called *droit du seigneur,* if it were practised, stated that an overlord had the right to spend the first marriage night with a serf's bride. In Chrétien de Troyes' *Cligés* Jehan is a distinguished engineer who builds marvellous castles with many clever devices. Jehan remains, however, a serf.

Peasants and serfs often served in military capacities and were then known as *serjanz.* If a *serjant* distinguished himself in his lord's service he might be given a spot promotion without much

---

on the strength of which alone Guillaume de Salluste assumed the title of Guillaume du Bartas, raising his social status.

hesitation, and be graduated into a knight, or baron. The most celebrated case of this sort is that of the seneschal of Henry I of Champagne, who had never paid his fee for manumission from serfdom. He advised Count Henry not to give to a supplicant what the man did not have. Count Henry turned on him and reminded him that he was still technically a serf. In addition, he ordered the seneschal to pay at once his freedom fee, to be handed over to the supplicant who had asked for the favor.

The passing from one social class to another was greatly increased by the many free and serf peasants who were able to set up business in a nearby town and to become burghers. A wealthy overlord who was eager to establish a new town, for one reason or another called a *villeneuve*, would offer inducements to settle there. Many of the new merchants were tradesmen from other locales, but many also were certainly peasants beginning new business ventures. A lord could set up a clever serf with a *fenestra* (shop) arranging that the new merchant would give him a percentage of all he gained. A new merchant was, therefore, quite often a former serf.

An inevitable result of the rise of class mobility was that many plots of land granted in fief demanded only *serjant's* service to be paid to the overlord. Eventually a well-to-do individual might be obligated to pay a complicated series of services to his lord — both *serjant* fees and knight fees. However, one could always hire a young and impecunious knight or *serjant* to render knight's or *serjant's* service when required, for a good cash payment.

Another mode of egress from peasant status was through the clergy. Since it was not easy for a rural lord to secure the services of a priest for a chapel on his estate, a good way of getting around this was to send a serf's son to school, with the understanding that when the son was ordained he would return to his lord's land. This, however, could be contested, and it often was. Sometimes the state of ordination was ruled not to be inferior, and as a result the priesthood removed a young man from servile status. For example, a bishop of Paris who had been of serf status was succeeded by a priest of the baronial class. Thus the Church was a great leveller. Perhaps, even more interesting, a distinguished monk or friar need not even be concerned with the history of his family. Saint Bernard and Saint Hugh of Lincoln were of baronial origin, but the father of Abbot Samson of Bury St. Edmunds was a peasant.

## Peasants' Life

Various descriptions of a peasant's life exist, especially detailing the distinction between peasants and serfs, but we feel sure that the protagonist was in most of these instances a serf. Here is an amusing scene from the *Roman de Renart*.

> Renart the Fox had convinced Ysengrim the wolf that he was an English minstrel who had lost his *viele* (fiddle). Ysengrim said: "You know what you can do? Come with me; I know a peasant who has a *viele*. Every night his neighbors come to his house; he entertains his children with it. There is hardly a night that I don't hear him. By the faith which I owe St. Peter, it is a good *viele* and an expensive one. If you come to Court with me you shall have it at all costs." Then they start out and walk along happily. Dant Ysengrim tells Renart how Renart has done him shame; he tells him this in his good French. Renart answers him in bad English-French. Soon they come behind the house of a monk (the peasant's master), right near where Ysengrim could find the man with the *viele*. Into the peasant's yard they both entered. They were much afraid. They lay beside the wall and kept listening all evening. The peasant amused himself; but when sleep overcame him, he went to bed at once. Ysengrim pricked up his ears and looked and listened. There was a hole in the wall which he had known for a year. Through a split plank he saw the *viele* hanging on a nail. The peasant family snorted and snored noisily until they were all asleep. A big mastiff lay beside the fire. Near their shake-down he had made his place, almost touching the fire. But the shadow of the bed did not let him see Ysengrim. "Brother" says Ysengrim to the pretended minstrel, "wait for me here and I will go see how I can get hold of it." "You leave me all lone here?" whimpers Renart. "What, are you that kind of coward?" "Coward, no, but me afraid that in this country if I be alone I be carried off. That's why I scared!" Ysengrim heard this and laughed. His heart grew a little more tender and he said: "For God's love, I never saw a hardy minstrel, a brave priest, or a wise woman. When she has what she wants, then she wants what she is complaining about." Renart answered shamelessly: "Sir Ysengrim if that Renart fellow was here then may he be hanged

on a rope." "Let that be," says Ysengrim. "I know all the roads. You sit on the ground. I will go fetch the *viele*." Then he went straight through the window like one who knew exactly the situation. The fiddle was hanging by straps. That night they had forgotten to put it away. Ysengrim climbed up and jumped through the window opening; then he went straight to the spot where the *viele* was hanging. He took it down and passed it out to his companion, who put it around his neck. Renart began to think how he could ruin Ysengrim. "I'll fix him" he said, "no matter what may happen." He went over to the window and pulled out the stick that propped open the shutter and Ysengrim was shut inside. He thought the window had closed of its own accord and he was much afraid for his life. He jumped against the shutter and because of the noise the peasant awoke. He sprang up astounded; his wife screamed, and so did the children. "Up with you. There are thieves in here." The peasant jumped and according to custom blew up the fire. When Ysengrim saw him at the fire he drew back a little, then seized him by the buttocks. The peasant shrieked; the mastiff was aroused; he grabbed Ysengrim by the testicles and removed what he could. Ysengrim still had a hold on the peasant's rear end but his heart was not in it, and he himself was in great pain. The man yelled for his neighbors, his relatives, and his cousins. "Help me, by God in Heaven! Devils are in here."

Through the open door Ysengrim saw many neighbors with axes and clubs, running in the street. He made a jump between the wall and the peasant, pushing the man so hard that he fell flat into a puddle. The wolf sprang out on all four feet, not knowing where to find his friend. He fled from the peasants. The man had fallen deep into the mud and was almost submerged. He was pulled out with great difficulty but was not well for a month. [4]

The passage above describes most graphically the set-up of a poorer peasant, probably a serf, who lives in a community behind a manor house. He has only one window with a hanging shutter, supported by two straps, and held open by a stick. His fireplace burns in some way nearly always. There are few furnishings, the most obvious of which is a flop bed for all the family before the fire. At the front door is a hollow worn spot where feet over a long

---

[4] *Le Roman de Renart,* ed. Ernest Martin (Strassburg: Trübner, 1882-87), Ib, vv. 2466-2596.

interval of time have worn a deep hollow in the earth. This is always full of dirty water. A fierce dog, of course, also lives here.

[The picture is not one, however, that makes us think of poor, persecuted serfs from old Robin Hood films. The serf has a *viele*, he does have family life, a fear of being robbed, and a will to fight back. There is an integrity in the character of this serf.]

The well-known Chentecler tale in the *Roman de Renart* describes a more prosperous peasant, who had a chicken yard. Renart happened to be coming near a town:

> The town was situated in a wood. There were lots of hens, cocks, ducks, mallards, ganders, and geese. The owner, Constans des Noes, was a peasant who was well provided. He dwelt near his enclosure *plesseiz*. His house was full of hens and capons; it had everything: salt meat, bacon and sides of hogs. The peasant was rich in wheat. His house was good. His garden was well stocked; there were good cherry trees and fruits of various kinds: apples, etc. There Renart often went for pleasure. The garden was well enclosed by oak pales, sharpened at the top and thick. It was further guarded by hawthorn vines.
>
> Dant Constans had put his chickens in there for protection. Renart made his way with head lowered. He had strong intentions, but the thorns turned him away from his intent, and he could get nowhere by crouching or springing. Much was he agitated and he moved his tail. He figured that if he jumped and landed from above he would be seen by the hens and they would crouch under the thorns. He went along lifting his head; at the bend in the hedge he saw a broken pale. He pushed it in; there where the pale was broken the peasant had planted cabbages. The fox went down in a heap but the hens perceived him when he dropped and they proceeded to flee. In a path beside the wood, between two pales, under the loop hole Master Chantecler had drawn himself up.[5]

Here is another passage from the tale of the Fox and the Raven:

> Dant Tiecelins the raven, who had been hungry all day, did not want to remain still. He left the wood of necessity and came sailing towards an enclosure, anxious to make an

---

[5] *Ibid.*, II, vv. 26-85. It is somewhat difficult to picture this loop hole and the pales, but I have made a careful translation from the original.

attack. He saw a thousand cheeses which were put to dry in the sun. The woman who was supposed to guard them had gone in the house. Tiecelins saw that it was time to get something and he made a swoop, snatching a cheese. The old woman then jumped out into the street, saw Tiecelin, and threw after him pebbles and stones. She cried: "Vassal, you will not get away with it." "Old woman," say he, "you can say that I am carrying it off whether that be right or wrong. I had a good chance to take it. A bad watcher feeds the wolf." [6]

These enclosures made with pales sharpened at the top must have dotted the rural landscape almost everywhere. They served as horse corrals, chicken yards, and surrounded gardens as well as little houses. In the *Yvain*, when the girls find Yvain asleep naked in the woods, one of them is sent back by her mistress with clothing and ointment. "Her horses she puts in an enclosure (*pleissié*) where she ties them up very strongly." [7] Obviously, thievery was a problem and there were no police. But there was also enough prosperity for something to be stolen — even from the peasants.

The dwelling of a well-to-do peasant farmer is not completely describable by any of us. Such a farmer must not have lived a life greatly different from a baron who also was engaged in farming his land. [Again, we must remind the reader not to make too arbitrary a distinction between overlord and peasant. A king's palace was not that much more comfortable than a serf's dwellings.]

Of course, no wooden houses have survived the age. We must draw our picture of prosperous medieval dwellings from the stone country houses which are still visible. One of these is preserved at Donnington-le-Heath, just outside Leicester in England and has survived in rather excellent condition. [8] It was a rather large house of a peasant farmer of some wealth, built towards the end of the thirteenth century, in 1284. This house helps us judge how the peasant of that time lived.

---

[6] *Ibid.*, vv. 852-88.
[7] Chrétien de Troyes, *Yvain*, vv. 2984-85, in *Christian von Troyes...*, ed. Wendelin Foerster, vol. 2 (Halle: Niemeyer, 1887).
[8] The local County Council is working to put this remarkable dwelling into shape.

A timber house could not be built more than one story high until the carpenters of the time developed a mortice and tenon joint that could hold safely the weight of an upper floor. Such a device probably was first designed for a siege engine — a movable tower — which could be pushed against a city wall, allowing the men on the upper platform to climb on to the wall. [War so frequently brings about inventions that are later put to less violent and more constructive use.] We know for certain that this carpentering feat was accomplished by the twelfth century — and then it must have spread everywhere in western Europe. There is a portrayal of a look-out wooden tower on the Bayeux Tapestry, so it is probable that this problem was solved, in a way, even in the last quarter of the eleventh century. The wooden ceiling and roof structures that we have surviving today from these early times are mostly in tithe barns and market buildings. There are a few ceiling timbers surviving from the twelfth century in bishops' halls, such as those at Hereford and Farnham.

A large manor house in wood or stone consisted of a central hall (the *palatium*), which had two rows of columns dividing the floor area into a nave, and two side aisles. At one end were two doors: one into an outside kitchen and the other into a shed where the bottles were kept (the buttery). These were the service doors. In an early structure in England the fireplace was usually in the center of the floor and there was a smoke hole above in the ceiling timbers. This feature was retained quite late by Germanic peoples. The Continental people, notably the French, preferred much earlier a fireplace built of big stones against a wall. An exit door was at the end of the aisle opposite the service doors from which one could get easily to the chamber, or chambers above (in a chamber building) where the inhabitants slept and stored their belongings. In the better type of house this chamber structure was entered by a stairway leading up from the hall floor.

A chamber building was apt to have two floors, and the principal chamber would be on the upper floor. A storage room of some kind, perhaps a wardrobe, with chests around the wall for clothing, or a work room where sewing and weaving were done, would be on the first floor. A manor house combined the hall and chamber building and was obviously the dwelling of the more wealthy. It was set in the centre of a large enclosing court which was surrounded by a high palisade with an outer moat that was usually dry. The palisade was a revetment against a low embankment which surrounded the manor set-up. Inside this courtyard, continuing around the embankment and its palisade, was a series of sheds. One was a stable, another a storage shed, another a place for washing, perhaps an infirmary, an outdoor oven, a kitchen, and a buttery (in an appropriate position away from the service doors of the main hall), and so on. Adam dou Petit Pont wrote an account in which he returns to his parent's dwelling and describes the manor and the circular row of service sheds around the rim of the palisade. A strong wooden gate which had a draw bridge for crossing the outer moat opened into the manor. Sometimes a *phala* or low wooden tower for containing weapons of some kind was also attached to a manor dwelling. [Protection was always prominent in people's minds. It must have been like life on the American frontier, where everyone was his own law.]

From what we have quoted from the *Roman de Renart* we assume that lesser peasants lived in rows on what we might call a *ruga* or street. Their huts were close together within their lord's protection. In Jehan Renart's *Escoufle* (c. 1225) an old peasant woman lives with her daughter in a lean-to against the master's barn, over which she has supervision.

As just seen, there were many kinds of peasants: some with independent wealth were almost like small farming barons while others occupied a hut in a row of similar houses, along a muddy road and close to the lord's own manor complex. One peasant might even have a lean-to against a larger building. The siding of such houses was made of battens applied perpendicularly. The chinks were filled with daub and wattle, though holes were not uncommon. A window could have only a hanging shutter before it, propped open by a stick. Fires in these communities were undoubtedly plentiful; but not much was required to rebuild, for labor was communal.

*The Furnishings and Dress of the Peasants*

There is in existence a rather charming list of the tools and equipment which a peasant should have before taking a wife. It applies, we expect, to the middle class of peasant — probably the prosperous serf. He has duties to perform on his overlord's land;

but he seems to be occupying a farming patch, apart from a crowded community. This list, usually referred to as *L'oustillement le vilain* (the equipment of a peasant) I shall translate almost in its entirety. It is a precious record of the daily life of a peasant.

    A peasant who is about to marry will be much blamed if he is not properly provided with the necessaries. He must have a house, a grain shed (*bordel*) and a hay barn (*buiron*). He must have wood for the fire, tools for digging, and bacon for a party (*feste*). Every morning he should go to the spring for a full *buire* (pitcher) of water. If he drinks enough of this he will not get drunk. A man who is often drunk cannot keep his belongings. The peasant will need beans, cabbages, turnips (*raves*), garlic and leeks, scallions and onions; he must have a tub for bathing, a cart for hauling, a carter's saddle, neck band ((*forrel*), saddle strap (*dossiere*, in which the shafts fit), breeching (*avaleoire*), trace (*trais*), breeching strap, horse cloth, and reins (*meneoire*), pot-hook of iron, and a *craisset* lamp in winter. He needs also a trivet, a saucepan, a big andiron, a pot and its ladle, where the pot herbs murmur away, the grill, and the meat hook to pull the meat out so that it may not burn. He needs tongs and a bellows to blow up the fire, a mortar, and a mill — a pestle. So is it necessary for him to have an axe, sharp and with a handle, a planing hatchet (*doloire*), and a chisel freshly sharpened, a double tanged mattock (*besague*), a drill to make holes, a tool to make a mortice both in stone and in wood; a plumb line and a compass. [This is not said jokingly.] He must have also a fish spear (*foisne*), and a scraper (*roisne*) a small knife (*canivet*), a device for fishing, and a basket to hang from his neck in which fish can be placed when there are a lot of them.

    The peasant must have also arms to guard his land, a mail coat (*coterele*), a helmet, a club (*maçuele*) and a stick (*gibete*) shaped like a crook, a bow, a lance, and a sword in case of a fight. A rusty sword should be at the head of the bed, and there should be no foolishness or haste in using it. A man can be killed very quickly, no matter who is right or wrong, by a small arrow (*saietele*). This sort of fighting is not good for a small occasion. The peasant must have an old shield hanging on the wall. Even if it is not new and freshly ornamented it is nonetheless sufficient protection. He must hang it around his neck to defend his land. But take care it is not used sooner in exercise; for he is foolish who would strike the first blow.

Some are quick at this who would do just as well if they were last.

The peasant should also be careful to return on time to his house, and his dog should be so trained that he will not bark at night if he does not have a reason. This countryman should have chests (*huches*), baskets and earthen pitchers — and a cat to catch mice to defend the chests. There should be a bench before the fire and a table to be set up for eating; there should be a cheese safe (*chasier*) strung up on high near the rafters for keeping cheese, and a ladder to get up to it; also a trivet (*trepier*), and a cauldron in which to make one's gruel when it is the proper time in Lent and in Advent. In March let him have gathered enough willow sticks (*withes*) for attaching to the harrow. A goad for sticking the ox should not be forgotten, and he must carry, if he is wise, behind his crupper a hook knife or a little sickle for trimming the willow sticks, when he has need, and a spade or steel hatchet to root up bushes. Let everything be done for gain, and he will be a wise man. If he needs a harrow (*herche*), a handbarrow, a weeding hoe (*sarcel*) or a pruning knife (*fesche*), to remove thistles, let him have them. He will want a sickle, an awl, a curry comb, a bread knife, a steel cleaver (*jarce*) whet stone (*keus*) and a steel for putting an edge on his tools. He needs sharp needles, cutting scissors, shoes, boots (*estivaus*) [these were high-shoes or buskins], leg coverings (*chauces*) and boot tops (*housiaus*), a *cote* and a *surcote*, a hood, and a hat, a belt, and a knife case, a bag (*borse*), and an alms-purse (*ausmonoere*). He must have mittens (*moufles*) with lots of leather, freshly made, against thorns when he is serving his overlord by making a hedge all around his house. He will need a sieve and strainer, suspended by a thong. He must have a bed frame to lie on and a kneading trough (*met a pestrir*). He requires an oven and fire-rakes.

In case his beard is singed he must make no fuss. He should be of good mien and make good cheer, for any trade is good when one can gain by it. If he requires a salt box, and behind his fire a malt drying bin, he should not mind storing these up. He must be ready to lend to a neighbor when need arises. Pestles and a mortar he ought not to hold lightly; a sack, a bushel measure, a flail, and a rake, a pick, a wedge, and a shovel. If his house has all these, he will certainly be able to help his overlord. Yes, by my head, it would be troublesome for him without these. If he does not have them he will have to go find them. Drinking cups (*hanas*) deep plates (*escueles*), platters (*pla-*

*tiaus*) and basket containers, large jars and small are needed. When these are cracked do not throw them away, for that would be silly.

The father, before a child is born, should have plenty of cloths and straw. If the child is a boy (*vallet*) let him look for a tub (*auget*) in which the child can be bathed all stretched out, and he will grow up the quicker. When it is a little girl (*baisselete*) get her a smaller basin (*minette*) for that is best (*la maistrie*). And, if he wishes, let him find a cow with milk which he can use without delay to nurse the child when it is needed. For if the child is not appeased, it will cry all night and prevent others from sleeping when they lie down — and the next day they must do work (*l'ouvraigne*).

That is why I say that fools should be forewarned by what the wise say. A man who marries, if he has not the proper equipment, will never be considered prudent. He who can only take has nothing to lend. But it is true that he has no worry about a thief who may break into his house, or who may take from him by some device. For that reason I am not going to try to have anything!!! [9]

This somewhat witty little piece is more than just a list of daily-life tools. There is philosophy of a kind as to what is best. It obviously shows a spirit of self-reliance unlike anything we know today, but also an accompanying lack of social control. One should not be too ready with "edged tools."

The lines on child care, especially the part concerning the need for supplementary feeding, are most interesting. An excellent idea of the care and the accoutrements which could, if necessary, be given to a new-born infant among the well-born is seen in Marie de France's *Lai Milon*. In it an infant is being carried on horseback to its aunt, who lives far away in Northumberland. The party stops seven times every twenty-four hours, and each time attendants remove the swaddling clothes, bathe the infant and have it fed by a wet nurse. They then put on fresh swaddling clothes and continue. This is not unlike the sort of care which infants received still a few years ago and now once more after a generation of attending to the

---

[9] A discussion by Urban Nyström and a printing of the two manuscript versions of the poem, are to be found in "L'oustillement au villain," *Soumalaison Tiedeakatemian Toimituksia: Annales Academiae Scientiarum Fennicae*, ser. B, 46 (1940), 51-71.

child whenever it cries. We may assume the practice among the peasants was the same.

The dress of country people, whether they were free peasants or serfs, must have been influenced by their conditions of work. The peasant man is featured in many a low relief carving. He wore a *gonne*, a sleeved garment fitting over the head, usually of undyed wool, which came just above the knee, and he had a belt of some kind. The belt buckle would seldom be of metal. On one end of the leather would be a slit and on the other a thong with knots at short intervals. The wearer of such a belt hooked the proper knot into the slit, and this held very well. There could be a tie belt, of coarse cloth. The sleeves of the *gonne* were quite loose, extending to below the elbow. A *chaperon* or hood was worn and we infer from extant carvings that this was not attached to the *gonne*. The lower part of this hood lay along the top of the shoulders and the hood was usually pulled up over the head. A wide brimmed hat was often worn as a protection against sun while in the fields, or moving about much in the open. A peasant's legs were most often wrapped with coarse woolen cloth and this wrapping was held tightly in place by a long strip of leather which was cross-gartered up the leg and fastened just above the knee. On the tympanum of the Church of Saint-Ursin at Bourges, which is still preserved at the Prefecture there, one can see peasants working with hoes, etc. Their legs are wrapped in cloth, and at times this hangs baggily down the legs without any cross gartering.

The usual dress for a working woman was also a coarse *gonne* with loose sleeves extending down the forearm. She would wear a belt, usually a single one with a tie buckle. Her hair was in two plaits down the back and she seldom wore a wimple or anything else on her head. On a cold morning she might wear a pellice, or fur-lined gown, with no sleeves. Working in the overlord's house she would wear a wimple and a band around the head.

The men, of course, wore long drawers — the *braies* — and perhaps a shirt. The *gonne* could be slashed from the crotch down, but this was not necesary when the peasant's work did not involve riding. The woman, we know, had no underwear of any kind, except perhaps a shirt. The shoes of both men and women were stout and rather high over the ankle. (Fifty years ago it was the fashion for most men and women to wear "high shoes" which had just such an ankle support. These were called boots in England.) The peasant's soles were of thicker leather and doubtless, in many instances, they were made of wood.

Marcabrun gives a rather charming description of a girl of the upper peasant class, in one of his *pastorelas*. A knight comes upon a young peasant woman (half peasant, that is) seated on a *perron*, or mounting block. He addresses her with an improper proposal:

> The other day beside a hedge I found a shepherdess, half peasant and half upper-class, full of gaiety and sense. She was the daughter of a peasant mother. She wore a head covering, a gown (*gonella*), and a fur-lined garment, and she had a well woven shirt, shoes, and stockings of wool. [10]

To one who knows his medieval dress it is evident that this girl is not just a peasant; that is how the knight recognizes from her dress that there is an "upper class strain" there. She definitely has an undershirt and it is a carefully woven one. It has a third thread woven in on the diagonal (*treslissa* 'third thread'). (The modern garden *trellice* is so called because following this type of weave there is a third strip of wood which is on the diagonal.) She has on her *pellice* or warm garment, and she wears woolen stockings and shoes, not boots.

Another marriage fabliaux, the thirteenth century *Dou valet qui d'aise a malaise se met*,[11] gives us more sidelights on a peasant family and their belongings. The title in English is "The Young Fellow Who Falls from Comfort into Trouble." It is a kind of anti-marriage story and the characters are certainly peasant folk of the better class. The young man has worked hard enough to outfit himself in a good suit of clothes. Next he wants a wife. He makes up to a girl, who speaks about it to her mother. The father agrees and so the mother gives a little extra push to the affair. The boy counts up how much he has just spent on his clothes: a *cote* (main garment) 14 sous, his boots (4 sous), his *braies* (pyjama-like underdrawers) and undershirt — especially well sewn — at 24

---

[10] Marcabru, *Poésies complètes du troubador Marcabru*, tr. J. M. L. Dejeanne et A. Jeanroy (Tolouse: E. Privat, 1909), p. 135.

[11] In Antoine de Montaiglon and Gaston Raynaud, eds., *Recueil général et complet des fabliaux du XIII$^e$ et du XIV$^e$ siècle* (Paris: Librairie des Bibliophiles, 1872-90), II, no. 44, pp. 157-70.

sous and 6 deniers, his mantle (10 sous and a half), a pair of shoes for Sundays (4 sous), attachable soles to go on the bottom of his feet (9 deniers for three of them), a belt and a pair of white gloves (6 deniers). All these things cost him 47 sous six deniers which gives a good idea of what a better-class peasant would pay for his clothes.

However, he has only one outfit and he has not had it washed yet. "I have worn them so long that they are almost rotten." This last is an exaggeration, we are sure. When he tells his relatives that he wants to marry they say that he does not have enough property and that no well-fixed man will want to give him his daughter. "You have no lodging where you can take her, and there may be children soon." They say he should go serve a master somewhere. He insists he will not serve another peasant.

One of his relatives promises the newlyweds a small room together. The priest who announces the banns collects ten sous for him, and this is the cost of the wedding. The young man borrows another ten sous with the promise that he will pay this back out of the wedding gifts (*revisdailles*). The groom now buys his *afichiés* and *juiaus* (fancy things? jewels?). The day after the wedding the gifts arrive: wine and bread, and about 8 sous. With these bits of money the two purchase a pot and sauce pan. Then they receive some lesser gifts: a piglet and two hens.

Because of this livestock they cannot have the promised apartment. The bride weeps and says she wants a little house where they can put their chest and their bed as they will. They have to sell all their clothes and borrow from a usurer some 30 sous. At the end of the year she is pregnant. They are unhappy. He has to work for someone all day long. When he returns at night he must blow up the fire. He regrets his former single life. She responds with spirit, although she is not well: "You *puans pendus* (stinking wretch)! When I left my father's house I was well clothed. I had a good fur underjacket (*pellice*), *surcote* (petticoat) and frock (*sourquenie*). You have sold them all."

Particularly interesting are the prices that the young man paid for his clothes. Then sous amounted to half a pound, or one hundred and twenty silver pennies or deniers. This sum filled an entire purse, and at current wages amounted to about four days' work. Wedding gifts, received the day after the wedding, often took the form of 120 pennies in a purse.

This tale is a little cruel, but it reflects in poignant detail the frustrations of a little family of the lower class who aspired to be "clean and decent." [There is a timelessness to their aspiration, which we can recognize in the "situation comedies" not infrequently seen on television. It bespeaks a universal human longing to embody in their lives those images of living up to a social expectation of what is appropriate or successful. There are in all societies the less fortunate socio-economic classes, whose stable commitment to seemingly small values forms the foundation of the society. Robert Coles, whose studies of the American lower classes have recently awakened us to the solid values of those people, would have relished the opportunity to explore the life and meaning of the medieval peasant.]

*The Country Priest*

We could have spoken of the situation of a country priest of the peasant type in our previous chapter, but it will give a more unified picture to write of him here. Again we must return to the *Roman de Renart* (12th century). The author of the story was, of course, anticlerical [or perhaps, just cynical], although he was probably a priest himself; but this amusing little account was certainly somewhat close to existing conditions. Renart is taking Tybert the cat to a priest's house to find some rats and mice:

> "Tybert, do you know what we are doing? Among those houses there lives a priest who has lots of grain and oats, of which the mice are very fond. They have already consumed a good measure of them. I was there a short time ago and I got ten of the hens. I have eaten five of them already and the rest I have put in storage. This is how we get in. Pass through and eat what you want." But this wicked creature was lying all the time, because the priest who lived there had no oats or barley; there was no problem about that. But all the town complained of him because of a woman whom he kept who was the mother of his son Martin of Orleans. He had much goods, but he had no ox or cow — only two hens and a rooster. Little Martin, who later became a monk, had set at the hole in the enclosure two snares to catch Renart the Fox. "May God spare for the priest such a son who could make such a fine trap to catch a fox or a cat."

"Tybert, go on through," says Renart. "Dammit, what a coward you are. I'll wait for you here near the hole." Tybert rushes in quickly and the snare catches the idiot by the neck. Tybert pulls and draws back; the more he pulls the more it tightens. He tries to escape; but no luck. Martin, the little clerk, springs up. "Over here, *bele mere, bel pere,* help, help! Light up and run to the hole; the fox is caught, fool that he is." His mother wakes, jumps up and lights her candle. The priest holds on to his front with his fist and springs at once from the bed. Tybert has a bad time; he receives a hundred blows before he gets away from that house. The priest strikes, the concubine also, and Tybert has to use his teeth, as we have learned from our source account. He sees what the priest has in his hand and with his sharp teeth and claws tears off one of the testicles. When the woman sees what she has lost her grief becomes more severe. She calls herself miserable three times, and then faints dead away. Because of the grief which Martin shows when his mother faints he lets the cat go. The cat has bitten through the cords with his teeth. At last he was well avenged upon the priest who has been thrashing him. He would have got his revenge on Renart if he could have got hold of him. But that character has fled hastily without waiting further. As soon as he saw Tybert in the trap and heard Martin call "Up with you," he did not want to stay. "Ah" said he, "Renart, Renart, may God never save your soul. I should be punished for the number of times I have been tricked by Renart the Fox. And for that priest, the evil *cocu,* may God give him a bad lodging and very little bread, both to him and his filthy slut who attacked me today. After what happened today he will ring with only one bell in his parish. May no wealth ever come to Martinet his son, since he beat me so hard. May he not be dead until he has become a monk and been destroyed by theft." [12]

A pilgrim could be a peace-maker or "marriage counselor" among the class of society that is portrayed so heartily in the *Roman de Renart*. After Hersent (female wolf) and Hermeline (female fox) have been fighting a most terrific clawing battle (they have both been thrown out by their husbands), it is a pilgrim who helps. [Perhaps the fact that he had a liminal or marginal power in medie-

---

[12] *Renart,* I, vv. 819-916.

val society, bespeaking a transcendent quality, gives him this authority.]

> Dame Hersent was big and strong and she holds Hermeline under her with great strength. She has pushed her against a tree trunk and might have strangled her and killed her, when there came along a pilgrim limping down the road. He finds the ladies fighting. He seizes one of them (Hersent?) at once and lifts her up by the hand. "Up with you," he says, "Do no more of this." When he had separated them he admonished them very gently, asked them whence they came and where they were going. They told him everything, because he was a holy man and a priest. He gave them good advice — that each should return to her mate. Each should ask for forgiveness and want to be loved and held dear. He made Dame Hersent go to Ysengrim for peace, and he conducted Dame Hermeline to Renart in his den. He was so saintly and religious that he accorded them both and then made peace all around.[13]

The villain or peasant class was, on the whole, strictly illiterate and many of them bore ill luck with a stoic grace. They were at the bottom of the totem pole, but they were quite capable of defending themselves by shrewdness and quick wit. They knew nothing of the Universals or of the niceties of the schools; but, if these episodes which we have just reviewed are any indication, they respected saintliness and they appreciated discipline in the clergy.

*Summary*

The peasants' lot was similar to that of any lower class. For example, in private wars they were the first to suffer [as we have recently seen with our lower classes in the Viet Nam war]. Many, however, knew how to play off their lord against his rivals, and those who were lucky or had ambition could move up from the peasant class in various ways. They could use the escape route afforded to competent men-at-arms. They could learn a useful trade which would make it profitable for them to migrate to a town, usually with the overlord's permission. Those who remained on the

---

[13] *Ibid.*, vv. 3169-96.

land, which were the vast majority, could buy release from their condition of servitude and become independent farmers if they could accumulate enough money or land. They could even marry above their rank. The majority of these peasants, however, must have been unable, or unwilling, to alter their circumstances.

## V

## THE TOWN DWELLERS

In our reflection on medieval man's self-understanding we are brought very soon to a contemplation of his experience of town life. This may seem a little irrelevant to a philosopher, but man's estimate of his fellow beings depends very considerably upon how he sees them in large groups and how he can earn his living among them. In view of this the present chapter must not be considered too long. At the same time it is not going to be easy to keep the philosopher's attention when he is obliged to pick his way laboriously through descriptions of the layout of towns, their many kinds of dwellings and working places, and the places of amusement. I must write also of man's comforts, or perhaps lack of them, and especially of his houses. Of considerable importance are methods of trade and commodities and goods, and the extent to which these were influenced by an important minor race, the Jews, for they directed so much of the financial routine. We must discuss somewhat the daily routine, marking of time, gambling, tourneys, types of money that were employed, ideas of profit, how people lodged, how they ate, what they taught their young, and the positions occupied by women. This is a considerable amount of material, and it is unfortunate that so much of it comes under the one heading of town life and the bourgeoisie. But the bourgeois furnished the stage upon which most of communal life is set, and we must seek the medieval man in this setting.

### The City and Its Buildings

In the Middle Ages people lived in cities for two obvious reasons: protection and the easier enjoyment of the few comforts that were available. With a constant lack of stability in the local governments and with rivalries stimulating private wars, any community, even though it contained only one family, had to be prepared to slow up a marauder. A walled town was approximately a square mile — about a mile would lie between two opposite walls. About the most effective layout of streets was the *castrum* plan, which was inherited from the large Roman military camps that had dotted Western Europe. There were two main arteries crossing in the center, with a town cross at the intersection, and roughly four entrances to the cities: a Northgate, an Eastgate, a Southgate, and a Westgate. The chief variation from this was when the position of the river, of steep hills of an island, or of forests, made natural contours that could be more easily followed. Oxford, Winchester, and Exeter, are all examples of the *castrum* type of city.

The main arteries through the town were the chief routes of traffic. The many side streets formed only a network of districts where individual trades could be clustered together. More often than not they were *culs de sac*. Innumerable alleys and footpaths connected them. From the summit of the wall which went around the town the Captain of the watch could have good surveillance and be ready to respond to trouble. The present writer has clearly in mind the city of Ragusa (now Dubrouville) which has its twelfth-century walls in splendid repair, to their full extent. There is one main artery, through the center. The other little streets, like the bones of a fish coming out from the spine, extend from the central street to the wall.

An accurate view of the interrelation of such little streets is seen in medieval Winchester. The fullers' section (Brook Street) has now been excavated down to the twelfth-century level with its wooden houses. A network of dwellings and little paved alleys are all fully visible, and will be commented upon here, shortly. In a densely settled town such as Winchester most of the central streets were paved with small flint stones, fitted well together, extending quite deep into the ground. The main artery of some of the important cities was part of an ancient Roman road, and it had been paved to last through the centuries. But many, many side roads could still be of packed earth or mud. Where there was no pavement there was undoubtedly a large hollow in the ground before any principal entrance door. The peasant village described in our previous chapter was only a peasant settlement, but it should be noted that such a hollow formed a puddle even when it was not raining.

Houses were made almost entirely of wood in the twelfth century. There were, of course, some prosperous houses and shops of stone, whose number was much increased by the thirteenth century. Most of these private buildings were two stories high, although a large proportion of them had three floors. They were usually attached, with walls common with those of the next neighbor. Drainage was mostly by a slight ditch in the center of the roadway, in which the water kept moving sluggishly when the rains were heavy. There were some open drains, privately maintained. Fortunately many of the larger towns had natural creeks or streams which flowed through the built-up area into the river close by. This was true of Wall Brook, Long Burne, and the River of Wells in London. These absorbed much of the drainage from the streets and the private ditches.

As we must expect, the character of these tightly built streets was "perpendicular." There was little place to rest except on a door sill or on the side of a small cart. However, every built-up area had to have some horizontal places for gatherings and lounging. Some of the cross roads and gate areas had open markets, and there was space inside and outside of the many churches and public halls. A large manor complex of a noble or very high man also might have a flat space in front. Examination of the Paris *taille* roll of 1294 tells us where the "best" people, the wealthiest burghers, lived. The tax which they paid is marked on the list and we assume that those who paid the higest tax rates were the richest. These folk lived around the Greve. The Greve was the open air wine market; but its charm for residents was that it was close to the Seine River, above the lower end of town where noise and odors must have been annoying.

In London somewhat the same kind of preference must have prevailed. Westminster was an approved area. It too was close to the upper reach of the river and it was more removed from the stale air and the bustle of the wharf district below London Bridge. An added inducement was the presence of the King's principal palace at Westminster (on the site of what is now the Houses of Parliament). The *Camera Picta* (or Painted Chamber) of the royal household was the King's best private room. This had three fine large windows on an end wall overlooking the Thames. The King's landing quay was just below and to the right.

The large residences of kings and other wealthy people could be dwelling complexes, surrounded by a wooden palisade (which became a stone wall at a slightly later date). Inside this bailey or enclosed area, after crossing moat and drawbridge, and going through a strong fortified gate, one saw directly the great hall building. If of wood, this structure was commonly one-story, but sometimes it was a stone building with an undercroft, which made it necessary to enter by a broad stair. This hall building was termed a *palatium* (palace). Westminster Hall in London and Winchester Hall, are good examples of this feature. The undercroft of the great stone hall at Paris can be seen today on the lower floor of the Conciergerie.

In the great hall the king, or lord, gave audiences, ate on feast occasions, and here many people could lounge. It often had a private chamber at one end. Then there was a chamber building close by, most often of two floors. In this, the sleeping apartment was above; the bottom floor could be the wardrobe, for storage of clothes, or it could be occupied by guards or by other members of the Court. There was often a smaller great hall which was used by the lord or king on lesser occasions, usually called the Little Hall. There was such a lesser hall in Bishop Henry of Blois's castle at Winchester and the English king had something similar in his Westminster enclosure. The kitchens were in a separate ground-floor structure; there were usually additional first-floor hall structures for the Queen or the owner's wife, with a Chapel below, and for others who had to be lodged there. In a complex of this kind there was almost always a keep or donjon. This tower could be used as the lord's sleeping building, if he were fearful; it could also house his treasure room; and his wife and daughters might be lodged there, for it was a secure place.

A baron's complex such as we have just described could be located within a town, or it could be maintained outside the town walls. It was also possible to find two or even more such complexes within the walls of a principal town. Within the walls of London there were two of them: Baynard's Castle and Montfichet, in addition to the king's White Tower of London.

Marie de France's *Laustic* gives us the impression that two such complexes existed side by side, for the dwelling of a married knight had a common wall with the complex of a bachelor knight. The wife of the one, who apparently was lodged on the upper floor of her husband's donjon or tower, could look over the intervening wall and see the chamber of the bachelor who, we assume, slept in a chamber building within his own premises.

However, most of the lesser barons or knights, as well as merchants of the wealthier kind, must have maintained large first-floor halls. Such large houses were usually flush with the street; but they might have a small court in front and be set back a little. These well-to-do first-floor structures were very common indeed, and many of the stone ones have survived today, although the inner arrangement of rooms has usually been altered. In England it has been the custom to refer to these fine structures as "Inns" although they were primarily intended to be the town house of a baron or very wealthy man. In France they were designated by the term "Hostel" (later hotel). On the ground floor these structures could have a series of archways with or without doors filling these archways. On the upper floor there was a fine long room going across the facade. In addition, one or more small interior chambers could open off from the long room.

In the *Ile et Galeron* of Gautier d'Arras the heroine, posing as a needlewoman, rents dwelling space inside one of the lower ground-floor arches of a rich man's house. Guilhem, the protagonist of the *Flamenca*, rents such an apartment as a dwelling, and is able to introduce diggers into it during the night. They dig a tunnel from his quarters to a bath across the way, and were able to carry out the dirt as they worked. Since that was Guilhem's living apartment, it was easy for him while there to do as he pleased.

At the back of one of these archways might be a spiral stair leading up to the master's apartment on the upper floor. This was the case in the so-called *maison des Templiers* at Beaugency, in the Romanesque house at Saint-Antonin, and in the *maison romane* at Perigueux. The master's big hall up above could have a shallow wooden balcony with two little end doors leading out on to it; this was true at Perigueux and at Pudsey's Hall in Durham.

One of the shops on the ground level might be operated by the proprietor of the building. Tackley Hall and the Golden Cross Hall in Oxford were of this kind. The doorways onto the street level are still visible in the modern basement. The raising of the street level has made these underground today. This same altering of the ground level is also found at what is called the Angel Hotel in Guildford. Some house experts have suggested that these street archways were originally on a subterranean level and that one entered there by descending a front stairway. This was possible in some cases, but I think that in the inns just recorded the street level rose. [Every city develops its own midden, on which it slowly rises. For example, New York is already in some places a full "story" higher than in the beginning.]

Tackley Hall at the foot of Cat Street in Oxford may well have served as a large lecture room on its upper floor. The lower floor, with its archways, was for shops. This is the earliest university lecture hall that I know. Frequently a small first-floor hall type of house had not more than two archways on the ground level (today replaced by nineteenth-century shop fronts). Such a house is the Jew's House at Lincoln. The archways on the lower level were rented out to other merchants. Some claim that the Jewish money lender in question who owned the building occupied these lower premises as an office.

A few illustrations of town scenes have survived in thirteenth- and fourteenth-century manuscripts. They show a conglomeration of just plain towers, first-floor halls with archways below, and what we call a tower hall. In this last case a room with an entrance leads up to a top floor, perched on the top of what might be thought of as a tower. In this kind of structure the top floor is very secure, indeed, because hostile intruders were unusually vulnerable as they climbed the very long stair. The Tour of Jehan Sans Peur in Paris (fifteenth century, in private hands now) is a fine example of this.

The vast majority of the shops and houses of a town were small and in rows. When made of wood these houses had cambered beams across the ground floor. The merchant kept his stock, and often his own manufacture, in this undercroft room, which might have a fireplace. His actual selling was done from benches ranged before the opening into the street. When such a merchant went into liquidation his benches were frequently broken there by indignant creditors. The merchant then was *banchi rotti* (bankrupt). The small merchant's own living quarters were in the room above the street.

This could be reached by a small spiral stair tower against the inner wall. (I remember seeing this feature in a now destroyed shop on the High Street at Exeter.) Often the living quarters were reached by a narrow stair on the outside wall. At times an extra room was on a second floor above, under the rafters. This was the *soler*, and was often rented. This upper room is seen in the *maison romane* at Chaise-Dieu, and in another such house at Chartres. A stone shop of this kind had the undercroft opening into the street, and then possibly a separate entrance with stair leading up to the first floor.

These houses were all in sequence, attached to one another. The location of the kitchen and other necessary service sheds is a problem. Where possible there was a courtyard in the rear. In a few of the surviving houses it is quite obvious that there was a kitchen on the ground floor, but in all towns there must have been many cook houses or public kitchens serving cooked food cheaper than it could be sold on the hoof. FitzStephen in his account of London noted such a cook house or public food shop at Dowgate wharf. It is extremely likely that many of the burghers made use of these cook houses when they could. After all, an active kitchen is very hard to maintain in "shut-in" premises. I feel sure that much cooking for meals was done in the average fireplace which was maintained in all such houses in the *sale*, or living room.

### The Good Life of the Town

All towns had plenty of taverns. From some of the *chansons de geste*, notably the *Giole*, we can be assured that customers descended by an outside stair to a basement level where they found a tavern. Little portable tables were set out there, and one or more big kegs full of wine that could be broached. A drawer was in constant attendance. Each patron purchased a candle end as he entered, called for the drawer, and drank as he saw fit. Most taverns had little food, often serving one fixed meal. A few, as in the *Trois aveugles de Compiegne*, could give their patrons a private room somewhere, for eating and even sleeping. Warmth, wine a plenty, some food of a kind, and the attentions of a woman could be enjoyed in such a place. But the chief entertainment encouraged was dicing — the dice (three of them) being thrown from a special cup on to a table top. Many beds were set up when necessary for both men and women in the same area.

Cities could offer places of higher entertainment for knights and ladies of the upper class. I will translate closely from the romance of *L'Escoufle* by Jehan Renart (early thirteenth century).

> After searching for two years to find her lover Guillaume, the young lady Aelis, goes to Montpellier to settle for a while, accompanied by her attendant Ysabele. Ysabele says: "Let us go live in Montpellier and rent a house there which will suffice for us, I will earn for both of us by making towels, and wimples..." Aelis adds, "I will work too. I will make jewels of gold thread and of silk. No other girl knows as much as I do about orfreys, belts, ties. I have skill in these things. We will go there and nothing more to be said." They did not delay and when they got to Montpellier they took a house and were concerned with arranging it and furnishing. Ysabele sent for furniture and household gear, and mattresses. There was a court in front of the house and a courtyard behind.
>
> From then on there was no delight *(deduis)* except to call upon the charming young lady *(la france pucelle)*. The news goes around the city that the most beautiful woman in the kingdom had arrived from Lorraine. Very quickly she got the trade of the burghers and the knights. Never since Montpellier was founded was such a lovely creature seen. She soon won the favor of the knights, and of the young men. This was because of her good sense and because of the jewels which she made for them such as they ordered. And those who were charmed by her lovely eyes thought they were more than counts; they paid her without counting out their money.... She got much money.
>
> Know that a good woman, beautiful and worthy is a real treasure. She did not care to go to a church to pray. It made her the more honored that she loved, feared, and served God. She lived as she deserved, by washing the heads of high ranked men. She knows very well how to manage everything that a woman should know how to do. Her companion Ysabele was also most successful. Her tufted mattresses and her beds embellished very much her lodging. There was not in Montpellier such another place for pleasure and delight. In seven or eight cages were birds hanging at the windows. The whole house and its upper balconies were full of people on festival occasions. The girls told romances and tales; there was no limit to the other games: chess, draughts, and dice. So many charming narratives were recited that all were obliged to listen.

Every morning Aelis caused to be scattered through her house fresh rushes and herbs. She was intent upon doing whatever was pleasing to the people.... Her arrangements and her amusements were much esteemed by those who frequented there.... They were finally persuaded to move to the Castle of Saint-Gilles, serving the Count and his lady. They broke up their household. The two girls caused to be taken away all their equipment, giving some to the neighbors: to one they gave a mattress, to another cushions, cauldrons, pots, trestles (for tables), and table tops. Then they put all their garments into bags, their shirts, tunics, mantles, pelices, surcots. They paid all their bills *(escos)*. They were convoyed and bidden farewell by all their friends.[1]

Just how do establishments of this kind fit into the life of a medieval city? It seems evident that these girls were not engaged in any sort of prostitution. They made a charming milieu for many of the young people in the town. We can assume that it was possible for certain merchants of the higher type to make their shops and living rooms so attractive that clients would flock there as to a kind of club. I personally have seen this sort of thing in modern France. Mlle. Eugénie Droz, when she conducted her book shop and publishing establishment at No. 25, rue de Tournon, in Paris, maintained a constant open house to scholars of Romance philology. She served them tea and told them the news of those who had already called upon her.

A kind of idealized medieval town, where the good life abounds, is described in certain works of the time, as in *Durmart li Gallois:*

... the streets are large and wide, and all paved. The town is clean, wealthy, wide, and full of amusements. There are many houses well built, halls with windows, crypts, vaults, and cellars, chambers, *loges* (balconies), and attic rooms, mills, and clear streams *(fontineles)*. Many are the clerks and the burghers, well dressed and courteous. The city is not unfurnished. Some 140 knights lived there who have their lodging there. This city is the capital of that area and well supplied.[2]

---

[1] Jean Renart, *L'Escoufle,* ed. H. Michelant and Paul Meyer (Paris: SATF, 1894), vv. 5452-6089.
[2] *Li Romans de Durmart li Galois,* ed. Edmund Stengal, BLUS 116 (Tübingen: Laupp, 1873), vv. 4400ff.

We have spoken of the types of houses, the churches, the wealthy complexes, and the towers. Some of these towers are still standing in Italy, notably at San Gemignano. They contained a sleeping chamber high in the air, and certain other rooms useful for treasures and security. These, however, were by no means so common in France. There was a special kind of tower house in France, of which we have already spoken. It must have been a center for the social life of the city. The Hotel de Jehan Sans Peur in Paris (although closed to visitors now, and of the fifteenth century) is a building of this kind. There are a number of similar structures throughout France, at Burlat, at Le Puy, and so on. Modern owners of these magnificent old structures often have inserted a new floor between the ground-floor and the upper apartment.

All these houses had their floors paved mostly with brick or tiles and strewn with straw and rushes. Such straw must have been lying about everywhere — much of it in the streets. The rooms were insufficiently lighted, with the few small windows, and in the colder months everything was dreadfully cold. There were no panes of glass in the twelfth century, except for those in a few ecclesiastical structures, like Le Mans Cathedral. As we have observed in the quotation given from Jehan Renart's *Escoufle*, bird cages of wicker were often hung in the open windows. Also little baskets containing-sweet-smelling substances could be hung there which would make living a bit more pleasant. Because of lack of running-water plumbing, the streets and the rooms of the twelfth century had a constant odor of feces and of decaying flesh. There were some clean, finicky people in the Middle Ages, but they were vastly outnumbered by those who did not much care.

In the *Escoufle,* there is a description of an informal "lodging house." The protagonist of the story is Guillaume who arrived in the town of Saint-Gilles, somewhat penniless in his search for Aelis, the heroine. He went to High Mass where, before the chancel, he met a rich burgher. When Guillaume had said his prayers the burgher spoke to him, asking whence he came and inquiring whether he was employed. The young man said no but that he would like a job. He was not afraid of anything by which he could earn a living: he could make bread, a fine bed, and he was very able in the care of falcons and of dogs. The burgher was very pleased with him; he inquired when he arrived in town. He replied "today, and

I have no lodging as yet." "If you want one such as I have, very near here, you can have it." They left together and at the lodging the burgher sat at table with two of his neighbors. They had brought some wine with them. Guillaume served them, and the host sought to retain him. He agreed on a wage of 50 sous (600 deniers) a year. One of the other burghers took him aside and assured him that he would do very well, for this was a place *(repaire)* much frequented by pilgrims and other people, and since he was so agreeable he would come out well financially. Guillaume stayed there for three months and at no time was the house without a guest. He removed their saddles and bridles for those clients who had no serving man themselves. Joking and chatting, he prepared their beds at night. He was not bothered when there were a great number to care for. No good man stopped at the lodging who did not give him something.[3]

*Commerce*

One of the essential reasons for the existence of the town, as we have already stated, was buying and selling. There were many benches along the fronts of the shops of the side streets where this was done. There were also benches and tables set up in the "horizontal" areas for this purpose. Those who dealt in very valuable objects: goldsmiths, money-changers, etc., were apt to be congregated in an area which could be overlooked by the *serjants* (warders) from the keep or donjon, or from a principal gate, or the town wall. The elite market could be on a stone bridge, which was the case at Paris — the *Pons Magnus* or Grand Pont. In a letter written in 1175 Gui de Bazoches speaks of Paris:

> There are two suburbs right and left. From each suburb a stone bridge extends to the town. That bridge which is called the Grant Pont is crowded, rich, full of trade *(emax)*, teeming, sighing, abounding with ships, wealth, innumerable goods; it boils with ships, sighs with riches, abounds in goods. This place does not have an equal. But the "little bridge" is for those strolling, disputing, dedicated to Logic.[4]

---

[3] *L'Escoufle*, vv. 6504-6604.

[4] From a lecture made at l'Académie des Inscriptions et Belles-Lettres, February 9, 1877, pp. 38-39.

## THE TOWN DWELLERS

At Troyes, an important stop for those going down into Italy, the money changers were congregated on the streets and in a place adjacent to the Viscount's donjon, at the western end of the town. At London that quarter of town which was near the White Tower was the safest. The Provost's guards or the Viscount's armed men could be available in a few minutes in the event of bold robbery.

Here is a fictitious description of the wealth for sale in the market quarter of an imaginary city (of Ladt Gaut), which Gawain visits.

> The streets were paved with heavy stones *(gries)* and square stones *(quarrels)*, from the lower town up to the castle and they were richly set. But all that is nothing compared to the other wealth that was there. When I give an account of this you should not be astonished, for there were many manufacturers working in that town. Some made cloths, other dyed them; some were fullers, other dyers. Some of the workers made shoes and still others painted them. Certain ones did boots *(botes)* and others high shoes *(housiaus)*. The furriers beat their skins; this one executed them; another stretched them. Still another cut them and this one sold them. There were lots of workers. One made bridles, and another saddles, painted with azure, rich and fair. Another did shields, sharpened lances and polished metal; you could not find a single shop where merchandise was not being manufactured. Mail coats there were of many kinds, which you could find if you looked. Another made helms and another polished them. One forged hauberks (mail coats), and this one swords. Metal *chauces* (leg coverings) were well fabricated which you could see hanging at the shop openings *(fenestres)*. You could find everything there that God wished to be sold: brooches, belts, rings, large purses, cloths of silk, ivory combs. What shall I say? No one could estimate the riches. One sold pepper and wax, another pitch and cumin, — incense from Alexander, boxes of unguents. These last were for lying doctors. They say they know physic, who concentrate on fools full of guff *(musique)*. One does it to deceive his mother and makes a fool believe by his cozening tongue that he can cure him of dropsy. Only someone full of melancholy thinks to be healed by a physician. They know very well how to lie and cover up their falsehood.
>
> Now I will tell you of those who work cloaks of gold and great cups of silver, spoons, chalices, which are sold to priests in churches. This fellow changes money, this one

strikes coins; yet another makes purses, and one makes dice. This chap over here fabricates both narrow and broad orphreys (gold braid), of several kinds, attractive and fair. These girls manufacture ribbons and braid *(freseaus)*, inner belts *(braiels)*, outer belts *(çaintures)*, silk cloths. If any one would stand in the street he would see marvelous things all day long. Some men turn bowls of hard wood *(masors)*, covered vases *(juistes)*, boxes and eating bowls *(escueles)*, this one makes grails *(graius)* and troper stands. [We assume that the grail is an ornamental bowl of large size.] This one does nails and horse shoes, another does *hapies* (?) and locks; still another makes jars *(orceus)* and fasteners. One fellow turns out pots, still another cauldrons; another does stew pans *(paieles)* good and bright; the work was not all the same *(unie)*. This chap makes casks and that fellow binds them [with hoops?]. Another fabricates headstalls and curry-combs, pegs *(chevilles)* and gussets or pods *(gouces)*. Still additional people sell bread, others wine. There are some who deal in birds and fish; pork and venison can one find in the butchery.[5]

 A similar but less lengthy description of the trades is in Chrétien's *Perceval*. It is frequently said that these were stock descriptions, but they were not false fabrications. These lists represent what (admittedly) tradesmen would be doing in any wealthy town.

 If the area within the walls of the town was not packed tight with dwellings and commerce, people living on the fringe just within the walls could have been almost in a rural setting. Near a house there might be a little granary and a barn, and a garden patch close by. To be sure, even where this was not possible within the walls, many burghers maintained close association with their crofts and farming enclosures nearby, outside the town wall. Their civilization was after all rurally based, which is the opposite of our society, whose rural life is urban based. It was not so easy to bring in farm products through the principal town gates (the city fathers exacted a heavy tariff), but where there was a postern, a little door in the wall, usually close to an ecclesiastical building, opportunities were not hard to find.

 This is evidenced particularly in the fabliaux where monks who are primarily associated with agriculture outside the walls seem to

---

[5] Raoul de Houdenc, *La Vengeance Raguidel*, ed. Mathias Friedwagner, in *Sämtliche Werke*, II (Halle: Niemeyer, 1909), vv. 1806-79.

move quite frequently into their cloisters which are within the walls, usually on the inner edge. I have in mind a group of buildings at Reading Abbey, which reminds me of certain international boundaries such as those in the Pyrenees between French and Spanish areas. The mountaineers engaged mostly in herding and were not restricted very much in the matter of moving over the Pyrenees between allegiances. Smuggling among medieval clerics, as among the inhabitants of the Pyrenees, was an honorable profession.

A very important section of town was the Jewish quarter. Jews were quite essential for international commerce and for banking and credit of any kind. Not only did they have access to easy money, but they were also a businesslike people. They could not have prospered or even existed if they had not been protected by the lord of the town. In France and England the Jews lived in clusters, or in quarters, not far from the town civil authorities. (The common concept of a Jewish ghetto in some inferior part of town was not true at all.) In Winchester the intersection of Jew Street and High was the principal business center. Winchester was an international business town with its great Fair; and for much of the Middle Ages it was a capital city.

It is difficult to pinpoint any given house as a Jewish domicile, but I am going to do just this, hoping that it is true. Let us take the so-called House of Isaac the Jewish moneylender in Lincoln, which we have already mentioned. The entrance door at the centre of the façade had a much higher opening than is now the case. (A man on horseback could ride directly in without getting off.) This leads into a long corridor which takes one through to the courtyard at the rear. This would be excellent for an owner who did not want to be stopped as he entered his front door. In the courtyard there was certainly a stairway tower against the rear wall of the main block which brought one up into the *sale* or hall. Adjoining this room was the chamber. The fireplace which was in the *sale* had its chimney rising directly from over the outside entrance door. The two rooms on the ground floor, on either side of the through-corridor, may have had connecting doors with the corridor; but I rather think each of these rooms was a separate entity with an archway opening on the street. These could have been rented to separate tenants who had no concern with Isaac the Jew. I know there has been romantic fantasy about these rooms in which the bonds of indebtedness were supposedly kept; but much of this is only fantasy. There was no filing in the modern sense of the word, and valuable papers would not be kept where they might be easily stolen.

*The Routine of Town Life*

As the sun appeared on the horizon a medieval town came to life. The watchman in the gate tower made a burping sound on his long horn and not many minutes after that the usual routine of noises engulfed the area with a roar. Men and women shouted for every conceivable reason. The *regrattiers* (hucksters) had their food and other goods to sell. Criers advertised the taverns, often with a sample of their wines in a bowl which they tapped with a stick. There were many varieties of birds and animals kept on the roof in the back courts of houses, and one squawk was soon followed by a hundred more. All day long quiet reigned nowhere in a medieval city. Crowds and noise were not just tolerated; they were esteemed.

Usually one prominent church tower sounded the "hours" (roughly every third hour) by which the people kept to their routines. Prime was rung approximately at 6 o'clock (modern time), Tierce at nine, Sext and mid-day vaguely coincided; there was no ringing at three, and Vespers sounded at around six. At Vespers it was customary for most families to take their supper which was the second big meal of the day. Curfew, which was a signal to put out the fire and think of going to bed, varied with weather conditions and with the season of the year. Compline rang at nine p.m., Matins at mid-night, and Lauds around 3 a.m. (cock-crow); but these were really monastic hours and not observed to any extent by the people of the town. It is understood that, as with our modern daylight savings time, when the daylight was shorter the three-hour daylight intervals were shortened; in the months of longer light they were stretched out a bit. The clergy who rang these town bells made use of a water clock for telling their time.

Since the routine hours of the day were marked so inexactly there was little precision to a person's routine. After rising, sometime between sunrise and the first hour, it was probably customary to take a draught of wine, ale, or perhaps even water, and then the average man put in about two hours at his daily work. Many went to church for prayers followed by Mass. Sometime between 10 and 11 a.m. they knocked off and prepared for the first big meal of the day. When the bell rang Sext it was proper to rest — some lay down, and some just lay around. By approximately 2 p.m. they took up their labours again. This was often referred to as *relevee*, or the second rising of the day.

We will imagine that most workers then put in three or four hours of activity, stopping in time for a little recreation before Vespers, which meant their supper. This could be followed by entertainment, from minstrels or others. These people got a great deal of pleasure from chatting together, singing together, and listening to arguments.

It is probable that almost every male carried with him a dice cup which held the usual three bone dice. These they liked to roll whenever there were one or two partners and a flat surface. Sometimes they played for "most points" but they had also a more popular game which was called *hasart*. The upper and lower sum totals which could be counted up on the three dice were known as *hasart* points. If all the points which you rolled came to fifteen or more, or to six or less, the man rolling the dice won. If he did not get an *hasart* total on the first throw and this came on the second then the opponent scored. When no *hasart* was rolled on either of the first two throws then the man with the dice continued to roll. If he eventually got again the total of the throw he lost.

A specific detail of this game is called the Chance. Your adversary names any total number that he wishes, lying between the six and the fifteen. He gives you this "chance." If the thrower gets this "chance" on his next roll, he wins — otherwise the dice pass to the other man and the throwing begins all over again. The rules of this game are explained in the *Libro de ajedrez y tablas* of Alfonso el Sabio, but not too well.[6] Undoubtedly our expression to be "given a chance" has reference to the "chance" throw at *hasart*.

Those attending a prolonged feasting, lasting a number of days, might take long walks every day or two, to work off the excess of food and drink, strolling from castle to castle. This is pictured in

---

[6] See Charles A. Knudsen, " 'Hasard' et les autres jeux de dés dans le *Jeu de Saint Nicolas,*" Romania, 63 (1937), 248-53.

Chrétien's *Yvain*. [In passing we might say a word about prolonged feasting. Food for medieval man was a commodity that was present sometimes in abundance and sometimes not at all. There were very primitive forms of preservation (e.g., drying of meat), and when there was plenty the community took delight in enjoying what was there without any notion of "waste not, want not." This was common to most people before Christian admonition against gluttony was made by the Puritans the order of the day. For while medieval man himself sought moderation in all things, he was not that far removed from his days in the primeval forests of northern Europe. There he lived much as the American Indian, whom we know to have practiced the same customs of feast or famine.]

It is definitely true that on the holy days one did not work. In the Anglo-Norman Life of *St. Edward* a penalty sickness was suffered by needlewomen who sewed on St. Edward's special day — they got a kind of quinsy. In nearly every week there could be some two holy days observed (other than Sunday). On these occasions games were played on the river and in other horizontal areas. There were ball games which, in the illustrations drawn in manuscripts, resemble very much cricket — with some imagination they resemble baseball. On special occasions there was cock fighting and bear baiting. FitzStephen describes all these in London in his *Life of St. Thomas of Canterbury*. The young squires were apt to practice tilting, with their guardians sitting by on horseback, watching. The boys in the schools participated in the ball games. At certain festal occasions there were exhibitions of boating on the water when crowds watched from balconies and roof tops. In cold weather many made skates from the shinbones of horses.

On special occasions there were tourneys. These were primarily for the baronial class; but it is to be expected that many of the townspeople looked on. These could be held in certain appropriate meadows outside of town, where the lists (barriers) were set up and the action was supervised by a class of people who are referred to as heralds. Chrétien de Troyes's *Cligés* mentions that an important three-day tourney was held in meadows midway between Oxford and Wallingford. *Loges* or informal shelters were set up for the occasion. These could be constructed by driving four good-sized poles into the ground, as a rectangle. On top of these, temporary rafters were placed and probably were then covered with boughs and leaves. These sheds made excellent viewing stands and kept the viewers out of the sun.

Of course, where a tourney was held outside the town near the town wall it was easy for spectators to stand on the top of the walls, and they could watch from the towers. The heralds, on a signal, began to call in loud voices: "To arms, to arms, flower of knighthood. Acquire the love of God by the love of ladies and arms." [7] A tourney was cried. [8] After the tourney was over there were always merchants around who purchased suits of armor and horses which had been acquired by the victors from the defeated.

We must now return to the merchants, who made up the wealth of the town, and their stalls. It was a very thorny problem indeed to justify "buying cheap and selling dear." In his Commentary on Psalm 70, St. Augustine rebuked the merchant for his deceits, but he then admitted as morally valid the merchant's defense that he travelled far to collect the goods. Again in his *City of God* St. Augustine accepted the idea that one could charge according to demand. But the Canonists, the Glossators on the *Corpus Juris Civilis*, at Bologna, who were fathered by Gratian, accused all profits derived from sale as *turpe lucrum*, or "filthy money." The problem was to determine the just price. Either the buyer or the seller could complain that the just price had not been observed when there had been paid less than one half of the just price, to be determined by consultation with a *bonus vir* or just man. This is the decree of *Laesio enormis*. Rufinus (1157-59) in his *Summa* and Huguccio in (1188-90) came to the aid of the theory of free trade. Both laity and clerks can sell when this is done from need. Huguccio specifically permits sale also to gain money to support one's family. (This does not include the clergy.) No one could be *honestus* if he sold for false greed. In view of these restrictions it was a very moot point whether clerks could indulge in buying and selling.

The view originally held in Roman Law was that a just price was determined between the seller and the purchaser by mutual bargaining, and this, of course, was the average procedure between

---

[7] "Les Enfances Garin: A Critical Edition," ed. Jack David Brown, Diss. University of North Carolina 1971, 36r, vv. 1924-26.
[8] *Li Romans de Claris et Laris*, ed. Johann Alton, BLUS 169 (Tübingen: n.p., 1884), vv. 1293-95.

the medieval merchant and his customer.[9] [This process of arriving at the "just price" through a give and take seems to us to underline again the kind of practical faith in the communal life, where there is no attempt to distinguish sharply the relationship of the seller to the buyer, but a willingness to see that life is a mutual enterprise in which we all have a common investment.]

But this label of *turpe lucrum*, "sordid gain," was applied for the most part to the *regrattier* "peddlers" and the travelling merchants who carried their goods for sale from town to town. Most of the tradesmen living within a city manufactured their own wares and thus "improved them" materially. These tradesmen had formed guilds since at least the eleventh century. At Paris the rules and regulations of these groups were compiled by Estienne Boileau in his *Livre des mestiers*, in which he lists a hundred trades. Many of the guild members were not permitted to labor by candlelight, or after Vespers, unless the nature of their work required them to wait until provisions were brought to Paris from the country. Holidays were specified. Some of these were observed by all; others according to the nature of the individual's trade.

Some of the trades were considered more noble than others, and their practitioners were therefore excused from menial work such as the *Guet* or watch. Among these were: makers of arms, illuminators, sculptors, stationers or book dealers, embroiderers, goldsmiths, and apothecaries. Still other trade groups were considered unworthy of manning the watch: tavern keepers, skinners, and bath keepers.

At Paris a Provost of the merchants had a court before which violators were obliged to appear. It was necessary to pay for the privilege of practicing a trade within the city. Foreigners, that is, tradesmen from outside the town, had to do their business there by acting in conjunction with a local guild member. As we can judge from the *Vengeance Raguidel*, already quoted, the medical practitioners were included among the tradespeople.

The fairs were set up by the local overlord, usually on advice, or for some special reason. Such a fair as the one on St. Giles Hill in Winchester would last twenty-four days, or maybe more, and could be of great importance. The one on St. Giles Hill brought

---

[9] See John W. Baldwin, "The Medieval Theories of the Just Price," *Transactions of the American Philosophical Society*, NS 49 (1959), part 4.

very important money changers from France, the Low Lands, and other distant points. If one wanted to travel in Italy, one could purchase a letter of credit, or tallies, from a French changer say, from Troyes. The change merchant sent his half of the letter, of the tallies, by special messenger to his relative or partner in Troyes. When the purchaser reached that point he might make a further purchase of credit on change in Modena, Bologna, or somewhere else. (All this is described in the *Speculum Ecclesiae* of Gerald the Welshman, who was making a journey to Rome.) When Gerald was returning on this occasion he gave tallies or letters in Bologna and they sent on a boy with these to Troyes.

Big fairs flourished best in those areas where Jewish merchants and bankers were plentiful. As we have remarked earlier in this book, close knit family relations made it possible for Jewish bankers to support branches from city to city in which they had perfect trust. There were "permanent" fairs in many places where trading and change were maintained on specified city street areas, as at Troyes; but the more general merchants, with great variety of goods, liked to move about, going to fairs when they were promised adequate protection by the local Counts. Of course, the Pont au Change at Paris was a permanent fair area; but the Lendit or Foire Saint-Denis was held at a certain time of the year only, near the Hospital of Saint-Lazare, on the grassy median between the Rue Saint-Denis and the Rue Saint-Nicholas not far from the town of Saint-Denis. Local merchants often complained when they were obliged to shut up their place of business once or twice a week to move their stalls to the *Campelli* or some other suburban quarter.

In addition to banking, the common task of a money changer was to convert money from another area into local money. They sat, prosperous, well-dressed merchants, before a heap of deniers and *maailles* from the local mint. As a traveller approached with a money belt, a large *aumosniere* (purse) or even a chest from the other land, the changers inspected these, testing some pieces, and then they converted them as demanded. For their fee, and to figure the necessary discount, they removed a certain number of pieces from the customer's pile. When Wistasce le Moine sought to convert his Francian money as he came back from Spain the changers demanded such a discount as fifty per cent. (This, of course, was intended by the author of the poem as a slander on

Philip Augustus' newly established coinage.) Wistasce would not allow this and got even by a magic trick.

In England at this time *all* money bore the English King's name and face. There were different mints, however, two of them being ecclesiastical: Durham and Bury St. Edmund's, where the Bishop and Abbot had special participation in profits of their mints. In Northeastern England, during the reign of Stephen, a few Earls had their own coinage. In Wales at Rhuddlan, the Abbot had the right to use his own dies of the King's face. The pennies minted in all these mints, bearing the king's name and face, were called sterling. British coins had a superior silver content and each one was equivalent to about four pennies of those struck in the mints on the Continent. Gerald the Welshman remarked when he had only eight Dijon pennies found in his possession that these were just about equal to two pennies sterling.

The English did not mint a halfpenny or a farthing until the time of Edward the First in 1278. For the halfpenny they divided a penny in two, along the line of the cross. For the farthing they split the penny into four. Such a farthing or *maaille frelin* in French was very light, and a considerable sum of them looked like metal trash. The fabliau of *Les deus Anglois* jokes along these lines. An English minstrel wants to buy a lamb from a French farmer and he says he will pay the entire sum in farthings. Both parties snicker at that.

In France and most of the Continent the silver penny or denier was accompanied by a *maaille* or minted halfpenny. It was smaller and the alloy was a little less pure. The French peasants had very little minted money, so they dealt mostly in these *maailles*, or halfpennies, and in *partis*. A *parti* was a *maaille* cut in two by a chisel! In the dice game portrayed in the *Jeu de Saint Nicholas* in a tavern the peasants are gambling with *partis*. They do not understand the gold *besanz* which have been stolen from the custody of the image of Saint Nicholas. They call these red pennies (*rouge denier*). The minstrel in the *Huon de Bordeaux* cries to his audiences to come back the next day. He bids them bring each a *maaille* tied up in his garment — and to remember that the *maailles* of Bordeaux were not very good. (Note that they had no such things as pockets.)

Nearly every baron of a considerable domain, every important abbot, and most of the bishops in France had the privilege of striking their own coins. This meant loss of business for the money changers. As you got farther away from the district where your coins had been struck these were discounted more and more. It paid to have them changed into the local specie. Of course your money had to yield up a few coins to pay for the rate of exchange. The individual coins were subjected to some scrutiny too to see if they had been badly clipped.

Considerable sums of these deniers could be kept in a belt around the waist; those that were intended for general use were placed in a large cloth wallet that hung at the belt. The usual sum for such a wallet was 10 sous or 120 deniers. Pickpockets who had knives with a sharp hook on the end could easily cut a purse and catch the coins in their hands.

Remember that the only coins in general use anywhere were silver pennies (*deniers*), and halfpennies (*maailles*), and a small number of farthings. Poor people had their *partis* and the luckier and richer folk might have some gold *besants*, from Constantinople, but more frequently from Moslem Spain. In King John's time a *besant* was equal to 24 sterling pennies. Multiplying by four one can see how much a *besant* was worth in French *tournois* money.

In the fabliau called "The Three Blind Men of Compiegne" (13th century) a mischievous student goes up to the three blind men and says that he is giving them a *besant*. They rejoice. They do not know just what it is worth, but they return to the town and go to a burgher who serves food. They say they have plenty of money. He prepares them a dinner in a *soler* upstairs and then agrees that they might spend the night there. In the morning, at paying out time each thinks one of the others has a *besant*. Fortunately the joking student is nearby; he pays, and turns the joke in another direction.

The fabliau of "The Three Hunchback Minstrels" also has to do with money. At Christmas time they come to the house of a wealthy hunchback bourgeois, as they want to spend the season with one of their own kind. He takes them in for the moment — up the stairs of his nice stone house (the author notes that his house had such a front stairway) and he sets them down at a good meal; they had *pois au lart* and capons. Afterwards he gives each one twenty sous of *parisis* (the king's money) — that is one pound — and then forbids them to ever appear at his door again, unless they wish to be thrown into the river. At this point the master of the household has to leave. His wife keeps the three minstrels in order to hear them perform some more. Suddenly her husband is seen returning. There is a "hand barrow" on the floor beside the fireplace loaded with three boxes; the minstrels are suffocated. She then hires a half-witted porter to throw one of them into the river for thirty pounds of deniers. He does this but then he comes upon the second hunchback. He is convinced that this is the same dead man (come back). He is persuaded to dispose of him "again" in the same way. Then he sees the third minstrel. He throws him into the water likewise. At this point he meets the hunchback husband of the lady. He whacks him on the head with a large pestle and disposes of him in the same way. The "widow" now gives him the thirty pounds and lives happily ever after. For our present purpose note the stone house with the steps, the hand barrow sitting in the main room by the fireplace, and the pound of *parisis* which the husband gave to each singer after that first dinner.

## Houses and Their Furniture

We have already given a rather systematic description of the types of houses that one would find in a town. We are handicapped by the fact that, though most of the houses must have been of wood, we can describe mostly only stone buildings — from extant structures. There is, of course, the page from the Morgan Library which shows King David watching Bathsheba in her bath, for which the maids are bringing cauldrons of hot water. The upper floor in that case in a kind of *loge* with very little wall on the façade towards King David. This two-story wooden house is another argument to be added to those we have already mentioned that wooden houses of more than one story existed in the mid-twelfth century. The medieval texts make rather frequent mentions of the *estres* of a house. This term must refer to the upper parts of a house as they are viewed from outside: the roof, the upper windows, the *loges* on a top floor. There are many, many occurrences of this term: "Uriens was at the highest *estres* of the palace, at the principal openings." [10]

---

[10] *Claris*, vv. 18963ff.

A wooden house could have long rows of windows without weakening the structure because the weight of the roof in such a building was borne by the huge oaken end posts at the four corners. The floors of dwellings, wood or stone, must usually have been of tile or brick. We cannot rule out the suggestion of wooden boards, but there were no saw mills at that time and wooden planking had to be sawed by hand without any mechanical assistance. The flooring was practically always covered with straw or rushes in every conceivable kind of room. We know this to be a fact; but it is interesting to quote some sixteenth century evidence. Paul Hentzner, a German traveller, attended a presence reception in Greenwich Castle in the 1590s. He says, "We were admitted by an order Mr. Rogers had procured from the lord chamberlain, into the presence-chamber, hung with rich tapestry, and the floor after the English fashion, strewed with hay, through which the queen commonly passed on her way to the chapel." [11]

A *chambre celee,* sometimes cited as a long narrow space, is mentioned not infrequently. What was meant by a *chambre celee?* In the *Yvain* Chrétien speaks of the allegorical figures Love and Hate living in the same house. Perhaps Love had shut herself up in some *chambre celee* and Hate had gone into the *loges* (outdoor galleries) which face on the street, because she wanted to be seen. [12] We assume that the *chambre celee* was some walled-off space, behind a stair, etc.

Town streets, except for the main streets, were extremely narrow. On festal occasions awnings and tapestries were hung across between houses, keeping off sun and rain, while at the same time making a rather dim and unpleasant "pit" between the houses, particularly if they were tall. We can imagine the stench on a hot, summer's day, with the space closed in and the street the usual open privy. Medieval man lived very close to his rudimentary functions, and was perhaps the wiser for it.

Of course, many of the smaller houses, especially the wooden ones, had only one floor. Such a house is described in the *Roman*

---

[11] Paul Hentzner, *Travels in England,* tr. Horace Earl of Oxford (London, 1797), p. 33.

[12] *Yvain,* vv. 6040ff., in *Christian von Troyes,* ed. Wendelin Foerster, vol. 2 (Halle: Niemeyer, 1884-99).

*de la Rose* (13th century). The lover cannot sleep, so he is advised by Love to go in the very early dawn to visit his lady's house. It is clear from the description that she lives in a one-floor wooden structure:

> When you cannot endure the miserableness in your sleepless bed, you will have to dress yourself, put on your foot covering, before daybreak comes. You will go quietly, whether it be in rain or in frost, straight towards the house of your beloved. She will doubtless be sound asleep and will hardly be thinking of you. For a while you will go to the back door, to ascertain whether it has been shut, and you will stand there on one leg all alone, in rain and in the wind. Afterwards you will go to the front door, and if you can find a split siding (*fendeüre*), or a window, or a keyhole, put your ear there and listen whether those inside are asleep, and whether the dear girl (*la bele*) is awake. I advise and recommend that you let her hear you lament and grieve, so that she will know you cannot rest in bed because of her. A woman should certainly have pity on someone who endures such sorrow for her, if she is not very hard.
>
> I will tell you what you should do ... when you leave to go home, kiss the door. Do not let anyone see you before the door, so leave before daybreak. [13]
>
> I also command and bid you that you must seem generous to the maid of the household. Give to her such a present that she will speak well of you. You should honor your lady and all who wish her well; you can get great reward when those who are close to her will tell her that you are nice and worthwhile. [14]

It can be assumed from this description that the lady lives with her people in a limited environment. Since the lover can go easily to the back door they have no courtyard. Apparently the wall of the groundfloor hall where they live and sleep is not lined with hangings. Probably they had only two rooms. They have one servant, a *bajasse*, maid of all work.

---

[13] *Le Roman de la Rose par Guillaume de Lorris et Jean de Meun*, ed. Ernest Langlois, SATF (Paris: Firmin-Didot, 1920), II, vv. 2508-42.

[14] *Ibid.*, vv. 2557-67.

## THE TOWN DWELLERS

It is very apparent from this, if it has not been obvious before, that the average town dweller lived like a bee in a hive. He had constant physical contact with his fellow men — and women. They lived wedged in together, and they slept in a minimum of space. [If it is true, as we would argue, that the spatial arrangements of our life shapes our understanding of the meaning of life, we should not be surprised that strong notions of privacy and the rights pertaining to individual choice never entered the medieval mind. The recent Supreme Court decision, for example, which argues that a woman has a private right to choose to abort the unborn fetus within her womb, would be utter nonsense to a medieval man, for whom the right was always a matter of divine will manifested in the social structures of which he was a small part. He could not possibly think of an ethical decision as an abstraction, divorced from the hard realities of living in such close proximity to conception, parturition, defecation, decay and death — the body functions of which his senses never ceased to be reminded.]

> For a long time they sat and talked
> Straightway are the beds all ready —
> Then they go to sleep when it is time. [15]

These beds consisted, usually, of a front board, a foot board and *espondes* or bed-rails with which they could speedily hook the front and end pieces (or frames) together. A *chaaliz* or frame (with bed cords) was dropped into the center and thin mattresses were laid in some number on this. On top of the *coutes* or pile of these mattresses were placed two sheets (*linçueus*), then a *couverture* — fur-lined with silk on top. This sort of bed could be assembled in a few minutes. The young men and boys of the household were trained to do this, and they filled the hall or *sale* with many beds when the number of people made it necessary. In the morning nearly all these were unhooked, and stowed away behind the hangings. The floor space was then clear for sitting, and eventually for eating, at which time the table trestles and boards were brought out.

The medieval man had very little furniture permanently in place. His clothes and other belongings were stowed in chests around the

---

[15] *Durmart li Galois*, vv. 9980ff.

wall. Clothes for daily use were draped on a pole or rail which was held in a bracket some four feet above the floor. At night the clothes taken off were draped over the floor board of the bed, which was often drawn close to the fire. There were no closets in the modern sense of the word — except a treasure room. The chest is sometimes referred to in English as a "press."

The reader may well be asking how we can be so positive about these furniture arrangements. The answer is that they continued in practice until the nineteenth century. Particularly in some memoirs, as the *Diary* of Samuel Pepys, they can be verified. When Pepys and his companions were lodged in Holland and on various other trips, they were in rooms with other people, not infrequently with people of the opposite sex. Samuel was very angry with one of his maids because she would not sleep in the room with him and his wife.

Passing into a bed which held a strange lady was not difficult, and not always resented. In *Amis et Amiles* (12th century) the daughter of Charlemagne crosses over to the bed of her beloved Amiles. His only question is as to her rank. She lies and the trouble that results makes up much of the story. (A girl was protected by her family and not by mere convention.) [To contemporary man for a woman to join a man in bed or *vice versa* is, *ipso facto*, an offer and acceptance of sexual congress. Perhaps it is our notions of privacy which breeds this universal judgement. Medieval man, living in a much less overtly "criticized" society, was freer to make rational judgements about close physical contact and had greater options of action. We suffer from our Pietist heritage.]

The floors were covered with unclean rushes, so it was preferable to use a thin mattress or a rug when sitting there. A lamp was often kept burning all night. In an average burgher's house the number of inhabitants could be as follows: the man and wife, the niece of the husband, three maids, three nephews, and three lower-class handymen.[16] We can wonder how so many people were bedded down. I suggest that the man and wife and the niece were in the chamber or bed-room. The three nephews bedded in the *sale* or hall.

---

[16] Antoine de Montaiglon and Gaston Raynaud, eds., *Recueil général et complet des fabliaux de XIII$^e$ et du XIV$^e$ siècle*, 6 vols. (Paris: Librarie des Bibliophiles, 1872-90), IV, 144ff.

The three maids could have slept also in the big hall, or perhaps in the kitchen below stairs, or outside. The three menials (*ribauz*) would lie on straw in the stable or some other outside shed.

The disposal of human waste was, to be sure, a constant problem. We have mentioned the *longaigne,* but this was very often occupied and too hard to get to. There is an almost inexhaustible series of comfort objects pictured in Lilian M. C. Randall's *Images in the Margins of Gothic Manuscripts* (Berkeley: University of California Press, 1966). These naughty little drawings or *babouines,* often with apes serving as the principal figures, were sketched by idle or mischievous pens on the margins of all kinds of serious works.

In some of these sketches the *pot de chambre* is portrayed very clearly as a vessel in the shape of a large chalice (fgs. 530, 533) with a stem that raises it to a desired position above the ground. The individuals in these particular drawings are not actually sitting on the vessel while defecating — they are poised above it. Urinals resembling slim vases are also seen in these sketches. The shape of the wooden toilet seat can be seen in an illumination on a manuscript of the *Cantigas* of Alfonso el Sabio.

*Meals*

We have been hinting in these pages about the nature and circumstances of the average meal. The food and lodging arrangements of a travelling couple are very well presented in the *Escoufle.* The protagonists, boys and girls, are fleeing together and they know that they are being pursued. As a precaution they

> ...never stop for the night on a main street or along the road side. (They are riding on two handsome mules.) The boy makes arrangements with the chamber maid and the household of their host that he may have his boots drawn off and also the saddles from the mules. (He sees to oats and hay for the animals.) They do not spare money in getting meat and other food, good wines and fish which he commands that they buy in plenty.... In the evening the boy has the pasties made for them to eat the next day when they are in the country.... He does not begin eating supper until his host is seated. His hosts and hostesses all marvel at the wealthy display.... After eating he calculates the expense with the host.... the girl takes out her

purse and pays.... they have the hosts make their beds with their own hands.... the boy causes the salt and the cakes (*gastiaus*) to be wrapped in a towel and has the skins filled with good cold wine or *raspé* (very weak wine). In one part of the food wallet are kept the pasties, in the other is a *fouace* (hearth bun) with cold meat or roast chicken. Then the boy closes the bag so that no one can remove the meat or anything else... When sleep comes over them he goes up to Aelis — they drink and then go to bed. The next morning they get up very early and ride till prime (six o'clock). When the hour of dinner approaches, if they can find a spring on their road, either in the open or in a wood, he says: "Dear girl I suggest we stop here for dinner".... When they have spent their day either in the field or the wood they mount their mules who are fat from the fine grass and they go to their night's lodging.

On a certain day (their last together) they removed their outer clothing and lay in a field. He removed the head stalls from the mules, he placed the wine skins in a stream to cool, he spread out the towel and his cloak for the tablecloth; the girl washed her hands in the spring; the boy draws out a chicken and a pasty from the wallet.... Finally they pack up again, and they become separated when he pursued a kite which had snatched away their purse of money. [17]

It is very often mentioned, in many texts, that for a picnic lunch a capon, a *gastel*, and a henap to be filled with wine, were ample.

We have said that it was common for the first principal meal to be taken at ten-thirty or eleven in the morning, followed by a sext (rest) at around noon; the next principal meal was at Vespers, our six p.m. In a house the trestles were brought out at those meal times. Benches were placed beside the table board which was covered with a fair white cloth almost touching the ground.

We have almost no information on the breakfast or an early breaking of the fast, but there is something about this in Ramon Lull's *Blanquerna*. The father Evast is annoyed because Aloma, Blanquerna's mother, sends him to school in the early morning on one occasion "with a breakfast (*almorsar*) of roast meat; [and] for later she gave him a custard (*flaon*) that he should eat in school if he felt hungry." Evast said that "for children one should not give

---

[17] *L'Escoufle*, vv. 4480ff.

for early breakfast (*almorsar de mati*) anything but bread, so that they might not lose the desire for eating at the table at the dinner hour." [18]

[Such a breakfast is very much like that of ancient Rome. There a cup of water, a piece of bread, and a bit of cheese prepared the average man to leave his house and do his business in the market place. One wonders whence came the Anglo-American tradition of the heavy breakfast.]

A fine evening meal (at Vespers), a little on the elaborate side, is described for us in one of the fabliaux. A bourgeois comes to a town and can find no one to lodge him except the village priest. This priest is a grasping fellow; he takes pains to give him a good meal, but for this he must pay five sous (60 deniers), for each item.

The miserly priest in question wanted to charge his guest five sous for each item of the meal. Ten sous are mentioned frequently elsewhere as making a full purse (*aumosniere*). [19] May we assume from this that five sous represented half a purse full of coins?

The passage which we now cite is where the priest's household is preparing the dinner:

> There were not many in the normal complement of the household so they asked two cousins of the priest to come; they were attractive and knew how to serve properly.... They cooked two hens. The meat course was very agreeable for the rabbits and the geese were already prepared, and the fish. Gille, who was attractive in person, made two pasties, and a cake (*gastel*); Dame Avinee selected the fruit.... The priest peeled the almonds. Some one pounded the garlic, another ground the pepper, and thus they made a very good *soivre* sauce. A third washed the eating bowls (*escueles*), a fourth set out the benches and the stools. In two basins bright and shiny they brought the hand-washing water.... Afterwards the chaplain washed his eyes, his mouth, and his hands. Then they took their places near two candelabras of copper; in each of these there was a large candle. The courses were served one by one. First there came bread and wine. For the second course they had

---

[18] Ramón Lull, *Livre d'Evast et de Blanquerna*, ed. Armand Llinares (Paris: Presses Universitaires de France, 1970), p. 13.

[19] Montaiglon and Raynaud, V, 320.

pork and rabbit; then were brought the young birds — and afterwards the cakes (*gastels*), followed by capons with the *soivre* sauce and the fishes in strong pepper. Last of all come the pasties. Then Dame Avinee brought nuts, other fruit, and cinnamon, ginger, and liquorice — many a good herb and many a spice. They drank red and white wine (*vermeil et blanc*).[20]

To make this dinner menu clearer we will repeat the items in sequence: bread and wine, pork and rabbit, fresh birds, capons in sauce, fish well peppered, pasties, nuts and fruits, ginger, liquorice, and both red and white wine.

This *soivre* sauce was a kind of garlic sauce, made with leeks and garlic, and onions.[21] (One did not usually eat meat without bread.)[22] The nature of the *gastel* has long intrigued us. I have suggested that it was a kind of shortbread containing only flour, honey, and shortening. There was no baking powder at this time. The *gastel* could contain an egg: "The *gastel* which is in there which the *bajasse* just made, is very wide, and made with eggs."[23] Conforming to what was presumably a common practice, Thomas Becket took spices after eating as a remedy against nervous indigestion.

Dogs were so common in most medieval houses that bones were dropped on the floor rushes where the dogs could gnaw them. [Again this is a practice closely related to classical custom. For example, in the New Testament the Canaanite woman reminds Jesus, "The dogs eat the scraps that fall from their masters' table."[24] Children and some adults may still feed their dogs from the table, but what was once taken for granted is now considered bad manners.]

I have spoken frequently thus far of the *escueles*, or eating bowls made of metal or of wood. Our modern word *skillet* derives from *escueillete*, a small dish. Usually two people ate out of one bowl. There were a few sharp knives lying on the table cloth for cutting, and salt containers, sometimes in elaborate shapes such as

---

[20] *Ibid.*, II, 52-57.
[21] *Claris*, vv. 24302.
[22] *Ibid.*, v. 2309.
[23] Montaiglon and Raynaud, V, 199.
[24] Matthew 15:29, *NEB*.

salt boats. Such a container, a *seller,* is what we mean today by a (salt) seller — now spelled cellar. Drinking was done from henaps — fine big goblets of the chalice kind. Such hena(p)s were passed from guest to guest and filled each time from a small wine-skin. In one corner of the *sale* would be the *henapier,* a small chest for storing the many cups. At Vézelay, in the nave carvings, there is a carving of bread being broken over a *henapier* chest, which looks like a small side-board. The loaf of bread is round in shape, like a large bun.

After such a meal the tables would have their long cloths removed, but these were not always taken away immediately. A guest might loiter with his arms and other things laid on the table and relax and perhaps listen to a minstrel. This is depicted in the *Flamenca* and in many other tales. The table boards would be removed when the beds were brought in for the night.

*Schools in the Town*

We have said almost nothing so far of the education of the children of the merchant class, which varied considerably according to the prosperity of the family. A very wealthy merchant such as Evast, in the tale by Ramon Lull, can be mentioned first. Evast's son Blanquerna was carefully brought up, nursed by a wet nurse until about the age of three, then permitted to run and play with other children without any constraint except that of nature until he was eight. At that time he was subjected to the rules of the *Doctrina Puerilis.* He was taught, in vulgar tongue, doctrine and an understanding of the articles of Faith, the Commandments, and the Seven Sacraments, the Seven Virtues, and the Seven Sins. Then he was given a *mestre* or guardian — a young clerk. [I am reminded of the classical *paidagogos* (*lit.* "child-leader") who took the boy to school. For example, Paul the Apostle writes that the law has become our *paidagogos* to Christ.] [25] This clerk took the boy to church and superintended his behavior there. They would go together to school.

Blanquerna learned enough grammar so that he could speak and understand Latin, and then he studied enough logic, rhetoric, and

---

[25] Galatians 3:24. Greek: "...paidagogòs...eis Christón...."

natural philosophy to appreciate the elements of Medicine. After learning *The Book of the Principles and Degrees of Medicine*, in order to know how to care for his own health, he studied elementary Theology. Pirenne says that beginning in the second half of the twelfth century towns began to operate little schools for the sons of tradesmen. This is the first manifestation of lay education in the medieval period.

The town authorities had the right to nominate the schoolmaster, but theologians also had some supervision from external ecclesiastical authority. This is illustrated by what we have quoted about the instruction given Blanquerna. The most advanced countries in economics were Italy and Flanders where such schools were certainly maintained. The growth of commerce required of course, more and better schools. By the thirteenth century it was a general practice for the merchants to keep books in single entry. Double entry was later devised in Italy. Money lending became quite general. So much property was tied up in land that many loans were made just to keep one's capital liquid. Italian bankers began to flourish as much as the Jews, and they needed educated clerks. The Fairs of Champagne, nonetheless, where Jews were very plentiful, were the headquarters of the banking industry and so the Jews still led the way in business training.

In this chapter we have scarcely mentioned the education of middle-class women. After their childhood they were almost always instructed in sewing, weaving, and embroidery. Some learned a little about singing and the elements of reading. It was common for a girl to be married at the age of fourteen. By rights she was considered an adult at that age; but Lambert d'Ardres in his *Historia Comitum Ghisnensium* narrates how the little countess, wife of his overlord, still played with dolls and went swimming in the kitchen fish pond to the delight of many onlookers.

There were exceptions, however, and Baudri de Borugueil had some correspondence of a poetic nature with learned women. An important center of female education was the convent of Le Ronceray at Angers. In this convent a group of young girls received a literary education while intending to return to the secular world. They were, of course, students — not nuns under ecclesiastical discipline. The amatory verses which Baudri wrote to them were common leonine hexameters or couplets. Apparently these poems were not just exercises in imitation of Ovid; they represented genuine relationships.[26] In the early twelfth century Hilarius, a pupil of Abelard, also wrote love lyrics to these young ladies of Le Ronceray.[27]

*Summary*

[This brings us to an end of this rather long chapter on the town dwellers. Reflection upon what we have discussed and its relationship to medieval man's self-understanding highlights several points. First, man is perhaps best analyzed *qua* man in the context of the "city," by which I mean the image of a self-contained, organic, socio-cultural entity. The Greek *polis* (on the basis of which Aristotle said man is a *politikē* or "political animal") is the paradigm of *human* existence, and the medieval town reveals this universal truth in a peculiar cultural context that is our concern.

Second, there is a common character to town life that reaches into the classical past and forward into what has been called the "walking city" of early nineteenth-century Europe and America. It was rapid transportation along with other technologies (e.g., the flush toilet, central heating, the elevator, telephone and telegraph, etc.), that made possible the "megapolis" of the twentieth century, and thus created a *discontinuity* with the town life of previous millenia. This break precipitated a new image of man. It is almost commonplace, therefore, to say that eighteenth-century man had a more common sense of identity with twelfth- and first-century man than he would have had with us of the twentieth century.

Third, the boundaries between the town dweller and the rural countryside were more easily penetrated seven hundred years ago than they are today. Man's alienation from nature was not so developed that he failed to recognize the source of the raw materials of the town crafts, the original form of his food, and his utter dependence upon the caprice of natural events. He did not have to rush from work on late Friday afternoon to his "camp" in the country to recapture his primordial roots, in an earlier existence, to

---

[26] Peter Dronke, *Medieval Latin and the Rise of European Love Lyrics* (Oxford: Clarendon Press, 1965), I, 213ff.

[27] *Ibid.*, pp. 216-20.

the earth. Despite the town streets, the clutter of people and buildings, and the growing bureaucracy, medieval man was still there in the soil from which he sprung. This may lie behind both his engaging honesty and his thinly veiled barbarity.]

## VI

## THE BARONS AND KNIGHTS

Any description of the medieval baronial class is complex. They were not just the administrative class, because many of the lesser officials of town and organized society were of the middle class. They were not the only military group of the era, as the lower class sergeants were more frequently under arms. The barons were the vassals of the king and at the same time a military class. The lowest rank among them was lord of a manor.

The manorial system below the barons consisted of the peasants (including serfs) and those bourgeois who owed service of various kinds to the lord of their manor. In return these vassals received military protection, certain lands belonging to their lord, and the right to practice trades within his jurisdiction. Infeudation began as a serious social system in the ninth century when the "little man" required protection from the invaders which he could not handle himself.

### The Knights and Courtly Love

Almost always, in the period with which we are now concerned, upper class vassals were knighted. The candidate for knighthood knelt before his actual overlord, placed his hands, palms together, into the cupped hands of his overlord and promised him loyal service. [A recollection of this practice can be seen in the common custom for the active participants in a solemn liturgy in the Anglican or Roman Catholic churches to disport themselves with hands held, palms together, before them — a sign of their "vassalage" to Christ as Lord.] Gradually the Church had been making a religious service out of the dubbing of knights; but this was not firmly the case till the later Middle Ages. Then, for example, an aspirant for knighthood was encouraged to keep a vigil in a church over his arms all night long.

In the twelfth century the chief qualification for knighthood was the possession of full arms and a horse. In Marie's *Eliduc* the wife had been helped by a young man who is undoubtedly a bachelor in his late teens. He has helped her find the lady who is beloved by Eliduc, and as a result the wife promised to the young man that, if he would find her husband, "horses and arms she would give to him."[1] Shortly after that when the stoat had revived its mate with a flower she cried in haste "Catch him, throw at him, *franc humme,* don't let him get away."[2] The meaning of *franc humme* is too often dismissed. Since the protagonist was administering the lands of her husband while he was in England, she was the overlord who had the right to make the young man, her vassal, a knight or a freeman as she wished. We believe that by calling him a *franc humme* (free man) in this tense situation she was giving him his freedom. So, for his aid to her, he became both a non-serf and a knight.

In an effort to control excessive fighting zeal and brutality among these armed men the Church encouraged gentleness and service. What we call the Code of Courtly Love is still an enigma for scholars. Andreas Capellanus, drew up an art of love *(De Arte Honeste Amandi)* for Marie de Champagne. This stipulated the necessary requirements for a proper courtly romance: complete service to the lady, without any demurral, absolute secrecy and perfect loyalty. True love of the courtly variety could not exist between married people. This doctrine remained more or less in vogue among knights and their ladies for some two hundred years. [The fact that this relationship of love existed outside marriage perhaps leads contemporary thought to see in it something akin to an institutionalized occasion for extra-marital affairs. To make this judgement is to commit the unforgivable sin of historical scholarship: to interpret one period's customs through the *Weltanschauung*

---

[1] *Eliduc,* v. 984, in Marie de France, *Les Lais,* ed. Ernest Hoepffner (Strasbourg: Heitz, 1921).
[2] *Ibid.,* v. 1056.

of another's. Let us keep in mind that romantic love, which classical man considered a disease, has been unrelated to the social institution of marriage, existing for the purpose of socializing children, through most of the history of man. All marriages prior to the last century were "of convenience" — but by "convenience" we mean with the clear intention of perserving the society. Romantic love would be considered an unnecessary entanglement to this very sober business of maintaining the social structures through a solidly founded family. What happened in the twelfth century was that the "disease" of heterosexual, emotional attachment became acknowledged as the basis of a valued human relationship.]

Was the Code of Courtly Love originally a sort of game, a sensible practice, or was it an ideal that never really existed except in the common imagination? Some scholars have found its origins in Plato, others say courtly love developed from Plato's Arab commentators: Avicenna (980-1037) and Averroes (1126-1198). Certainly superficial resemblances to such doctrines as the Italian *dolce stil nuovo* of the thirteenth century, and thence Petrarchism — and even the Preciosity of the seventeenth century, exist. In stories where courtly love is featured the lady is invariably a married woman. (See the *Chevalier de la charrette* or *Lancelot* of Chrétien de Troyes for a perfect example of this love doctrine in literature.) Slightly older than this exploitation of what we can term courtly love is the type of love known as Ovidian love, which also flourished in the early romances of chivalry. Ovidian love generally demands that the lady refuse marriage, although the lover yearns to marry her. Love is described as a kind of malady, with symptoms that are always visible. In the thirteenth century, courtly and Ovidian love more or less merged in literature.

Young, unmarried people in the Middle Ages were in fact very young indeed. The lady might well be no more than twelve or thirteen, and the boy could be anywhere in his teens. Boys and girls of this age have always been, since the earliest times we know, sentimentally silly. This should be taken into account when estimating the true nature of the kinds of love found in medieval literature and their relationship to marriage.

There are three parts to a Church marriage: the Betrothal, the Promise, and the Consummation. It was entirely possible in the period with which we are concerned for the Betrothal to take place when the participants were still infants. The Promise was supposed to wait till the age of puberty in both bride and groom, and the Consummation, sexual intercourse, sealed the marriage [although in the later Middle Ages the Church emphasized the Promise, which gave it more control over the institution]. Considerable fuss was made over the Consummation. The bride was put to bed formally by her mother, and then the wedding party, led by the officiating cleric, marched past them into the bridal chamber. The cleric blessed them. When there had been no formal consummation, the bonds of marriage, it was commonly thought, could be broken with little trouble. The Church was not entirely in agreement with this idea, but it was certainly expressed in medieval literature (see the lai *Le Fresne* by Marie de France). In later times the *charivari* was probably a continuation of this march of guests past the bed. Probably the throwing of rice today has some relationship to these customs. [It is obviously related to an act of sympathetic magic: the scattering of seed, which the act of ejaculation in intercourse was precisely considered to be.

If this overt fascination with the marriage bed seems to us repulsive, or at least in "bad taste," we must keep in mind that medieval man did not isolate himself from the natural functions of the body — either in himself of others — as we do. There was no privacy which permitted the children to grow up ignorant of the "primal act" between their parents. Furthermore, we have no evidence that their psyches were irreparably damaged by witnessing this scene, as Freud predicted for his late Victorian patients. In fact, it is evident that they saw in this the promise of fertility and the hope of the future family.]

### *The Barons and Their Dwellings*

Henceforth I shall speak of the upper-class fighting men as "barons," or the baronial class. In rank these men could be dukes, marquis (rulers of a march or disputed bit of territory), counts or earls (senior rulers in shires or counties), viscounts (actually the sheriffs of counties), or *sires* — lords of single manors. *Baron* was a title that could be applied to any one in these orders, and also to any knight.

The term *chasé* was used frequently for one who held a single manor and lands. A *vavasour* was one who did not hold his fief directly in the feudal line. This was what you might call "subletting." An *aloez* was one who held his lands without any service or rent due to an overlord. An *avouez* was a lay knight who held jurisdiction over the laymen in a fief which was headed by a church lord (bishop or abbot). The knights, to be sure, even when they held no civil jurisdiction, were the "genteel" class. A young man, of an upper-class family, who aspired to be a knight was called an *escuiier* (squire) and it was usual to find him attached to the service of a knight. The word *vallet* was not an indication of an office or rank, as all boys in the age group of eight to fourteen had that designation, and, of course, many of them were engaged in all types of lesser service. A *bachelor* was a young man of fourteen to twenty who was not necessarily of the military class. The word *liege* when applied to an overlord or to one who served under him meant that only military service was involved, as there was no land rent or any other kind of obligation, and derived from an old Germanic word meaning "free." A liegeman was generally expected to give forty days of military service each year to his lord unless he could provide a substitute.

The men of the baronial class usually had obligation to furnish protection to their vassals, so they naturally lived for the most part in fortified structures. The simplest building of this class was a wooden blockhouse on top of an artificial mound. Such blockhouses are represented in the Bayeux Tapestry and can be viewed and measured from the post holes of their vertical timbers which are still visible on some very old mounds. There was undoubtedly a moat encircling the bottom of the outside of the mound. A gate house of a simple kind stood at the outer stair which led up the slope.

This sort of simple structure was succeeded rapidly in the twelfth century, and even in the eleventh, by motte and bailey keeps. These had similar arrangement; but the donjon proper was a stone tower, round or otherwise, of three or four floors. This structure soon developed a circular wall of stone around the foot and often had a draw bridge from the summit of that wall to a small door on the first floor of the tower. Then the space between the circular or curtain wall and the tower itself began to level out and this became a courtyard, filled with many chickens, a fish pond, and various other noisy creatures. This structure became the fullfledged motte and bailey castle of stone. (The bailey was the courtyard.) The groundfloor of the tower was for storage and service of various kinds, perhaps even torture! The first floor up in the tower was the main *sale*, or hall, and often the circumference of the *sale* was quite small. If the *sale* was a little larger it might have a few service rooms on one side. A stair close to the wall, mounted to the floor above, which I usually call the women's apartments. There the lady and her girls slept before a nice fireplace. There were *gardrobes* (toilets) at one end of the floor, and there might be a chapel on the wall. The floor above the women's apartments would be for servitors and guests; the roof was used often for defense. At Conisburgh near Sheffield there is a fine example of a twelfth-century "castle."

In the next stage of castle development, the court or bailey around the tower becomes much larger, and includes other buildings. A small manor house in which the lord and his family can live more comfortably is set against the inner wall. The lord almost always lived in the manor's chamber and entertained in the *sale* of this manor.

He may, however, have found it necessary to keep his wife (or perhaps his daughter) in the second floor up of the donjon tower, for her protection, or in order to check any amorous adventures towards which she might be inclined. The romances of the twelfth and thirteenth centuries are just full of this kind of description. The women's apartment in the donjon was about twenty feet up allowing ten feet to a floor. The heroine in Marie de France's *Yonec* falls this twenty feet after her wounded hawk lover flies out the window. Flamenca is incarcerated in such a place, and so were very many other heroines.

In Marie's *Laustic* two knights have their donjons or towers almost side by side. That is, there is a common wall between their baileys. One of the knights is married and the other is not. The married knight has reason to fear that his wife has a roving eye, so he takes no chances. He keeps her in the upper room of his tower and he goes to sleep with her there at night. The single knight is certainly sleeping in his manor on the first floor up. (The ground floor would have been for service purposes.) From her apartment on the second floor the lady can gaze down into the bachelor's sleeping room. They apparently toss objects up and down to each other. There is no reason, we suppose, why two fortified dwellings should *not* be side by side, and Marie is most explicit about this case. These twin dwellings could have been some distance out into the country, or they might have been in a "horizontal" area within a town.

The larger type of fortified dwelling is what is traditionally today called a castle. The castle is a fortified town, perhaps a mile in radius. It has streets, though not necessarily many. The overlord's tower is at the highest end of the town beside the wall. It is surrounded by quite a large bailey in which there should be a manor house, kitchen building, perhaps even a buttery and a pantry shed, maybe a church, and a few other halls to house knights, clergy, and others. Such a complex as this could require a strong gatehouse. A narrow street leading up to this would be named Castle Street. A good-sized moat and a drawbridge crossing over it to the gatehouse complete the picture.

Yvain encountered this type of castle when he was chasing Esclados the Red after the mortal battle at the Magic Fountain. Esclados spurred on to his Castle, the town in which he lived, through the silent streets and reached his donjon moat. He rushed across the drawbridge (which was down), avoiding a block of wood which was called a "trigger." Yvain rushed after him, his horse hit the trigger and the steel (or reasonable facsimile thereof) door fell, quickly cutting Yvain's horse in two. The lord Esclados passed through the room of the gatehouse, the exit door closed tight, and Yvain was stuck in that room between the two doors. Lunete who, I suspect, lived in the room over the hall of the gatehouse, came down and accosted Yvain. This kind of arrangement is pictured in one of the manuscripts of the *Yvain* and it fits well with what I have seen in actual castles of this size.

A manor house can be a castle on a smaller scale when it is in open country. Many of the thirteenth-century house ruins in England are commonly called castles, but they are just fortified manors. Stokesay "Castle" in Shropshire, and Eynsford in Kent are fortified manors. (Contrast these with genuine castles such as Hedingham in Essex and Castle Rising in Norfolk.) Such a country manor was built inside a large bailey, and the whole was surrounded by a moat. There would be also other buildings: kitchens, chamber buildings, chapel, but not necessarily a keep or a donjon, as at Framlingham, Suffolk. A manor was fortified for its own protection, while a castle was a fortification intended to hold a certain region from attackers.

A most interesting country manor in England was Warnford in Hantshire, not far from Winchester. It is a groundfloor hall with an attached chamber building of two stories. In a groundfloor hall the large hall rests on the ground and its ceiling rafters are of oak timber. A fireplace is at one end and two service doors are at the other. One enters from side doors.

A first-floor manor is readily adapted to a town site. Its ground floor has service rooms and storage; its big hall is a half story up. The lower chambers with vaulted stone ceilings on the ground level were more private. The people congregated in the large hall with a raftered ceiling. One finds in reading a romance or *chanson de geste* that for a private talk two people often withdraw to a *chambre voutie* (vaulted room). A small first-floor manor could also be attached to a row of houses, in a narrow city street. I have seen only one such manor house in France, at Cologne in Gascony, now a large wood-shed.

Medieval man did not pay much attention to views or to roominess in his dwellings. The essential factor for him was protection. Private belongings could easily be stowed away in chests. Of course, the lighting in medieval dwellings was seldom good, although tapers on standing candelabras were burned day and night. There was not a great deal of reading except in the open air. Often a family group would gather in a court or garden and one of the members, a young girl preferably, would read to the others. This sort of scene occurs in the romances of Chrétien de Troyes. [Perhaps in this regard we can speculate on why fighting was not so much an evil necessity, but a style of life for medieval man. There was very little to do for amusement and very little occasion for the refinements of culture. Life was often short and cruel. It can readily be seen, therefore, how there were not nearly the aspirations for the future that would hold in check the joy of a good battle and the glory of victory or the honor of having died on the field rather than in bed.]

### The Apparel of the Barons and Knights

People of the upper class during these centuries lavished much attention on their clothing. Expensive furs of *myniver* or of *cisemus* (delicate, most expensive eastern European dormouse) were soft and silky, and fairly well matched together by the furrier. (Remember that it was cold indoors, so the warmest clothing had to be worn in the house.) Formal mantles, gathered on the right shoulder, were particularly expensive for both men and women. When a minstrel received great applause it was usual for him to have many such mantles thrown to him; but the patrons were too lavish then, and this was considered an abuse. "Wild man, don't hurt me," said an old minstrel to Huon. "...I pity you. Take in my pack an ermine loose robe and a padded mantle of scarlet. Cover your flesh, then come and sit down and drink this good wine." [3] The minstrel gave Huon an ermine *peliçon* (fur garment), a *chemise*, *braies*, and a mantle of siglaton (cloth with very large coin dots or 'seals') on top. These were garments worn by a gentleman.

An upper class person began dressing by putting on his *braies* or baggy underdrawers. Then he might add a shirt of fine linen with long sleeves. On top of this perhaps was worn a fur garment called a *peliçon* with the fur against the body, a handsome *bliaut* or *cote*, and finally his mantle. As an example of fine textiles and furs I must slip in this little description from the *Elioxe:*

> The king gives marvellous clothes, sealed cloths (siglatons) and samites, scarlets, and greens, peliçons of myniver and grey squirrel fur.... There were many samites, many Escariment cloths, many cloths from Halape, interwoven with shiny gold, rich brocades, sealed cloths, rich greens from Ghent, many a stuff from Africa, fine dark velvet, and the furs were myniver and sable; the attach cords were worth many a besant. [4]

Many of the rich cloths that were used by the wealthy for their clothing, were brought from the Near East. I illustrate by two passages from Marie's *Le Fresne:*

---

[3] *Huon de Bordeaux, chanson de geste*, ed. François Guessard and Charles Grandmaison, APF 5 (Paris: F. Vieweg, 1890).

[4] The edition of "La Naissance de Chevalier au Cygne" known as the *Elioxe* is edited by H. A. Todd, *PMLA*, 4, nos. 3 & 4 (1888-89). This reference is to vv. 3080-85, 444-45.

> In a kerchief of very fine linen they wrap the fine child and on top of it they put a cloth with seal designs *(paille roé)* — her husband had brought it from Constantinople where he was. They had never seen another so good.[5]
> ..."I had our cloth carried with her and the ring you gave me when you first spoke to me."[6]

Cloths of this kind were characterized by Eastern designs that have now been identified. Fragments of such cloths are in the Victoria and Albert Museums in London and at the Musée de Cluny in Paris. To be sure, most of these remains of early rich cloths, parts of capes and chasubles, have been taken from the coffins of high ecclesiastics; but we assume that medieval taste in secular garments was of the same expensive kind.

During much of their daily routine the barons wore chain armor. The principal section of this armor was the hauberc, a coat of chain mail with a slit front and back at the crotch to enable horseback riding. Only one hauberc of this kind has been preserved from Europe before the fourteenth century, a hauberc at the Royal Museum in Stockholm, tightly rolled up and never placed on exhibition.

We possess, of course, a vast quantity of representations of this kind of armor from bas-relief carvings, from drawings, from the Bayeux Tapestry, and from other sources. The pictures of feudal lords on their seals (which can usually be dated) are the most informative. This hauberc, or mailed shirt, was worn over a padded *gamboison* or quilted undercoat. The mail coat was often of single thickness. Sometimes it was double thick so that a sort of flap could lie inside the visible external part of the coat. Very cautious knights doubled this flap, making a triple thickness. In the early part of the twelfth century the mail sleeves extended loosely to the wrist — later they began to extend over the hands, like mittens.

In the early part of the twelfth century the legs of knights were wrapped with cloths and cross-gartered like those of a peasant. In the later half of the twelfth the knights began to wear *chauces* (stockings) with wool on the rear and mailed links on the front.

---

[5] *Le Fresne*, vv. 121-26, in Hoepffner, *Les Lais*.
[6] *Ibid.*, vv. 474-76.

These were called mailed *chauces*. In the earlier times ordinary heavy leather shoes were used.

The mailed coat or hauberc had a hood called a *coiffe* which could be pulled up over the head. When desired a separate rectangular strip of mail (trapezoidal in shape) was usually fastened by leather thongs under the chin and into the *coiffe,* leaving only the cheek bones unprotected. This was called a *ventaille.* Over the *coiffe* a round helmet, like a pot, was placed and tied under the chin by thongs. This had a *nasal,* a projecting piece of metal wich extended from the lower forehead over the nose. When capturing a knight who wore such a helmet, it was usual to grab him by the nasal. In the last twenty years of the twelfth century, and into the thirteenth, box-like helmets began to be used, resting their weight on the knight's shoulders, with gratings in front. The effigies of King Richard I show such a helmet. Over the mail it was customary to wear a light *cote* of wool for decorative purpose. Spurs, with a single prick which could make bad wounds in the horse's side, were worn on the heels.

The knight wore a sword on his left side and carried especially a heavy lance and a kite-like shield with his arm slung through a transverse strap. The shield was of wooden boards *(linden)* covered with leather which was usually printed with some designs. Although registered heraldic devices were not in regular use until the midthirteenth century, the favorite design of a prominent knight was commonly recognized. In the eleventh century, and sometimes in the twelfth, a knight might carry one or two light lances *(espietes)* which he could hurl efectively against a target. A mace (iron club) or a battle axe might hang at the knight's saddle bow. The heavy lance *(lance)* was carried upright, held upon the *fautre,* which we assume was a felt cloth attached under the saddle.

## Styles of Combat

There are some excellent accounts of fighting with heavy equipment. We will cite one which describes a judicial trial by combat, in 1127, between Guy of Steencoorde and Herman the Iron. Guy was accused in the murder of his overlord, Charles of Flanders:

> Everyone present went out to the manor of Reningelst near Ypres. Guy had already unhorsed his adversary and was

keeping him down with his lance point just as he wished whenever Herman tried to rise. His adversary crawling closer disembowled Guy's horse with his sword. Guy slipped from the animal and rushed his adversary with sword drawn. Now there was a bitter struggle with alternating thrusts of swords, until both exhausted by the weight and burden of arms threw away their shields and hastened to gain victory by resorting to wrestling. Herman the Iron fell prostrate on the ground, and Guy was on top of him smashing the knight's face with his fists. But Herman, prostrate, little by little regained his strength from the coolness of the ground, and by cleverly lying quiet made Guy believe he was sure of victory. Meanwhile, gently moving his hand down to the slit in the hauberc where Guy was not protected, Hermann seized him by the testicles, and summoning all his strength for the brief space of one moment he kicked Guy from him with his legs; by this tearing motion all the lower parts of the body were broken so that Guy, now prostrate, gave up, crying that he was conquered and dying.[7]

The technique of keeping one's adversary on the ground by use of the lance head is most informative. The skill needed for the charge on horseback is best described by Ussamah. A knight fighting from his horse against an adversary similarly supplied began in this way. The lance in the right hand was tilted forward and the lower part of the shaft was held by the right elbow, tight against the body. At this point both adversaries dropped their reins on their horses' backs. The animals knew what to do: they lunged forward. By very lucky aim one of the knights might hit his adversary on the cheek bone which was not covered by a *ventaille*, helmet, or *coiffe*. (This did happen in 1559 when Captain Montgomery slew Henry II of France, but this was unusual.) The usual technique was to drive the lance into the other's shield and push the adversary backwards over his pommel (rear saddle bow). He was then unhorsed, and this probably was what Guy did first to Herman in the battle given above. But any knight who was nimble would time his defence better. The instant the enemy lance point struck his shield, he would lift the shield high over his head. This might well snap the other's

---

[7] Adopted from the translation of Galbert de Bruges' *The Murder of Charles the Good, Count of Flanders*, by James Bruce Ross (New York: Columbia University Press, 1960).

lance, or at least would break their lunge against each other. The knights could try again. This sort of fighting would be beautiful and thrilling to see.

Both knights could ask for other lances if the ones they had were broken. Sooner or later the action would be tiring and the two men could then continue with their swords, either both on the ground or both astride their horses. The first episode was described as breaking a lance together.

Perhaps some readers will recall that in Marie's lai *Milon* both the young knight and his father were remarkable fighters; but the older man lost his lance on that first plunge. We can see why: he was some twenty years older. I will give a rendering of this scene.

> He put himself into the ranks opposite the younger champion, and the two came together. Milon struck so hard that he shattered the other's lance truly, but he did not push him off his horse. The young man then tried and knocked the older man off *his* mount. But he noted under his adversary's *ventaille* the grey beard and hair. He was sorry that the older man had fallen. He took the empty horse by the bridle and gave him back as a present. He said, "Sire, mount. I am very sad that any man of your age should suffer such outrage." Milon jumped on and was quite pleased. [8]

A battle or a tourney consisted of a series of these single combats, until finally the last triumphant knight was proclaimed champion. Men who fought in this way were extremely sturdy individuals. William Marshal after some of this kind of battle had to go to a blacksmith to have his helmet removed — it had been driven down over his head. Knowing how much permanent damage can be done in the twentieth century to a prize-fighter by constant pounding on his skull, we may well wonder how the medieval knight could bear up, in the long run.

It was not the rule for a knight to bathe after such strenuous exercise. It was customary to make use of a sweat cloth for rubbing the body down after vigorous activity. The legendary Veil of Saint Veronica was, to be sure, a cloth of this kind, which medieval man naturally thought would be used to refresh Jesus' face. Such a

---

[8] *Milon*, vv. 413-29, in Hoepffner, *Les Lais*.

sweat cloth or veil became many centuries later, the ancestor of the modern handkerchief. Blowing one's nose in the Middle Ages, and early in modern times, consisted in blowing into the hand or on the ground with the aid of the fingers — which were then wiped as best it could be done. [9]

*The Games of the Upper Class*

Most younger men in the twelfth century of the Middle Ages were inveterate dicers. They rolled three dice of bone from their hand or from a cup — on a table or on the ground — whenever they had the spare time. They played for most points and at *hasart* (which we have described).

Older men are frequently described as playing chess. We shall give details of their game from the *Tratado de ajedrez* composed in 1283. The black pieces of ebony play against the white of ivory. The pieces were the King, and the *fierce* or standard bearer (later becoming the Queen), which normally moved only one square diagonally or straight, irrespective of any other pieces that lay between; it cannot take another piece on this initial movement. The knights could jump two squares to the right and then to a third in any direction whatsoever. The rook was played as today; one square at right angles, in any direction. The *alfin* could move six squares away and no more; it could take the piece on the square that it reached. The pawns move as in modern chess. If a pawn reaches the base line of the opposing side it became a new *fierce* or standard bearer. The chess boards were quite large (and the pieces as well). It is often mentioned in literature of the time that a chess piece was thrown in anger, injuring seriously the person it hit.

Some high-born players wished to learn the game seriously and did not seek to be flattered. Ruodlieb writes in the mid-eleventh century about a king who had just been defeated by Ruodolieb's pupil:

---

[9] Antoine de Montaiglon and Gaston Raynaud, eds., *Recueil général et complet des fabliaux du XIII⁰ et du XIV⁰ siècle* (Paris: Librarie des Bibliophiles, 1872-90), I, 114.

The king asking for a chess board ordered it placed before his seat and he bade me sit on the couch to play with him. I kept refusing saying that it is a fearful thing to play with a king. He saw me not daring to oppose him. I praised his playing, seeking to be defeated by him, saying, "How does it harm me to be beaten by a King? But I am afraid, lord, that you would soon be angry with me, if Fortune so aids that victory comes to me." The King, smiling, said playfully: "You must not be afraid of this, my dear fellow. If I am never defeated, I will have difficulty in becoming more skilful. I want you to play with me as strictly as you know how to play; for I wish to learn the unknown plays which you will make." Thereupon, the king and I set to playing studiously and, as he pleased, victory came to me three times, while there were an excessive number of his princes looking on. [10]

Another game which was played most frequently, perhaps more by people who did not worry about their dignity and intellectual status, was draughts or *tables*. This was related to what we call backgammon or parcheesi today. The two pieces played make progress according to throws of the dice.

It was a familiar practice to bet large sums of money on all these games, including chess. When money ran out, the unfortunate player would remove an article of clothing or something more valuable and try to pawn it with any one else present. This gambling fever was very strong among all classes of society, though somewhat less among the clergy [or so one might hope].

[It may well be that clergy are open to more criticism about their passions, and that in fact they were no worse and perhaps somewhat better on the average in their freedom from obsessive gambling, and the vices that go with it. However, it is noteworthy that there are constant complaints throughout the Middle Ages, of both an official and unofficial kind, about the frequenting of taverns and the fondness for gaming on the part of the clergy. It is just possible that priests, called to serve the transcendent present within the material stuff of life, have a more than usual temptation to stop short of a sacramental outlook and merely become sensual in life style.]

---

[10] "Ruodlieb Plays Chess with the King," in *The Oxford Book of Medieval Latin Verse*, ed. F. J. E. Raby (Oxford: Clarendon Press, 1959), p. 183.

## Forms of Wealth

[The matter of gambling and the sale of one's clothing leads naturally to a consideration of the nature of wealth in this period. There was no great level of sophistication in economic affairs, although the beginnings of what later formed the basis of modern economy were there.]

A table top or cover which resembled a chess board could be used as a counting board. It is understood that in calculations where Roman numerals were used, as was universal in the Middle Ages, addition was done with counters on a board, and not with pen on parchment. In most cases the counting board markings must have resembled a tree — that is, a perpendicular line in the center with a number of short crossing lines, representing units, tens, fifties, hundreds, etc. Sums were figured on such boards by placing counters on the appropriate lines. At the close of a lengthy calculation, the counters were counted and the sum marked down in Roman numerals. The board, as I have just described it, was called a "tree." It is certain that either a checker board, or a board covered with a "tree" as just described, was in use for very large calculations and this was the Exchequer — the very large board used in the room where taxes were received from the sheriffs or viscounts.

When the finances of the French Kingdom were organized during the absence of Philip Augustus in 1190, it is mentioned that Adam the King's clerk stood in a room of the Temple at Paris three times a year, in the presence of six men good and true of Paris, and of a designated seventh person, receiving the taxes brought in by the bailiffs and royal provosts.[11] It is to be assumed that every clerk stood beside just such an Exchequer table doing his vast sums.

During the reign of Louis VII (1137-79) these tax monies were received by a clerk in the Louvre; but the Templars in their new stronghold (after 1146) stored the money. Normally the King was present himself on these occasions when taxes were brought in. The dates for the payment of taxes were the Octaves of Saint-Remy,

---

[11] "In receptionibus averi nostri, Adam clericus noster, presens erit et eas scribet," in Ferdinand Lot and Robert Fawtier, *Histoire des institutions françaises au Moyen Age* (Paris: Presses Universitaires de France, 1957-), II, 185.

All Saints, Candlemas (*Chandeleur*), and Ascension.[12] Conon, the Provost of the church at Lausanne, mentioned at the funeral of Philip Augustus in 1222 that Louis VII when he died had an annual revenue of only 228,000 livres, while Philip Augustus was leaving to his son, Louis VIII, a revenue of 438,000 livres a year.[13] Henry II in England had an income of 17,000 pounds annually.

Under Philip Augustus, Louis VII, Louis VIII, and in the first part of the reign of Saint Louis, the Royal Court, which gave appeal decisions, was made up of Bishops, Abbots, Counts, and other Barons, and the King's chief officers. The material on which they based their decisions was gathered by *viri sapientes, viri prudentes, jurisprudentes, consiliarii, judices nostri*. These members of the Court usually met at the four high Feasts of the year. After the middle of the thirteenth century this situation changed with the new appeal courts.[14]

We have just observed that the royal treasure was placed in such strongholds as the vaults of the Templars. Yet each noble of any rank, and probably most wealthy bourgeois, maintained their own rooms for valuables. Much of the valuables was goldsmithery: reliquaries, chalices, crucifixes, basins, and figures of saints. Many of these are still preserved in the treasuries of the Churches.[15] Alas, the barons of the Middle Ages were great robbers when they could steal under some cloak of respectability. They plundered in captured towns, so their private treasure rooms were supplied with much ecclesiastical gear.

When urged to take what one wished from a treasure room, one took moderately. There were, of course, many, many small carved ivories, and undoubtedly heaps of deniers and of besanz in which the visitor with special privilege was urged to dip a hand.

The upper crust folk in the Middle Ages, both clerical and lay, had a special virtue which was labelled *mesure*. We translate it "moderation." Those who acted with *démesure* in anything were destined to meet with trouble. In the literature of the twelfth and thirteenth centuries there is constant reminder of the perils of this

---

[12] *Ibid.*, p. 196.
[13] *Ibid.*, p. 159.
[14] *Ibid.*, p. 300.
[15] See Jean Taralon, *Treasures of the Churches of France*, tr. Mira Intrator (New York: George Braziller, 1966).

violation of *mesure*. [Perhaps this was related to the Horatian "golden mean."]

The medieval peoples were very fond of gems, which they knew how to set in cabochon only. They thought of most minerals as having magic, protective, and healing properties. Some years ago I examined the treasury list of King Charles V of France, as it was itemized by the goldsmiths after his death.[16] At that time the truly precious stones were rubies, emeralds, balas rubies, and pearls. The balas is no more than an ornamental stone today. It is now called spinel, which is isotropic (suitable for a burning glass), and which does not have the fire that is present in a true corundum ruby. A true ruby is uniaxial (splitting light rays except when they enter from one specific direction). The diamond is mentioned as precious, but it had almost no beauty in medieval times since it could not be cut and faceted. Many of the jewels in the twelfth and thirteenth century were just glass (which could be worked easily). The quartzes were much used in lesser jewelry: notably amethyst, prase, chalcedony, jasper, and the sardonyx or cameo.

A twelfth-century collection of finger rings, in a leather bag, was found by a ditch-digger in the mid-nineteenth century. Perhaps a lady riding along the highway had dropped this collection, to be found seven hundred years later. It contains several rings with sapphires (roughly bruited) as the principal stone; several with colored glass, and then various rings where there was no stone at all; a friendship ring with clasped hands, and others with engravings only.

It was a usual custom for lovers to exchange rings. Presumably a man placed on his little finger a ring from the lady's hand. She would put on her thumb a ring that he gave her. This practice is surely a forerunner of our engagement ring custom. Mentions of a wedding ring are rare, but here is one where the officiating priest puts the ring on the lady's finger. "The Archbishop afterwards takes a ring which was of massive gold and put it on her finger in the name of the Father, in the name of the Son, and of the Holy Ghost."[17] The ring could be sent as a love gift: "The ring I sent among my gifts is a token of love, so let us in all courtesy strive

---

[16] See my article on Charles V's treasury in *Speculum*, 9 (1934), 195-206.
[17] *Elioxe*, v. 435ff.

to submit to Love's law." The heroine replies: "My reputation does not know the law you mention, and indeed does not wish me to learn such courtesy."[18]

*Travel and Modes of Transportation*

Travel by the upper class was mostly on horseback. (The lower classes did not travel.) If one were travelling independently he required a sumpter, that is a horse or mule which had a special pack saddle for carrying baggage. This pack animal was led by a boy, an attendant, who would be riding on a *rocin*, a sturdy animal who could take much punishment. The master was apt to be mounted on a *palefroi* (palfrey) which could be of Spanish breed.

For fighting, the knight preferred a large kind of horse, similar to our Clydesdales or Percherons. A knight's fighting animal would be led on the right hand by a boy on his *rocin* when the owner was not readying for action. A mule was often used as the principal mount, particularly by ecclesiasts. The mule had no tendency to trot, which could be disagreeable.

Unless one was an armed knight, it would be preferable to travel with a large group. Clothing could be placed in sacks which were then hooked on to the pack saddle of a sumpter.

When a rider mounted a spirited horse, there were various kinds of paces which one could put the mount through: "As they came back they did the French pace."[19] Horses could be protected by armor: "He mounts on a Spanish horse all covered, neck, crupper, and breast."[20]

The harness then was very similar to what our grandfathers, and even our fathers, used for their horses, but most of our readers, unless associated with horse racing, will not be familiar with this. In the twelfth and thirteenth centuries straps and laces were not secured by metal buckles with a metal tongue, but were tied. The horse's headstall was tied under his head by a knot. The bellyband

---

[18] Peter Dronke, *Medieval Latin and the Rise of the European Love Lyric* (Oxford: Clarendon Press, 1965), II, 428.

[19] *Li Romans de Raoul de Cambrai et de Bernier,* ed. De Glay, rprt. of 1832-48 ed. (Genève: Slatkine Reprints, 1969).

[20] *Li Romans de Garin le Loherain,* ed. Paulin Paris, 2 vols. (Paris: Techener, 1833-35), vv. 7317ff.

also was tied underneath. The saddle had two parts: the pommel and the cantel, which were referred to in Old French as the *arçons*. The stirrups were approximately the same as those used today. A rider always wore a spur on his right heel. This was somewhat cruel: the rowel or wheel type had not yet been devised. The rider had a spike point, and this he pricked into his mount rather liberally — drawing blood we can be sure. Most of the harness, including the reins, was of woven material, and there were bells and other pendants arranged along its strips.

A usual day's travel was about thirty-five miles, the result of seven hours of riding at about five miles an hour, unless there was need for special haste. One might put in three hours in the saddle in the morning, then have a good meal, resting at sext or the sixth hour. When getting a good start, it was possible to go for four more hours, after *relevee*. At approximately our six o'clock it was time for supper. After this the travelers were entertained by minstrels or engaged in conversation.

Carriages were not used until the late fourteenth century, and then only for short distances. A cart, of course, was out of the question. The remaining method of travel, aside from "shank's mare," was by ship.

There were four principal kinds of ships: the *esneque* (*esneke*), the *cogge*, the galley, and the *dromont*. The small coasting vessels which are represented in the Bayeux Tapestry crossing the English Channel, were *esneques*. These were what we today would call "long boats," with a single mast that could be stepped in the center. A steering oar on the starboard (or "steer board") side had a tiller-like head. For protection from the weather there was the fore-castle; a similar one aft was the rear-castle. The master of the ship stood before this rear-castle and operated the hoist or windlass (*grindas*) which raised and lowered the single sail. There was probably an implement called the *luff* which we cannot identify exactly. It may have been a kind of pole for pushing the yard arm, when desired, against the wind. The *New English Dictionary* translates luff as "perhaps a contrivance for altering a ship's course, often in the phrase, to wend or turn the luff."

The White Ship which was lost in crossing the Channel in 1120, with all on board including the King's sons, was an *esneque*. The reader may recall that the unfortunate death of William and Richard, the only heirs of Henry I, threw the whole question of the English succession into doubt, bringing on the issues surrounding Stephen and Matilda, which were resolved only upon the accession of Henry II. The nature of the vessel carrying Henry I's sons is only incidental, although the fact that they were all drunk is not.

I have said that the Channel was crossed in these boats by William of Normandy. There was another heavier type of ship, but not much larger, the *cogge,* which was more rugged and capable of combat. Its lines were roundish, and it was most difficult to capsize. A *cogge* could sail very close to the wind, and had space below deck. It was not a speedy craft, but in holding a position against an attacker, speed was not especially desirable.

In the Mediterranean the preferred vessel was the galley, which descended, of course, from the galley of the Romans and the Byzantines. It could be maneuvred at great speed, and ramming the enemy was its chief fighting advantage. The galley had long slim lines. It was propelled by oarsmen — three or four seated on a bench for each large, heavy oar, a row of which ran on each side. A walking deck ran down the middle, between the oarsmen, and guards with cats-o'-nine-tails walked there ready to flog any sluggard. The timing of the oarsmen was synchronized by a man beating on an anvil. The captain stood in the stern and barked his orders.

When King Ramiro of the Asturias was preparing to steal back his wife who had been captured by the Moors:

> ... he sent for his son Dom Ordonho and for some of his vassals who, he knew, would be keen for a hazardous adventure, and they got into five galleys, for he could not use any more. He could not take any galley slaves except a few who knew how to operate the galleys; he had his nobles row instead of the galley men. He did this because the galleys were few in number, and he wanted to take as many gentry as possible, that the galleys would go more dedicated to that mission which he intended. He covered the galleys with green cloth and he sailed with them through San Johane da Foz. There the banks of the river on each side were covered with green foliage. He pushed the galleys up to the bank under their branches. Since they were covered with green cloth they were not visible. [21]

---

[21] "A lenda de Gaia" in Kimberly S. Roberts, *An Anthology of Old Portuguese* (Lisbon: Livraria Portugal, n.d.), pp. 56-57.

Evidently green paint was not available.

In the famous naval battle outside Acre in 1189, a Christian galley with King Richard on board fought to prevent a Saracen *dromont* loaded with supplies from revictualling the town. The Saracen *dromont* had green cloth draped on one side. In that battle Richard's galley was propelled by fierce galley men, whom he threatened to kill if the enemy ship escaped. It did not, and was captured in most savage style. Some of the galley men swam under it, cutting ropes and making holes. Others boarded with bared knives; they cut rigging as well as throats. Powdered talcum was flung about to blind, heavy stones were thrown on the deck to break the planking, as well as Greek fire. (Greek fire, apparently a Byzantine invention, was in bottles which when broken, released the chemical and burst into flames.) Eventually the defenders jumped overboard and swam for shore. But they were slaughtered ruthlessly except for those who were spotted as operators of *mangonels* (the catapults used to throw boulders in beseiging walled cities) and talented in similar ways.

The plan in a naval battle was to draw the enemy down wind, crossing to the shoals of the shore line, where he could not maneuver easily. The opposing side kept in deeper water as far as posible, so that they could tack about and strike the defeated enemy again.

There was a celebrated naval battle in 1204 between the French and the English. The English sailing out from Dover harbor did just as we have indicated. They drew the French ships from behind, before they could maneuver free. This is said to be the first prominent naval battle in modern times. In this battle both the French and English were using *cogges*.

The *dromont* was actually a transport ship. It was very large and heavy, said to be capable of holding from 500 to 1000 people. In that event personnel must have been crammed into every inch of space. There are no *dromont* preserved, of course, but we can reconstruct one from the low relief on a column at Pisa, and from descriptions such as that of Joinville in his *Life of Saint Louis*. There are facts also in Bishop Jacques de Vitry's account of his voyage from Genoa to Acre, and in Ibn Jubayr.

Joinville, speaking of the Genoese vessel in which King Louis IX was travelling, says that it was valued at more than four thousand livres. He adds that this ship had five hundred people on board. When a storm increased it became necessary to take down the sides of the King's chamber. No one wished to remain therein for fear the wind should carry him into the sea.

Such heavy ships are difficult for us to reconcile with our concept of the Middle Ages: "On the sea we found a *dromont* with *bretesches* (fortified walls) and castles; it was enclosed (*fremés*) good and fair... to the upper floor (*estage*) someone goes with him to hear what it is like; within it he leans out the window."[22] An overall length of 400 feet is mentioned in the passage just cited. *Dromonts* as large as these often had three masts — the one forward carrying a fore and aft lateen sail, a kind of jib. The rear-castle, often referred to as the *maison*, was a veritable house of two stories, doubtless with two rooms on each floor. Apparently the King and Joinville were sleeping in the upper rear cabin; the Queen was in the adjacent upper cabin or room. The Queen's ladies were in the lower floor chamber below her. Partitions could be removed in time of trouble. Probably in the first-floor chamber below the King rested the double tiller — the two steering oars joined together. Exclusive of the rear cabin, I assume that there were three decks to such a ship; the top one, open to the sky, may well have had an awning over it, stretched from the principal mast aft to the rear castle. The top deck forward of this was not so covered. The second deck, below, must have carried the horses forward (under the fore-castle) and cargo on the rest of it. There must have been a number of very small cabins with ventilating slits opening on to the upper deck above. Was there still another deck below this, a kind of steerage? If the *dromont* carried as many as five hundred men, there must have been more space. Still farther down, in the bilge, must have been where they had the cooking stone, on which burned a fire day and night and where food was prepared. Perhaps the bilge water in this compartment made the fire seem safe.

Vitry mentions the spaces which he reserved, and paid for, to accomodate him and his party on their way from Genoa to Acre:

---

[22] *Blancandrin*, vv. 3002, 2895; in *Blancandrin et l'orgueilleuse d'amour, roman d'aventure du XIII*[e] *siècle*, ed. Franklin P. Sweetser (Genève: Droz, 1964).

I paid for five spaces for myself and party, viz. a fourth part of the rear-castle on the upper deck in which I would eat, and would study in my books during the day, unless there were a storm on the sea; also I reserved a chamber in which I would sleep with my comrades; I took another place in which my servitors should lie and prepare my food, I had still another space in which my horses which I was transporting could be put. In the hold *(sentina)* of the ship my wine, biscuit, and meat, and other victuals sufficient for three months I stored.[23]

A smaller boat or barge was towed behind the *dromont* to hold less desirable people. Joinville's account dates from observations made in the mid-thirteenth century. The reader may notice the invention of the double tiller by that time.

Further furnishing of the ship might be of some interest. We have good reason to assume that the toilet seat for the ship was at the head of the ship, just beneath the bowsprit. In the ship depicted on the Pisa tower there is only a second mast forward of the mainmast and sail, which bears a kind of lateen sail. All sailing, of course, had to be made with the wind blowing the sails dead ahead. There was very little tacking or wearing. There was a windlass or windas (drum with spikes on it) for hoisting and lowering the heavy tackle of the sails. Certainly there must have been some one with a luff in his hand to trim the sails. Where there were horses on board, either in *dromont* or in *esneque* it was necessary to have a gate that could be opened or shut in the gunwale. In the case of an *esneque,* that type of transport ship was called a *huissier,* a transport with a gate.

On various occasions in English maritime history a fleet of ships rendezvoused in the harbour at Dartmouth. This was the case when the English and Flemish ships collected before sailing to Portugal to join with Afonso Henriques in an assault against Moslem-held Lisbon. Another important naval base in the south of England was Portchester. This spot, higher up the peninsula than the present Portsmouth, consisted of a large bailey or enclosure dating from Roman times. A Norman castle and other structures necessary to a medieval port town, including a fine church, are still preserved.

---

[23] *Lettres de Jacques de Vitry,* ed. R. B. C. Huygens (Leiden: Brill, 1960), p. 78.

The seamen depicted in the Bayeux Tapestry of the late eleventh century are represented as dressed in loose fitting *gonnes*, bareheaded and without shoes or stockings. There are no *braies* visible, but doubtless these were worn.

The master of the ship was pictured with a small quadrant in his hand. This was a metal quarter circle with which one could take angular measurements quickly in both astronomy and navigation. Somewhere in the rear castle many of the larger vessels had a rude compass which consisted of a thin piece of lodestone (magnetite) on a sliver of wood on the surface of a fluid in a shallow earthen dish.

While mentioning the crude forerunner of the compass, I include this section with an observation that is not totally unrelated to transportation — i.e., on clocks. What we know of as the mechanical clock was not invented until the close of the thirteenth century. It was fifty years before such a clock (clock=cloche=clocca) was known widely. Their wooden "works" were very heavy, and these instruments were for a long time used only in bell towers. It was not until this invention that the concepts of "minutes" and "seconds" were developed.

Some of the monasteries, but not the ships, had had water clocks for some centuries before the fourteenth. These marked the passing of an hour by a regulated dripping of water. The dripping was controlled so that in winter season the fall was more rapid during the daylight hours; in the summer months the fall was gauged so that the daylight hours passed more rapidly. Not a single water clock has survived, although one is pictured in a manuscript illumination. Those who have examined this illustration are not sure how it operated. [24]

*Hunting and Dancing*

The chief recreation of men of the baronial class, and of many others, too, was hunting: for red deer *(cerf, biche)* and for wild boar, wolves, and other large game that was available. Bird hunting was, of course, enjoyed. For this they made use of hawks and

---

[24] For a somewhat imprecise explanation of medieval clocks, see Alfred L. A. Franklin, *La Mesure du temps* (Paris: E. Plon, Nourrit et C$^{ie}$, 1887-1901).

falcons. The last wolf was killed in England in the 1500s; the last one killed in France was in the 1400s. The last wolf kill in the west was in Scotland in the eighteenth century.

We shall translate a few familiar passages from the *Lais* of Marie de France which will give an idea of the procedure during a hunt.

> That knight Guigemar summons his knights, his huntsmen, and his dog-masters. In the morning he goes into the forest... they get on the trail of a large stag and the dogs were then uncoupled. The huntsmen race on ahead; the young lord delays a bit. A boy *(vaslez)* carries his hunting knife and his quiver. He intends to get a shot if there is opportunity, before leaving. In the thickness of a great thicket he saw a hind with her fawn. This beast is a complete albino, and has the antlers of a stag on her head. She springs up at the barking of the dogs. He stretches his bow and shoots in her direction. She falls immediately. [25]

From Marie's *Yonec*: "The next day, in the morning, the lord gets up at daybreak and says that he wishes to hunt. The old woman escorts him; then she goes back to bed again, for she could not see the light of day." [26] From Marie's *Bisclavret* (Werewolf) we have the following:

> Thus did it remain for an entire year, until the king went hunting. He went straight to the forest where the werewolf was. When the dogs were uncoupled they found the werewolf and they ran after him constantly, both the dogs and the huntsmen. They almost caught him and tore him apart. But as soon as he saw the king he ran to him and asked for mercy. He kissed the king's leg and his foot. [27]

Men and women frequently dressed as though prepared for hawking. The fairy who comes to get Lanval, to carry him away to Avalon, enters the town in this way: "A sparrow hawk she held on her wrist and a greyhound followed her. An attractive boy was on her right hand, who carried an ivory hunting horn. They came in handsome fashion down the street. Such a great

---

[25] *Guigemar*, vv. 77-94, in Hoepffner, *Les Lais*.
[26] *Yonec*, vv. 301-06, *ibid*.
[27] *Bisclavret*, vv. 135-48, *ibid*.

beauty had not been seen before.... No man in the town, old or young, could fail to look at her as they saw her pass."[28] In the chamber, the private room of a house, there was very often a perch, a stand on the floor, where the favorite hunting bird could be set.

A well-to-do baron might very well maintain an extensive collection of hunting falcons. Once again we will turn to the romance *Escoufle* by Jehan Renart, of the early thirteenth century. As already mentioned, his protagonist Guillaume was working as an attendant in a hostelry that catered to visiting pilgrims in Saint-Gilles:

> One winter's day after he had eaten, he stepped out into the street. He wore a garland around his head of marigolds and rue. [(It was quite common in the Middle Ages for young gallants to wear a chaplet of flowers.) Rue has a special significance of grace which Shakespeare is well aware of in a number of his plays.] Guillaume saw falcons, hawks, moulted and unmoulted *(sor)* being carried in the street. The master falconer who was in charge had sent for a young fellow *(vallet)* who had not come. The master rode along after the others, alone, at a distance, and he was carrying on each wrist a moulted and an unmoulted falcon. "The Count has all the boys and the people he wants," he muttered, "and I cannot have a single servitor who will carry my falcons for me. I am certainly a fool when I put up with this and permit it. Now I myself have to carry to the river bank two falcons, and this is certainly wrong." Guillaume speaks up at this point and says: "Certainly, my dear master, if you would like my help for a league or two, or even four, I would go along for the sport and would learn to carry falcons." The master accepts him and suggests that he mount quickly. When he is mounted the master gives him the most tame of the falcons — but he knew on what wrist it should go — he was no tyro. They ride more than a league, and they never find a bird, nor ducks; they are all very irritated.... "I was crazy to select this stream," says the master, "It used to be full of good 'castings' against all sorts of birds. If our new young man had only seen our falcons fly we would go back. But how will we go back without our mallards and our herons?" The nightfall made it neces-

---

[28] *Lanval*, vv. 579-90, *ibid.*

sary for them to return home.... The falcon which Guillaume carries keeps moving its neck...he seems much disturbed. He who carries him, because he does not know what this means, holds the bird lower and more calm beside his thigh as best he could. The master who has fed him asks what this bird wants. He does not know. "Shall I let him go?" "Yes," the master said. "If you don't let him fly, as soon as he knocks down his prey, he may go far away." "Don't worry, I will follow him quickly. If he downs a duck or another bird, before he makes his circle in the air, I will pick up the fallen bird without delay." "Remove his strap, and let him go." ... He changes the falcon from one wrist to the other (from left wrist to right) in order to cast him to the right. [29]

This passage gives some idea of how a falcon could be launched. The most complete book on hawking is the wonderful *Art of Falconry* by Emperor Frederick II of Sicily. [30]

In the passage quoted from *Escoufle*, some importance it attached to the correct way to carry the bird. Citing in detail from Emperor Frederick's book:

> The falconer's upper arm should be allowed to hang loosely at the side of the body.... The lower arm is kept at a right angle to the body and the hand is extended in a straight line.... The outstretched thumb is laid on the forefinger. At this point the fingers are clenched to make a fist. The jesses or straps on the leg pass between thumb and index finger and then down through the middle and fourth finger. The leash is looped around the little finger. [31]

The point is made that such a bird does not like to look closely at the human face; so it should be carried so as to avoid this — opposite the shoulder. Frederick adds: "in this manner she can be

---

[29] Jean Renart, *L'Escoufle*, ed. H. Michelant and Paul Meyer (Paris: Firmin Didot et C$^{\text{ie}}$ [SATF], 1894), vv. 6682-6799, *passim*.

[30] See the translation by Casey A. Wood and F. Marjorie Fyfe, *The Art of Falconry, Being the De Arte Venandi cum Avibus of Frederick II of Hohenstaufen* (Stanford: Stanford University Press, 1943, 1961); for a less elaborate reference see *The Romance of Daude de Pradas Called "Dels Auzels Cassadors,"* ed. A. H. Schutz (Columbus: Ohio State University Press, 1945).

[31] *The Art of Falconry*, p. 144.

carried for some time with comfort and without danger of entanglement in her gear."[32]

The mews are where the birds moult. This change of their feathers usually begins in springtime.[3] The mews should be a good-sized room with at least one window, and a door. The floor is packed earth, covered with gravel or coarse sand. There is an upper and a lower perch.[34] A bathtub and other equipment are placed outside. The bird who is on a long leash can reach them through the door.

For hunting in wooded sections, in search of ground game, as well as birds, the favorite bird was the goshawk (or goose-hawk). The sparrow hawk was smaller and not so useful. (These are both short-winged birds.) However, the long-winged hawks or falcons gave more thrills to the observers. The best of these is the peregrine, which is the bird most often mentioned in the sources. These falcons bring down their prey by a single crushing blow which knocks the victim to the ground. A variant of the peregrine was thought of as a separate species in the Middle Ages, and was designated as the "true, noble falcon." Other fine falcons or long-winged hawks, are the merlin, which follows its prey into its lair, the hobby, and the lanner, or prairie falcon, which has a reputation for cowardice. The gerfalcon was trained specially to capture cranes. The hobby was most used against larks and was often termed the *alaudarius*. The mate of the merlin (larger than the male) is some 18 inches long with a 7-inch tail, and he is usually 16 inches with a six-inch tail. Because the male is commonly judged to be a third smaller than the female, the term *tiercel* ("a third") was often used to designate the merlin falcon. From these remarks it is evident that a goshawk and a peregrine falcon were the most desirable hunting birds.

From hunting we shall pass now to another pastime of the sophisticated youth: dancing. In the twelfth, and in most of the thirteenth century, we read about the round dance or carole, which is perpetuated for us in the rondeau. It is described among other

---

[32] *Ibid.*
[33] *Ibid.*, p. 98.
[34] *Ibid.*, p. 419.

places in the *Romance of the Rose*.[35] The participants seize each other by the fingers and move around in a circle while certain leaders perform in the center, either by singing or making special figures. We can assume that such a round dance never died out. Indeed it continued until the twentieth century, as "ring-around-a-rosy," among children [and would appear to have close affinity to "square dancing"]. It is said that Christmas carols began as dance performances by bands of young people in the fourteenth century.

In the latter part of the thirteenth century we believe there is evidence that a more formal type of dance, done in a hall indoors, to harp and guitar music, had begun. Here is a translation from the *Enfances Garin de Monglane:*

> They went into the palace where many a knight had the right to remove the tables; everyone began to dance. Instruments played to please them: *vieles* and guitars did what they could. Ladies and girls, sergeants and knights joined hands. Seven knights led the charming lady, and Flourette danced — as I heard tell — between two knights who held themselves well *(fier)*. When she saw Garin, whom she loved so much, she would not have continued with them for a chest of gold. The chap who was leading the bride in the front row put her back into the dance and left. Garin cut in on the bride who was light in heart.... Those who did not care to dance looked at Garin who knew how to perform his figure *(appointier)* so well that no one could match his step (ne povoit a son pas *arranguier*). "God," the girl said, "who judges everyone! Blessed Mary, please honor me so that I can have company with him, for if I had only one wish that would be what I would want." Garin led the bride so well to the sound of the instrument that it was a great pleasure to see him, for gracefully did he amuse himself.... When Garin had done what he wished, he went up to Authiaume and gave him the bride, asking him to take her... the boy did not refuse ...then Garin seized Flourette quickly by the finger. He set her into the dance; he squeezed her fingers... and she willingly agreed to all.... This dance *(feste)* lasted a very long time, until after midnight... Flourette and Garin were not sad; they would have liked to continue until dawn.[36]

---

[35] *Le Roman de la Rose par Guillaume de Lorris et Jean de Meun,* ed. Ernest Langlois, SATF, 5 vols. (Paris: Champion, 1914-24).

[36] Jack David Brown, "Les Enfances Garin: A Critical Edition," Diss. University of North Carolina 1971, vv. 1710-75.

There is just enough description here to be tantalizing. Evidently there was a line up, and certain couples stood out in front and performed certain figures, matching feet. There was cutting in and change of pairs. It has been suggested that a more stately type of dance arose at this time. a kind of polonaise in three-quarter time. This would push the origins of ballroom dancing back much earlier than the sixteenth century, which usually gets the credit.

*Summary*

[The medieval world was a violent place, and perhaps the clearest impression we acquire of the barons and that transitional class of knights that lie on the edge of the baronial caste is that they were people who lived close to fighting and pain. Society was not so constructed then that anyone could acquire the massive wealth of our contemporary industrial tycoons, and what they did have was more often the result of the plunder of war or, least likely perhaps, the luck of a few successful trading expeditions.

Yet they were a people who enjoyed the zest of living, and amid the tyranny of weather and grossly inadequate housing found the occasion to use their leisure in pleasant and sometimes even exciting pastimes. They particularly appreciated the beauty of color and line, even though we might find their taste now a bit garish. The upper classes of the twelfth and thirteenth centuries did not possess the sophistication that evolved from the Italian Renaissance or the classical revivals of the seventeenth and eighteenth centuries. Yet they were a refreshing people, not so far removed from the under class that they lost their sense of common humanity with them, and acknowledged that in death they, like the peasant vassal, would have to stand before the merciful Judge.]

## VII

## THE MINSTRELS*

[I suppose one might wonder why in a book of this nature a whole chapter is devoted to the minstrels. The answer lies, at least partially, in the fact that the minstrel is an expression of a certain healthiness in medieval society, a perception as to the nature of man which contemporary man fails to grasp to his own great loss. The minstrel was the culture's story teller, who in weaving his tale was able to provide identity and meaning to the lives of his hearers.

We are very much the victims of our technology, and we find it very difficult to "get above" our concern for production and success. Our world consequently is a very serious place and one that suffers severely from a loss of meaning and value. The minstrel was the "jester," the man whose vocation it was to keep the medieval man from taking himself too seriously, and yet he who recounted the songs and verse that give him an insight into "what it is all about." Poetry and music were not considered idle luxuries by the twelfth- and thirteenth-century man. He knew them for what they always are: the source of symbol and myth that charges our imagination and makes humanity possible.]

---

* This chapter is a lecture, with certain modifications, which was delivered at the Southeastern Institute of Medieval and Renaissance Studies held in Durham, North Carolina, in August of 1966. It was published in *Medieval and Renaissance Studies,* vol. 2, ed. John Lievsay (Durham: Duke University Press, 1968), pp. 146-66. It is included in this book with the permission of the Duke University Press.]

## The Nature of the Minstrel

Minstrels were public entertainers of different kinds. A large number of minstrels performed what we would call circus acts.[1] This group will be given some attention at the close of this chapter. I will not say much about the *histriones,* or actors, who recited monologues and took part in dialogues with elaborate gestures, because these belong to the history of the theatre. Gerald the Welshman spoke of their gestures[2] and, among others, Alexander Neckam has something to say about their costumes.[3] One of the continental versions of the *Beuve de Hanstone* shows a female character called Josiane disguised as a minstrel. She seems to be wearing male clothes (split in front and behind) with a belt, but on her fingers are rings set with stones — the rings resembling Saracen gold, bright and clear. In a loud voice she calls out: "Now listen to me, knights and serjants, girls, ladies, and children — to a new tune from the land of the Franks...."[4] The minstrels liked incongruity, badly mixed colours, and hair of a peculiar cut. Today we would say that they tended to be "far out," but it was a clue to their power in the society. The ministrel was a "liminal" person.

These entertainers moved from town to town, castle to castle, with their instruments often in cases, slung over their shoulder. Those who could play instruments used *vieles* (small fiddles), or plucked on zithers of various kinds held before them: rotes, psalteries, cithars, and especially small harps. Plucking instruments that somewhat resemble guitars were used in Spain. These can be seen in the wonderful illustrations which we possess in manuscripts of Alfonso's *Cantigas de Santa Maria.* There were some who blew on Pan pipes *(fresteles).*

---

[1] A most valuable reference for this subject matter is Edmond Faral, *Les Jongleurs en France au moyen âge* (Paris: Champion, 1910). I have used this source sparingly in a desire to keep my own approach as fresh as possible.

[2] Giraldus Cambrensis, *Giraldi Cambrensi Opera,* ed. J. S. Brewer, Rolls Series no. 21 (London: Longman & Co., 1861-91), IV, 41.

[3] Alexander Neckam, "De Nominibus Utensilium," in *Jahrbuch Rom. Engl. Lit.,* 8 (1967), 60-74, 155-73.

[4] Faral, *Les Jongleurs,* p. 292, cites this passage from B. N. fr. 12548. He comments also on the incongruity of clothing on pp. 64-65.

I shall begin by quoting from the First Branch of the *Roman de Renart*,[5] which, according to Lucien Foulet, was composed in 1177-78. The author is presumably Pierre de Saint-Cloud, who must have been a renegade priest indulging in strong satire; but satire, even when much exaggerated, can give a homely view of what the people thought and saw. The humor in this passage lies largely in the fact that Renart is pretending to be a minstrel from England. He talks in broken English-French. This mixed language can be instructive in various ways. It pictures how a Middle English speaker could "murder" the king's French — the French of Louis VII — and it describes the capabilities of a minstrel. It will be best for us to render this into a kind of pidgin English, keeping to the rhythm and idiom of the original pidgin French as much as possible.

Renart has been declared an outlaw, and he can be killed on sight. Naturally, he is a little nervous. He has also jumped into a dyer's vat, by chance, and has been tinted a lovely canary yellow. He thinks he will not be recognized, and this proves to be the case. His worst enemy, Ysengrim the wolf, does not know who he is. As the wolf approaches, Renart says with some trepidation:

> "I will talk to him whatever happens, and I will get some news about the Court."
> [Then he gets an idea. He will change his way of speaking. Ysengrim looks in his direction and at the sight of the unfamiliar canary-colored beast he raises his paw and crosses himself more than a hundred times. He too is terrified and almost runs away. Renart speaks first.]
> "Godehelpe, fine sir. Me no savvy your talk [*Non saver point ton reson dire*]."
> Ysengrim replies, "God save you, friend! Where do you come from? What country? You were not born in France and you are not anyone we know?"
> "Nay, sir, but from Britain. Me did lose all my money; me did look for my friend; me not find one can show me. All France and all Engelonde me have looked for friend to find. Now been so long this country have learned all about France. Me wish go back, go back Paris first, for have learned all about French language."

---

[5] *Le Roman de Renart*, ed. Ernest Martin (Strasbourg: Trübner, 1882-87), I, vv. 2323ff.

"Do you know any trade?"

"Ya. ya. I be much good minstrel [*ge fot molt bon jogler*], but yesterday I be robbed, beat, and my *viele* be took away. Me have *viele*, me know sing good *rotruel*, fine *lai*, and good tune for you who look like nice fella. Not have eat two whole days; now would like eat."

"What's your name?"

"Me do have name Galopin. And you sir nice fella, how call?

"Brother, they call me Ysengrim."

"You born this country?"

"Yes, I have lived here many a day."

"You know sump'n about king? ... You not got *viele*? I like serve everybody with my trade [*Je fot servir molt volentier tote la gent de ma mestier*]. Me know good Breton lai, 'bout Merlin, 'bout Noton, 'bout King Arthur, 'bout Tristan — Chievrefueil — 'bout Saint Brandan."

"And do you know the lai of Dame Iseut?"

"Ya, ya, Goditoet, me know all them."

Ysengrim remarks:

"You are very talented [*prous*] and you know a lot, I think. But by the faith which I owe King Arthur, if you should see, God help you, a red-headed scoundrel of the filthy parts, a liar, a traitor, who loves nobody, who deceives and tricks everyone... may God grant that I can get my hands of him... he would die right away. The king gave me permission; he even commanded it."

Some of the most amusing lines come next about the name of this unsavory character. These we must pass over [because of their obscene nature]. Renart then says in his "bad" French:

"He be in bad fix if you find him. By faith you owe holy martyr St. Thomas of Cantorbury, not for all the gold God had do me wish look like him."

"Apollin [a 'Saracen' god] would not save you, nor all the gold on earth.... Now tell me, sweet friend, about this minstrel trade which you have, could you use it at Court, so that no other minstrel could beat you out?"

"By my lord St. Jerusalem, never was such a minstrel like me."

"Then come along with me and I will have you know the king, and my lady the queen, who is a real nice girl [*qui tant par est gente meschine*]. If you want to come to Court I'll have you hired there."

"*Fotre merci* — T'anks! — me know much good tippling and known much 'bout lechery. Me will be much appreciated at Court. If could have *viele* me would say fine *rotruel*, sing verse of *chançon* for you, who do seem nice fella."

Ysengrim then remembers a peasant who has a *viele* hanging on a nail in his hut. The two go to steal it (as we read in a previous chapter), and converse along the way. Ysengrim speaks "en son françois" — Renart answers him "en englois." At this point we must abridge. They take the *viele* and Renart runs off with it. As the reader may recall, Ysengrim is castrated by the peasant's dog during the proceedings. Within two weeks Renart manages to master completely the playing of the *viele*. He next comes upon a poor animal, Poncet, who is seeking to marry his [Renart's] wife. The couple think Renart has been hanged. The bridegroom needs a priest and a minstrel — both are necessary to get the wedding properly celebrated. Renart admits that "he be good minstrel," knows lots of songs, and that he has studied at Besançon.[6] He will be grateful for the job: "Me know good song 'bout Ogier, 'bout Olivant and Rollier, 'bout Charlemagne with white flesh." Please note these distortions. Pierre de Saint Cloud is taking a dig at Oliver and Roland, and at Charlemagne with "la barbe chanue," the white beard. Probably Pierre de Saint Cloud was weary from hearing the *Roland* recited, and he knew that many others could laugh about it with him.

There is no need to quote further from the *Roman de Renart*, no matter how delightful we may find it. Some facts are evident from what we have translated: an average minstrel needed a musical instrument; he was accustomed to "living high" when he had a good permanent position, as at Court, and he had a large repertoire that he could recite from memory. Evidently a minstrel from England was expected to sing about King Arthur, Tristan, Merlin, and Iseut, the *Chievrefueil* of Marie de France, and Saint Brandon. Noton we cannot identify. This English minstrel was no Celt.

---

[6] *Ibid.*, v. 2756. Note that the jongleur school at Besançon must have been something to provoke mirth. At this time, to be sure, Besançon was controlled by the German emperor.

The minstrel was essential for a wedding. He remained outside the chuch door and escorted the bridal pair to their home, walking and playing in front of them. In the *Amis et Amiles* epic the lady Lubias is escorted to Mass this way.[7]

*The Character of the Minstrel*

Ysengrim implies that the English minstrel will enjoy the lechery at the Court. This is a reputation that performers have had through all the centuries, and in the Middle Ages it seems to have been a correct one. In the *Moniage Guillaume* a thief makes observations on the lack of responsibility of a minstrel:

> When they have three sous, or four or five, they rush to the tavern to spend them, and they have a good time as long as the money lasts — with good, savory wine and pleasant meats. When the tavernkeeper sees that all is spent he says, "Brother, get some other place to stay, for merchants will be stopping here. Give me a deposit on what you owe." The minstrel leaves his stockings or his shoes, or his *viele* when it comes to the worst.... When he is out the door he looks for some place to recoup, from a knight, a priest, or an abbot. The minstrels have strange ways about them. They sing just as well to get a dinner as they would to receive forty marks.[8]

Many medieval writers have written on this venality of the minstrel, including John of Salisbury.[9] Alexander Neckam has an amusing observation. He comments on the excessive pride of many noble barons. He adds that many of them have no right to their haughtiness, for they are offspring of minstrels who have been too free with the noble ladies.[10] There is a good passage in the *Enfances Garin* of the late thirteenth century, where the hero Garin

---

[7] *Amis de Amiles, und Jourdains de Blaivies*, ed. Konrad Hofman, 2nd. ed. (Erlangen: Deichart, 1882), vv. 2325-26.

[8] *Les Deux Rédactions en vers du Moniage Guillaume*, ed. William Cloetta (Paris: SATF, 1906-13), vv. 1253ff.

[9] *Polycraticus*, ed. Joseph B. Pike (London: Oxford University Press, 1938), I, ch. 8.

[10] Alexander Neckam, *De Naturis Rerum*, ed. Thomas Wright, Rolls Series (London: Green, Longman, Roberts and Green, 1963), p. 312.

feels footloose and is looking for female company of the lighter sort:

> At the entrance to a wood he met a jolly minstrel who had but little money and who was carrying his *viele,* on which he played attractively. Garin said to him in a loud voice: "Friend, whence do you come? Don't keep it from me. By my oath, you look like a good companion who takes pleasure quite frequently. Do you know a good-looking lady in these parts who would like to have a love affair — lightly?" The minstrel replied: "One may have a lot of this if he knows how to talk to them boldly. If a lady refuses, one should then pursue her vigorously — to keep begging a girl who defends herself soon pays off [*c'est tantos avisee*]." [11]

To put it bluntly, one naturally made use of a minstrel to find a light companion; he knew lots of people, too. Garin on this occasion got what was coming to him. This minstrel, named Rogier *li gentius,* suggested a *really* nice lady who became the reason for most of the blood shed in combat during the remaining eight thousand lines of the epic. Eventually Garin married her.

## Types of Minstrels

I mentioned that there were a number of kinds of minstrels, so I shall now expand on this point. There were certain specialized types of minstrels. There is the narrator who sings the saints' lives, often in churches. This was the first type of minstrel to be accepted as decent by the churchmen, and, he was probably, at the base of all Old French literature. Here is a celebrated passage which concerns this kind of jongleur:

> A certain man named Peter Waldo, grown rich on taxes, approached a crowd one Sunday which had gathered before a minstrel. He was touched by the singer's words and brought the man to his home, desiring to listen more intently. The subject of the minstrel's narrative was how the Blessed Alexius had died a holy death in the house of his own father. [12]

---

[11] I am quoting here from a transcription of the *Enfances Garin* made for me by Miss Evelyn Vandiver.
[12] MGH, SS., XXVI, 447.

This was the *Life of Saint Alexius* (ca. 1040), which most of us refer to as the oldest Old French poem. Saint Aybert also was headed towards a religious life by a minstrel who sang in his father's house. [13]

> The jongleur's profession was the most degrading a clerk could have had; but it was also the most natural. It was a clerk's business to sing.... a certain singing master touting for pupils declared singing to be the foundation of all ecclesiastical functions. [14]

Earlier in this chapter we said we would consider the minstrel as a circus performer. A most extravagant exhibition of this kind was noted by Albert des Trois Fontaines for 1237: Those who are called minstrels did many things there in a vain spectacle. There was one who rode on a horse across a rope in the air, and there were others who, clothed in scarlet, rode two oxen, blowing horns, each of which was brought to the king. [15]

This exhibition was at the wedding on June 14, 1237, of Mathilde of Brabant with Robert, the brother of Louis IX.

> Joinville described the performance of three tumblers. They put a cloth on the ground before their feet and, from the standing position, they made a somersault so that their feet came again to a standing position on the cloth. Two of them also backflipped, including the oldest one. When he thrust his head backwards he made a sign of the cross, for he was afraid that he might break his neck. [16]

Stephen of Bourbon spoke of painted clowns "like those jongleurs who have their faces painted, which are called *artifices* in French, with which they tease and delude men." [17]

---

[13] Albert Lecoy de la Marche, *La Chaire française au moyen âge, spécialement au 13$^e$ siècle*, 2nd. ed. (Paris: Laurens, 1886), p. 445.

[14] Helen Jane Waddell, *The Wandering Scholars*, rprt. pb. (New York: Doubleday Anchor Books, 1955), p. 195, n. 53.

[15] MGH, SS., XXIII.

[16] Jean, sire de Joinville, *Histoire de Saint Louis*, ed. Natalis de Wailley, SHF no. 144 (Paris: Mme. Renouard, 1868), p. 526. (Adapted.)

[17] Albert Lecoy de la Marche, *Anecdotes historiques, légendes et apologues, tirés du recueil inédit d'Etienne de Bourbon, Dominicain du XIII$^e$ siècle* (Paris: Librairie Renouard, 1877), p. 279.

An astounding repertoire is listed in the romance *Joufrois*:

> You would see the jongleurs come forward and do many tricks. One danced a spur dance, and they watched his feet carefully to see whether he would stumble; another jumped through a hoop held high; still another did sleight of hand under his mantle; another threw knives while others had swords, leaning and falling on the sharp points without fear. There was much fine play in the presence of the Count, including the singing of ancient songs. [18]

Elsewhere, in a German source, we find men dancing with dogs, and eating fire, which they blow from their mouths. [19] The poet Rutebeuf remarked towards the end of the thirteenth century that "it is common everywhere, as all men know, that when someone puts on a wedding or a feast the minstrels hear of it and seek nothing better. They come from everywhere, some on foot and others on horseback." [20]

We can sum up a full repertoire on such occasions by quoting from Chrétien's *Erec et Enide*:

> When the Court was assembled there was not a minstrel in the countryside who knew any form of entertainment who did not come there. There was much joy in the great hall. Each one performed as well as he could. Some leaped, some danced, some did magic tricks, some narrated, others sang, some whistled, some played upon instruments, one upon the *gigue*, another on a *viele*, another on a harp, still another on a *rote*. One played the flute, another a shawm. They had tambourines, drums, bagpipes, whistles, and horns.... The minstrels were all happy that day because they were paid without stint. They got what they earned and many gifts in addition: robes of miniver, ermine, rabbit, violet cloth, and scarlet. [21]

---

[18] *Joufrois*, ed. W. O. Streng-Renkonen, Ann. UA, ser. B, 12 (Turku: 1930), vv. 1196ff.

[19] *Karlmeinet*, 287, 11.

[20] *Charlot le Juif*, in Antoine de Montaiglon and Gaston Raynaud, eds. *Recueil général et complet des fabliaux du XIIIᵉ et du XIVᵉ siècle* (Paris: Librairie de Bibliophiles, 1872-90), III, 223.

[21] Chrétien de Troyes, *Eric et Enide*, ed. Mario Roques (Paris: 1953), vv. 2035ff, 2106ff. For a similar gathering, see Wace's *Brut*, ed. Ivor Arnold, 2 vols. (Paris: SATF, 1938-40), vv. 10823ff.

I give another illustration, which narrates the routine of a purely instrumental player. This is from *Huon de Bordeaux*. The protagonist Hue has lost all his clothes while struggling in the water.

> Underneath a tree he found a man who was as we shall describe him. He had a harp on which he could play, and a *viele*. There was not another minstrel so good in all the pagan land. He had spread a cloth before him and on this he had four loaves of fine bread and a skin of claret wine.... He poured this wine into his cup but he would not taste it; he was weeping bitterly. When he saw Hue, naked as the day he was born, he was frightened. He called out, "Wild man, don't hurt me."
>
> "By my faith, I am quite wild," said Hue, "but I won't touch you. Please give me some of your bread."
>
> "You shall have it. I am sorry for you. Find in my pack an ermine-sleeved garment and a mantle of scarlet, with lining. Cover your flesh. You have good need for this. Then sit down, drink this fine wine, and eat. I cannot do so. Keep me company with the understanding that you will hear my sad story."
>
> Hue went forward, found the pack, took out the ermine, put it on, and wore a mantle on top. He found plenty of *braies* and shirts, and he took what he needed.... The minstrel told his tale.
>
> "Brother, I am an instrumentalist; among the pagans there is none like me. See my harp and my *viele*, which I play well, and I know how to use the tambourine and dance."
>
> His sadness was because his lord had been killed. He hired Hue to carry his pack and he remarked, "Whenever I perform in a burg or a city you will see me receive so many mantles that you will hardly be able to carry them.
>
> "You have your man," said Hue. He picked up the pack, placed it on the nape of his neck, and on top he loaded the harp and the *viele*. They set out towards Monbranc.[22]

You will note the rewards which this old man gets. Strange to relate, he does not have a horse. Surely he could have had one from some admirer. It was not unusual for wealthy people to re-

---

[22] *Huon de Bordeaux, chanson de geste*, ed. François Guessard and Charles Grandmaison, APF 5 (Paris: F. Vieweg, 1890), p. 213.

compense the minstrels with fine garments. Rigord comments on this:

> Once we saw certain great men give lightly [ad primam vocem] garments which had been designed with great care over a considerable period of time, which were ornamented skilfully in flower designs, which probably cost as much as twenty or thirty marks of silver hardly a week before. They gave them to the minstrels, ministers of the devil.... But the Most Christian King Philip Augustus, seeing that all this was vain and contrary to the salvation of the soul, remembering what he had learned from pious men, and when he had learned it, said that to give to performers was to sacrifice to demons. He promised that he would give all his garments to the poor.[23]

This must have been temporary prudery on the part of King Philip. Elsewhere we have read of his using minstrels for propaganda purposes.

*The Manner of The Minstrel's Art*

We return to those minstrels who narrated. An important point is to know how the narrators presented their wares. Did they sing them with a tune, or did they recite them with a monotone rhythmic chant? At the Medieval Academy meeting in 1965, Albert Baugh of the University of Pennsylvania read an excellent presidential address on the medieval romance in general. Incidentally he examined all the Middle English verbs which preface the beginnings of these romances. He concluded that usually there was mention that the poem was sung, but that in some instances the verb used means "said," not "sung." I cannot speak on Middle English, but in Old French, *dire* can mean "say," "play," or "sing." In the *Metalogicon* John of Salisbury has something pertinent to say about this,[24] although he is not as clear as his direct source, Quintilian,

---

[23] *De Gestis Phillippi Augusti* (Recueil de l'Histoire de France), XVII, 21.

[24] John of Salisbury, *The Metalogicon, a Twelfth-Century Defense of the Verbal and Logical Arts of the Trivium*, tr. Daniel D. McGarry (Berkeley: University of California Press, 1955), pp. 60-61. Peter of Blois observes how listeners could be moved to tears by a minstrel reciting about Arthur, or Tristan; see J. P. Migne, ed., *Patrologia Latina* (Paris: 1879-90), CCVIII, col. 1088.

who remarked that the reciting of verse "must be different from the reading of prose, because poetry is sung and poets claim to be singers. But this fact does not justify degeneration into sing-song, the effeminate modulations now in vogue. There is an excellent saying on this attributed to Gaius Caesar while he was still a boy: 'If you are singing, you sing badly; if you are reading you sing.'" John of Salisbury imitated this passage as follows: "Poetry should be recited in one way, prose in another.... Caesar, while he was still a boy, with fine sarcasm remarked to a certain person, 'If you are trying to read you are singing, and if you are trying to sing you are doing a miserable job.'" We can infer from this statement by John that the medieval minstrels, who were usually concerned with verse, sang or chanted their wares. In presenting prose they employed an inflected monotone, a sing-song. The habit of chanting in some way all lines that were *read* aloud persisted till the seventeenth century, and probably much later.

The musical forms used by the minstrels must be taken into account.[25] The basic patterns of medieval song and chant were derived from the Church litany, the rondel, the Church sequence, and the hymn. (We are accepting the thesis that secular music was based largely on Church music.) From the litany type came the melodies of the *chansons de geste* and the *rotrouanges* (which differ by having an end refrain) — also those *chansons* which had no refrain. The rondel form gave rise to the *ballade* and the *virelai*. Following the sequence type came the *lai*, used for narrative poetry, the *notula*, and the instrumental *estampie*. From the hymn were derived the *chanson* with refrain and the *vers*. These last two do not admit a strict metrical reading. You will recall that Renart, pretending to be the English minstrel, declared himself ready and willing to perform the *lai*, the *chanson*, and the *rotrouange*.

The tunes themselves could be freshly composed, or they might be old ones, adopted from either Church or folk music. Lay people were quite fond of the major scales in C and F. This may seem strange. Where the minor modes were used, the laity liked particularly the Aeolian or ninth tone, and the *Protus* and the *Tetrardus* —

---

[25] Fine references on this are Gustave Reese, *Music in the Middle Ages* (New York: W. W. Norton & Company, 1940) and Théodore Gérold, *La Musique au moyen âge* (Paris: H. Champion, 1932).

first and seventh tones. Popular tunes could have a longer compass, often going to the octave and higher.

Eventually some of the singers became known as *rois des menestrels*. Adenet, for instance, was Adenet le Roi. An earlier occurrence of this was noted in 1174, when a minstrel won a contest and was crowned king of the competition, in much the same way that we now have young ladies as queens: the Tobacco Queen, the Peach Queen, the Cotton Queen, and so on. By the thirteenth century a *roi des menestrels* was the accepted leader of the performers at a court, or at a minstrel school. Minstrels and heralds were often equated loosely. A *roi des menestrels* might officiate as chief of the heralds.

These itinerant chanters and singers had places of assembly where they convened and exchanged ideas and repertory. We refer to these places as jongleur schools, although we are not quite sure how much instruction there was. Such schools may have taught pupils to read and write the vernacular language, and in this event they may have been the arbiters of French phonemic spelling. A new poem which had recently been *anoncie* or *envoie avant* (the medieval equivalent of published) could be taught there to those who wished to learn it.

Jean Rychner's thesis is that in the case of the *chanson de geste* only the principal features of each narrative were taught, and that the individual singers expanded the basic plot, each one in his own epic phraseology, or formulaic diction. [26] Eventually, Rychner claims, a truly artistic version, which had been received enthusiastically by the public, would prevail and be written down. This may have been true in the early stages of some of the epics, but more and more scholars are now convinced that the prevailing versions of some of these are complicated, artistic, and contrived compositions in which attention was paid to rhetorical devices and, sometimes, to arithmetical proportions (following Pythagoras and Plato's *Timaeus*). Certainly the Oxford *Roland* was very elaborately contrived, and would have to be memorized without much improvisation. [27]

---

[26] For nearly a decade after its publication, this theory was held as definitive. Gradually it has been modified in the minds of many scholars, as I have indicated.

[27] The bibliography of the *Chanson de Roland* is immense. An elaborate analysis of the possible arithmetical arrangement of the sections of this epic has been examined by Robert Lucas.

In order to employ such artistic devices the composers of the *chanson de geste* and romances must have been clerks of a kind. Doubtless many of them, probably the majority, must have been "flunkies" who had not persevered in the schools but who had received simple tonsure at an early age. Presumably they had received voice training in the ecclesiastical schools. Such status as this did not apply, of course, to the acrobats, tumblers, and animal trainers who made up so large a part of the Minstrels' Corporations. It need not apply, either, to those who were purely instrumentalists, although it is probable that many such players had served their apprenticeship in Church music.

Recently I read through the Paris *Taille*, or tax roll, for 1296, which is the earliest preserved.[28] Only laymen, those who were neither noble nor clerical, were subject to this particular tax. I found a Richart the flute player living near the Porte Saint Denis. On the nearby Rue des Jugleeurs eleven names were listed, but none was designated a minstrel. Two were called *Mestres*, and there was a Henri who made *vieles*. I am aware of what Raoul Glaber and Richard d'Argence of Fécamp had to say about secular minstrels;[29] but I believe that the singers who were in lower ecclesiastical orders were very numerous. This Rue des Jugleeurs was quite close to a prime source for epic material — the library at Saint Denis. One had only to exit through the Porte Saint Denis, five miles beyond which was the Abbey. The monks had a fine library, and we have reason to believe it contained vernacular poems: epics and romances which could be consulted by an approved master minstrel. Adenet le Roi wrote that he read the plots of two of his epics there.[30] The composer of the *Moniage Guillaume* also remarked: "Would you like to hear a good song of worthy deeds? You will enjoy it. Every minstrel knows this. The tale is in a roll at Saint Denis, but it was forgotten for a long time. The fellow who put it again into rhyme was a good man."[31]

So far we have said very little about the actual procedure followed by a narrating minstrel as he took his place before a gathering

---

[28] Karl Michaëlsson, *Le Livre de la taille de Paris l'an 1296* (Göteborg: Almquist & Wiksell, 1958), p. 88.

[29] See Ch. de Beaurepaire in B. Ed. Chartres, XX, 153; also Raoul Glaber, *Historiae* (Rec. HF, X, 42), IV, 9.

[30] Adenet le Roi, *Bueves de Commarchis*, ed. August Scheler (Brussels: Clossen, 1874), vv. 5-15.

[31] *Moniage Guillaume*, v. 4.

audience. In a castle or manor house the preferred time was after the first or midday meal, presumably continuing through siesta and some time thereafter.

> After eating the minstrels *vielent* and sing. They tell romance and adventures, they play psalteries and *gigues*; the harpers harp. This sweetness is worth hearing. They make great joy until vespers. The count paid each one according to his labor, giving mantles, mules, palfreys, etc....[32]

The minstrel in the market place, or at the street corner, may have had a slightly different procedure. He could begin with a short prelude on his instrument while the crowd gathered. Then, as Pierre le Chantre informs us, the performer would try for a tune that might please. "If a tale about Landri does not get quick response, he breaks off immediately and sings about Narcissus, and if that does not suit, he begins another."[33] About midway through the narration of a fairly lengthy poem he would stop for the night. Here is the announcement of such a pause in the *Huon de Bordeaux:*

> Gentlemen, you can see that it is near vesper [about 6 P.M.] and I am very tired. I beg of you to remain fond of Auberon and Hue the Strong, and of me, and come back tomorrow after dinner. I am quite pleased when I see the evening come, because I want to leave. Come back tomorrow after dinner, and I ask each one of you to have a *maille* [half denier] tied up in the tail of his shirt.[34]

Seldom do we find so frank a statement, but in many poems we can suspect there was a pause for the end of the day, which was followed at the next sitting by a short résumé of what had preceded. Even in the celebrated *Roman de la Rose* this sort of thing occurs:

> The god of love then charged me, just as you will hear, with his commands — word for word. This romance de-

---

[32] *Les Enfances de Godefroi,* ed. Célestin Hippeau (Paris, 1874-77), vv. 109, 230-36; also Gautier de Tournoi, *L'Histoire de Gille de Chyn,* ed. E. B. Place, NSH 7 (Evanston: Northwestern University Press, 1941), vv. 4689ff.
[33] Migne, *PL,* CCV, col. 155.
[34] *Huon de Bordeaux,* p. 148.

scribes them well. Anyone who is in love should pay attention, for this romance will get better from now on [*que li romanz des ore amende*]. It will now be agreeable to hear, provided one knows how to narrate it. The end of this dream is very attractive and the subject matter is novel. If one will listen to the end I assure you he will learn the tricks of Love, provided he wishes to wait until I can expound the significance of the dream. The truth, which may not be clear, will presently be quite obvious when you hear from me the explanation — there is nothing false in this.[35]

These remarks come also exactly at the mid-point of the Guillaume de Lorris section. Was this a reassurance following a pause for the night, or did the narrator (or poet) know from experience that this was a point in the narrative where interest was likely to flag and he was afraid the listeners would steal away?

We have been rather vague so far in distinguishing between those who composed the narratives and those who merely sang them. Some of the minstrels, especially the clerks, were certainly poets, who communicated their wares to others as well who were only singers. Some of these authors were women, such as Marie de France; others were clerks too prominent to serve as common entertainers; and others were laymen of high degree, such as the Conte d'Arras, who wrote *Ille et Galeron* and *Eracle*. The troubadors in the south of France and the *trouvères* in the north belonged to this last category — although I feel that some of these also in their youth had had some clerical training. Many a lord made a little clerk out of his heir, only to recall him to knightly duties later on. Such was the case with Guilhem in the *Flamenca*.

The troubadour Guiraut de Borneil went to school in the winter (was this a jongleur or a Latin school?) and travelled about with his singers during the summer.[36] Here also is a passage from the romance *Claris* which may indicate a differentiation: "Before them were the singers and also *li plus mestre trouveor* who sang to them

---

[35] *Le Roman de la Rose par Guillaume de Lorris et Jean de Meun*, ed. Ernest Langlois, SATF (Paris: Firmin-Didot, 1920), II, 2057ff.

[36] Jean Boutière and A. H. Schutz, *Biographies des troubadours: Textes provençaux de XIII$^e$ et XIV$^e$ siècles* (Toulouse: E. Privat, 1950), p. 191.

of ancient deeds and informed them of the great fights which their ancestors made and how they won their lands." [37]

I believe that the master trouvères were jongleur school instructors. Remember, on the Rue des Jugleeurs at Paris there were two men called mestres: Mestre Henri le grant mestre and Mestre Alixandre le grant mestre.

The chanting of *chansons,* romances, and *lais* was not confined entirely to professionals. Knowledge of music was considered a social asset. In Thomas' *Tristan* the poet says of Iseut: "The queen sings softly; she tunes her voice to the instrument [which she is playing]; her hands are fair; the melody is good." [38] Also in the *Roman de la Rose* we find this: "If you have a voice that is good and clear, seek no excuse not to sing, if someone asks you. Good singing is very pleasing. It is proper also for a young man to know how to play the *viele,* and to play the flute and dance. One can go far with these." [39]

These passages refer only to casual performances. In Chrétien de Troyes's *Yvain* a girl of sixteen is in a garden with her mother and father and she is reading [*lisoit*, chanting?] in a romance, "whose author I [Chrétien] do not know. The parents take great pleasure in seeing and hearing her." [40] Probably this was a more sustained performance. There is something odd here. Sixteen was a little old for a girl to be staying with her mother and father. She should have been married.

Certain older men of the knight class are mentioned by the chronicler Lambert d'Ardres (ca. 1181), [41] e.g., "Arnoul de Guines [who] was very fond of tourneys and of young people, as well as of playful servitors and jests [*familiaribus ludicris et jocis*]." Robert de Coutances [from the Norman coast] told him about the Roman emperors, Charlemagne, Roland and Oliver, and King Arthur of Britain. Then there was Philippe de Montjardin [Aude, near Narbonne] who brought to the delectation of his ears the siege of Antioch, Jerusalem, the Arabs, Babylonians, and deeds done in the

---

[37] *Li Romans de Claris et Laris,* ed. Johann Alton, BVUS 169 (Tübingen: 1884), vv. 29, 614ff.
[38] *Tristan,* ed. Bartina H. Wind (Genève: Droz, 1960), p. 65.
[39] *Roman de la Rose,* vv. 2203-10.
[40] *Yvain,* ed. Mario Roques (Paris, 1964), vv. 5356-73.
[41] MGH, SS., XXIII.

Holy Land. Gautier de l'Ecluse [a Fleming from Sluis] taught him diligently about the English, Gormont and Isembert, Tristan and Iseut, Merlin, Marcolfus, the deeds of the Ardennes, and the construction of the castle of Ardres. You will note that the repertoire of each narrator corresponds somewhat with his native district.

*Summary*

[The minstrel then was one who entertained as a circus performer, and yet who also bore in his art the tradition of the people. He was then a subtle force for the establishment of a person's identity, attracting on-lookers by what seemed mere entertainment and yet reminding in his song what it meant to be a citizen of that district. This combination of simple fun and profound meaning has always proved a powerful force in the shaping of a people's character, and we hope that the reader senses then the importance of the minstrel to medieval man's understanding of who he was.]

## VIII

## WRITING AND THE MEN OF LETTERS

We have discussed the musicians of the twelfth-century Renaissance. It would be well to follow with some remarks on those who are thought to write artistically. The medieval man who wrote cannot be thought of as free with his pen, either in his thoughts or in the mechanics of putting words on vellum. Literary content was closely tied to traditional themes and concepts, and one did not lightly record his own thoughts in the face of the labor and expense of writing.

High above the west portal of the cathedral at Chartres there are two remarkable carvings, in the semiround, which show Aristotle and Pythagoras engaged in work at their writing desks. The desks have a somewhat mid-nineteenth-century appearance. They are set upon the knees; they are ornamented with holes and carvings which suggest a "Victorian" design. One feels that they must have had a tendency to come apart frequently, and that they were patched with glue. At the right-hand corner is the inkhorn inserted into a hole in the desk. It was undoubtedly an actual cow-horn. Fastened to the wall above the left shoulder is a pen rack with pens inserted through small holes; a round sponge or two for cleaning pens also rests on the rack. In the carving, Pythagoras has his pen in the right hand and a penknife for erasures in the left. This is not just chance. At the close of our chapter, we remind the reader that while Aristotle was creative Pythagoras was representative of a polished style, where the erasure knife must have been frequently used.

## Material Limitations

The vellum usually must have been ruled beforehand (with a sharppoint blind line) and the sheets were folded in the middle with four sheets to a quaternion. An author, when writing quaternion after quaternion, could gauge how many lines would be required to fill such a unit of space. (It is possible that when composing verse material, a poet had the precise length of his material estimated in advance: how many quaternions he would try to fill.) In composing such narrative poems as a *lai* or a romance, it is not improbable that the author kept track of the length of his work in this way. A quaternion could hold sixteen pages; at forty lines a page, this meant some 640 lines to the quaternion. Ten of these would hold an average-length romance of some 6,400 lines.

Combinations of letters were made with certain consistent ligatures and abbreviations; but in general it may be said that speed writing was not the rule — although I fancy that I have noted more evidence of speed writing in the holograph pages of such great writers as Thomas Aquinas. To be sure, most letters were made with two strokes each in a twelfth-century hand, which meant that the pen was lifted once within each letter. When a stroke was erased with the scratch of the penknife, it was necessary to rub the spot afterwards with a deer's tooth or something similar, to enable the grain of the vellum to take fresh ink without smearing. Of course, frequent dippings of the quill pen into the inkhorn also were necessary.

## Teaching of Writing

In his school training, our medieval clerk learned a great many passages and phrases by rote. This was particularly true in studying the psalter, which was the first text that most boys (and some girls) learned in their "psalter school," or first reading and writing classes. Proverbs and even street cries were also burned into the young clerk's mind. When he attended grammar school, most of the early sessions in the morning were devoted to taking down dictation from the *clerc lisant,* or teacher. A considerable amount of the practice composition which the pupils did in afternoon sessions were paraphrases of verse into prose or prose into verse. Latin texts also were sometimes rendered phrase by phrase into the vernacular, and vice versa. (I make a parallel here with the way Chinese students used to be taught their classics, by memorizing and paraphrasing.) In class sessions where canon law, or civil law, was taught, copying from dictation was even more marked.

Nearly all this dictation and copying was in Latin. On exactly what was done in the places which we like to call Jongleurs' schools, we are almost entirely in the dark. Writing, and probably composition, in the vernacular was certainly the purpose. It is logical to assume that what was done in the Latin schools was imitated closely here. For me, a most precious text is the *Donatz Proensals* of the Provençal troubador Uc Faidit, written in the mid-thirteenth century. It was a grammar of the Provençal language composed in Italy for Italian clerks who already knew some of that language. It was intended as a grammar which would enable them to write better Provençal verse.[1] This Provençal grammar in the Provençal language is followed by a very precise rendition of the same into Latin. This translation may have been done by Uc himself. We give a few excerpts in which we render the Provençal into English:

> You should know that all that which I have told you whose nominative singular ends in *-aire* and in *-eire*, and in *-ire*, end all their singular cases, except the vocative, in *-dor*. The vocative resembles the nominative, as has been said above.[2]
>
> And for this reason I have made so long a treatment about the third person of the perfect preterite, because there is greater confusion in this than in all the other persons, because for the most part the first person ends in *-i* and the second in *-ist* — about the perfect preterite of the indicative, you understand, where for the most part the first and second persons are similar.[3]

---

[1] Uc Faidit, *The Donatz Proensals of Uc Faidit*, ed. H. H. Marshall (London: Oxford University Press, 1969). The editor complains a little that it is concerned more with vocabulary and morphology that with pronunciation and syntax (p. 77). Good grief! How fortunate we are to have what has come down to us! To concentrate on syntax would have reflected our twentieth-century preoccupation with language instruction.

[2] *Ibid.*, p. 94.

[3] *Ibid.*, p. 140.

Many Provençal words are translated carefully into Latin in this book: *raspalhz* — 'what remains of straw'; *contrahz* — 'with weak hands or feet.'[4]

Since I believe that spoken Old Provençal was quite close to Old French, with slight phonological changes one could reconstruct from this the vocabulary for teaching Old French grammar with oral approach! We assume that this terminology may well have been used in the Jongleur schools.

*Style*

An elegant style in poetic composition was achieved by using models found in Virgil: his *Aeneid* for the grand style, his *Georgics* and *Bucolics* for medium and lesser style. This stylistic doctrine was analyzed and gathered into poetic arts of the twelfth and thirteenth centuries. Chief among these compilations were the *Ars Versificatoria* of Matthieu de Vendôme (c. 1175), the *Poetria Nova* of Geoffroi de Vinsauf, also his *Documentum de Modo et Arte Dictandi et Versificandi*, the *Ars Versificaria* of Gervais de Melkey, and the *Laborintus* of Evrard the German.[5]

It was at the Schools in Orleans that this stylistic doctrine was taught with considerable zest, and many critics considered this a peril to the souls of those who taught there and those who learned it. These student poets, trained in the style of classical Latin, were called Goliards. I now give some love poems by so-called Goliards.

One of the best of these love poems is *Dum Diane vitrea*. I quote this in a translation made by Peter Dronke:

> As Zephyr's sweet breath takes every cloud from the sky when Diana's crystal lamp rises at dusk, kindled by her brother's rose light, so the power of music lightens the minds of men, and transforms the heart, that it inclines to the vows of love.
> ... ... ... ... ... ... ... ... ... ... ... ... ... ... ... ...
> Oh how happy is the remedy of sleep, calming the storms of cares and grief! When it steals under the closed eyelids, it is equal in joy to the sweetness of love.
> ... ... ... ... ... ... ... ... ... ... ... ... ... ... ... ...

---

[4] *Ibid.*, p. 198.
[5] See Edmond Faral, *Les Arts poétiques du XII$^e$ et du XIII$^e$ siècle*, BEH 238 (Paris: Mellottée, 1924).

> After the tender interchanges of love, the matter of the brain is languorous. Thus in a new and wondrous wise the eyes grow dark, swimming on a float of eyelids. Ah how happy the passage from love to sleep — but even sweeter the return to love!
> From the joyous reins a smoke evaporates, condensing in the three cells of the brain. It mists the eyes, inclining to drowsiness, and fills the eyelids with its smokiness, lest sight should range afar. So the animal spirits, which specially in this show themselves our servants, bind the eyes.
> Under the gracious boughs of a tree, while Philomena sings lamenting, it is sweet to rest, sweeter still to play in the grass with a lovely girl. If the scent of many herbs perfumes the air, if the rose offers a bed, the nourishment of sleep is sweetly won, showered upon the languorous after love's play has faded.
> Oh in how many ways a lover's spirit is filled with uncertainties! Like an anchorless raft drifting across the ocean, those in Love's company fluctuate, wavering between hope and fear.[6]

These Goliards, or wandering scholars, imitated the rhythms of Latin hymns. They were doubtless students and scholars, unemployed by the Church, many of whom possessed genuine poetic talent. They show that there was some serious relaxation of the ascetic ideal. Very many of these songs are anonymous. The finest of these love poems are probably found in a collection known as the *Carmina Burana*, a manuscript which was discovered in the Abbey Benediktbeuern.[7] It dates from about 1300, but much of the poetry was composed in the twelfth century.

We do not want to give the impression that these Goliards were the principal users of the rules of Latin rhetoric at Orleans. Nearly all the Latin poets, and a very great number of those writing in the vernacular — in Old French, for instance — followed these superior rules of expressivity (figures of rhetoric). There were some thirty-five. One is *repetitio*, or repetition. Here is an example occurring in Marie de France's lai *Lanval*:

---

[6] Peter Dronke, *Medieval Latin and the Rise of the European Love-Lyric* (Oxford: Clarendon Press, 1965), I, 309.

[7] A collection of the *Carmina Burana* was edited by J. A. Schmeller (4th ed; Breslau: M & H. Marcus, 1904). They have been much translated into English; see Helen Waddell, *The Wandering Scholars*, 7th. ed. (London: Constable, 1934).

There was not in the town a knight in need of a place to stay that Lanval did not cause him to come to him, and serve richly: Lanval gave rich gifts, Lanval freed the prisoners, Lanval clothed the minstrel. Lanval performed many honours, he spent generously [remember *largesce* was a great virtue], Lanval gave gold and silver; there was not an intimate or a stranger to whom Lanval did not give. [8]

Amplification, or minute description of things, was another frequent ornament; another which is fascinating was etymologia, where an etymology, usually somewhat fantastic, is inserted — as when Wace describes the Angles as getting their name because they were *anglés* — "driven into a corner"!

Such ornaments occur also in the more rude *chansons de geste*, or Old French epics. Jean Rychner and others have elaborated the theory that minstrels who wrote most of the *chansons de geste* did so without written preparation. They knew the plot they were to follow, and they filled it in, as they went along, from formulaic expressions, or conventional phrases. Of course, everyone, including Rychner, admits that the *Chanson de Roland* was composed more elaborately than this. It is my firm opinion that most of the extant *chansons de geste* were not composed orally. Nearly all of them show too much care in rhetoric and in balanced plot structure. The *Roland* is a masterpiece in this respect. There is much evidence that it was rigorously balanced throughout according to the principles of proportion given by Boethius and Pythagoras. [9]

*Humor*

It is true that to prove an example of humor across a period of eight hundred years is hard to do; but many of the writings of the twelfth and thirteenth centuries are filled with it. This is especially true in the *Roman de Renart* branches, and in the fabliaux. Humor is in much of the early medieval drama, particularly in the *Jeu de Saint Nicolas* — and it can be easily seen in the *chansons de geste* and in the romances. There are certain types. The first of these is the use of nonsense language and of distorted speech.

---

[8] *Lanval*, vv. 205-16, in *Les Lais*, ed. Ernest Hoepffner (Strasbourg: Heitz, 1921).

[9] Mr. Robert Lucas' investigation has confirmed this fully.

A most famous passage of this kind is the one in which the statue of the pagan god Tervagan expresses his rage at the close of the *Jeu de Saint Nicolas:*

> Pales aron ozinomas
> Baske bano tudan donas
> Geheamel cla orlay
> Berec he pantaras taÿ. [10]

It may be completely fortuitous, or it may be imagination on my part, but I can recognize a tinge of Basque in this. It is very difficult to make up an imaginary language without some reference to an existing language. *Berek* and *bano* are Basque words, and note *Baske*!

There are numerous examples of these made-up languages, but another especially interesting example is in the *Miracle de Theophile* of Rutebeuf (mid-thirteenth century). Salatins is calling up the Devil for Theophile:

> Bagahi laca bachahé
> Lamac cahi achabahé
> Karrelyos
> Lamac lamec bachalyos
> Cabahagi sabalyos
> Baryolas
> Lagozatha cabyolas
> Samahae et famyolas
> Harrahye. [11]

A much later example is in the *Mistère du Viel Testament* of the fifteenth century — the Tower of Babel scene. The gradual change of language is introduced most cleverly. Finally one of the workmen (Gaste Bois) breaks into this:

> Oriolla gallariey
> Breth gathahat mirlidonnet
> Juidamag alacro brouet
> Mildafaronel adaté

---

[10] Jean Bodel, *Jeu de Saint-Nicolas*, ed. A. Jeanroy (Paris: CFMA, 1925), vv. 1519-22.

[11] Rutebeuf, *Miracle de Théopile*, ed. Grace Frank, CFMA 49 (Paris: Champion, 1925), pp. 6-7.

Another workman (Casse Tuilleau) continues:

> Quanta a queso a lamyta
> La seigneurie la polita
> Volle dare le coupe toue

This last is obviously intended to be a Romance tongue.[12]

Dante, of course, was in this same tradition. He has his giant Nimrod exclaiming: "Raphèl maì amècche zabì almi."[13] At that very point, Vergil as Dante's guide refers to the Tower of Babel. The broken English spoken by Renart when he is posing as an English minstrel is a prime example of dialect. A similar language is in the fabliau of the two English minstrels. They try to buy a lamb for one of the two who is sick. The purchaser mispronounces *aignal* as *asnel* and, of course, gets a newborn donkey instead of a lamb. Other languages, and other dialects, were funny to a proper-speaking Frenchman.

As one might expect, plays on words were also funny. There is the fabliau of *La Male Honte* where the proper meaning was "Honte's bag." Those who heard it out of context thought it was "The Evil Shame," a curse. Then there is the fabliau *Estula*. The dog of a certain household is named *Estula*. When two thieves have entered and are doing their nefarious work, the owner calls to his dog, "Estula!" One of the robbers recognizing the syllables for "Are you there?" answers, "Sure I am," and of course the burglars are caught.

Another kind of humor is that where an ordinary simple animal is spoken of as though having human traits and reasoning power. In Chrétien's *Yvain,* the lion (pictured by Chrétien as about the size of a big dog) is most polite and genteel. Yvain is very tired and faints. His sword slips from the scabbard and makes a small wound through the links of his hauberk on his neck:

> ...so that it caused the blood to flow. The lion sees his master and companion; never before had he had such an emotion because he thinks to see him dead; he begins to make such grief as I have never heard before. He

---

[12] Baron James de Rothschild, ed., *Le Mistère du Viel Testament,* SATF (Paris: Didot, 1878-91), I, 27.

[13] *Inferno* XXXI, v. 67.

twists about, he scratches, he cries, and he wishes to kill himself with the sword that he thinks has slain his good lord. He removes the blade with his teeth and sets it up on a log lying on the ground, with the end supported against a trunk, for he is afraid it will slip when he strikes against it with his breast. His desire would have been accomplished when Yvain came out of his faint. The lion checked his run while dashing at full speed to his death like a crazy boar who cares not where he hits.[14]

There is always the mocking of "dignity." Under this heading come many anticlerical jokes and stories. Priests are always made out as rapacious lechers. Indeed, this kind of humor lies also in the fabliau of Aristotle and the Persian princess, the beloved of Alexander. She prances by Aristotle's window as he sits studying, until in a moment of "sin" he reaches out and grasps her. We know that this results in Aristotle's being ridden like a horse by the fair lady. When Alexander sees this and twits him, Aristotle replies that if woman can do this to him, what could such a creature do to Alexander. We need hardly add that a good bawdy story of any kind was considered funny.

Some of this kind of humor was expressed by sign language only, which has degenerated today often to the point of not being understood, although still used. Chief among such signs is that of the so-called "fig" of which only a rare person knows the meaning.[15] An amusing expression of contempt was to force a captured dignitary to remove a fig from the rear end of a large animal with his teeth. In the late Middle Ages even Dante speaks of the "double fig" which when made by Fucci was equivalent to a rude and lewd invitation.[16]

*Aucassin et Nicolette,* which is one continuous humorous narrative, achieves humor in many ways. In the first place, Biaucaire did exist as a town. It was a most unmilitary town, with no fighting men and no defenses, and surrendered with hardly a blow to the invading forces at the time of the Albigensian Crusade. In the story

---

[14] Chrétien de Troyes, *Yvain*, ed. R. W. Linker (Chapel Hill: University of North Carolina Press, 1940), vv. 3506-25.

[15] Medieval man thought that the inside of the fig looked like the human anus.

[16] *Inferno* XXV, vv. 1-3.

of *Aucassin and Nicolette* this town is mocked as completely pusillanimous. There was in reality no count there at all. The chief humor in *Aucassin* is that the best fighter, Nicolette, is actually a delicate female; Aucassin (Arabic, al-Kassim?) is a craven. One wonders whether the famous confession of not caring about going to Heaven has some satirical meaning. The style of the Aucassin resembles children's syntax.

We close this catalogue of possible humor with the statement that a good sharp trick, played on an innocent victim was always a provoker of risibility. In the fabliau of the thieves *Barat et Haimet* there is a contest of expertness in pilfering without being caught. One thief goes up a tree and removes the nest from under a sitting female bird. But the other thief wins. He goes up the same tree and comes away with the *braies* (underdrawers) of his competitor without being perceived.

*The Professional Writer*

Guernes of Pont-Sainte Maxence was a good professional writer who wrote what can be called the first on-the-spot biography of a distinguished man. I am referring to his life of St. Thomas Becket. Guernes went to Canterbury to get firsthand material, which was almost a unique idea for his time. He really did research on his subject. In an epilogue of twenty-two lines which most scholars believe to be genuine, although it is found only in the Paris MS of the Life of St. Thomas, he has something to say about the circumstances of his employment:

> The Abbess sister of Saint Thomas, to her honor and that of the Saint, has given me a palfrey and clothings (not even spurs are lacking). I did not make a bad throw of the dice when I came to her house. Nor has she lost anything thereby. She will have her recompense; everywhere, among high and low, I will exalt her name. From here to Paris one cannot find a better woman. The nuns of her abbey have all been kind to me, each one with a gift. May the good Lord send them every day plenty of wine, bread, meat, and fish! And when their bodies are silent and abased may God have mercy on their souls. I will never again cry "Alas" — for I have served a proper lord, Saint Thomas. Because I have often grown weary rhyming about his passion, he gives me everything (all

joking aside): gold, silver, clothing in my saddle bags, horses and other valuables.... Odo, the good prior of Holy Trinity Abbey and his monks have rendered me much assistance. They maintained me for a year and a day, and advised me. Wherever I may go, far and wide, it will be to them that I will return.[17]

Another such professional poet was certainly Wace, who, we assume, was a teacher or *clerc lisant* at Caen. He was not on the quick side. Wace's *Brut*, with 15,000 verses, probably required four or five years for its rhyming, meaning that Wace may have begun this poem in 1150 or 1151, when Eleanor of Aquitaine was still the wife of Louis of France. Wace says that he completed the *Brut* in 1155. When he began this work, Geoffrey of Monmouth was still alive (he died in 1154). It is probable that Geoffrey knew about this undertaking; he may even have encouraged it. By 1155 the scene had changed: Queen Eleanor was a blithe spirit in the new styles of poetry which were in the air; and the *Brut* was something new. Layamon at the end of the century is our authority that Wace finally dedicated the leaves of this great poem to Queen Eleanor: "the third book ... that French clerk made, who was named Wace, and who gave it to the noble Eleanor, high King Henry's Queen." But she is mentioned nowhere in the text of the poem. We may believe then that Wace began his long adaptation of Geoffrey on speculation, aware that the folk around him were ready for this kind of narrative in a popular form. Henry of Blois, abbot of Glastonbury and bishop of Winchester, was at the height of his influence at the time. The *Brut* is a subject that must have suited his tastes. It was a forerunner of the romance, in form and style.

Wace was undoubtedly a hard-headed man, a moralist; he wrote elsewhere (vv. 65-70 in his *Rou*) after 1160: "Everything declines, decays, dies, comes to an end. Towers crumble, walls give way, and the rose withers. A horse stumbles, and cloth grows old; man dies, iron wears away, and wood will rot. All that is made by hand will perish."

Since our theme throughout this book is to present the medieval man's concept of man, it is not far from our point to close with this

---

[17] Guernes of Ponte-Sainte Maxence, *Vie de Saint Thomas* (Paris, 1936), pp. 191-192.

quotation. But I shall add another from Wace which is enlightening as to method:

> I have heard minstrels in my childhood who have sung how William long ago blinded Osmund and dug out the eyes of Count Riulf, and how he caused Ansketil to be slain by trickery, and Balzo of Spain to be guarded with a shield. I know nothing about them. When I have no corroboration of detail, I do not care to repeat nor do I wish to affirm that lies are true. [18]

In another passage, quoted earlier in this book, Wace seeks to verify the authenticity of the magic spring of Broceliant, which he finds to be a fake.

> I saw the forest and I saw the land. I looked for wonderful things, but I did not find them. I was a fool to go there, and I came away like a fool. I looked for foolishness, and I considered myself silly. [19]

Gerald the Welshman also had a thirst for accuracy:

> When Prince John had remained in Ireland uselessly through the whole summer and a part of the winter, the prince then crossed the water back to Wales and England. Gerald stayed with Bertran de Verdun, the seneschal, in order to do the study mentioned, gathering and digesting until the following Easter [April 13, 1186]. [20]

These men were capable and desired to separate fact from idle tale-telling. Fact and fiction were well separated in the minds of such men as Guernes de Pont-Sainte-Maxence, Wace, and Gerald, and legions of others in the Middle Ages. It was their misfortune that they lacked the books and the tools for sure verification. It should be noted, however, that such a man as Guernes, who was doubtless famed in many places, had to be subservient — he could not be *fier* in receiving his payments. Men of letters seldom had

---

[18] Wace, *Le Roman de Rou et des ducs de Normandie*, ed. Frédérick Pluquet (Rouen: Frère, 1827), I, vv. 1361-67.
[19] *Ibid.*, vv. 6395-6420.
[20] Giraldus Cambrensis, *Giraldi Cambrensis Opera*, ed. J. S. Brewer, Rolls Series no. 21 (London: Longman & Co., 1861-91), I, 65.

any means of getting payment except from the indulgence of their patrons and masters. This was a concept inbred in a feudalistic society. (I could say that it extended to the patronage of the eighteenth century, although others have a different way of explaining the relationship of Samuel Johnson and Lord Chesterfield.)

*Summary*

I believe that the medieval man's concept of human nature can be summed up neatly in these words: he believed that man would be as free as he willed, but always within the framework of Nature (which represents God's will). Man must not be rebellious against any authority (be it only a patron) which we are sure God has set over us. Eventual decay is one unavoidable facet of human existence.

Postscript

# GOD AND MAN

Vital to our study of the concept of mankind in the Middle Ages is an understanding of man's interpretation of Man and his soul as creations of God. These relationships were discussed by theologians and this study was a considerable part of what we call medieval philosophy. The schoolmen, or clerks, who developed these ideas had as their sources the little that they knew of Plato, St. Augustine, the Neo-Platonists, and Aristotle's *Organon* (the Old Logic).

*The Classical Origins*

Most thinkers in the Middle Ages considered the systems of abstract thought which sprang from the great minds of Plato and Aristotle to be divinely inspired. They reconciled the masterpieces of the classical thinkers as well as they could with the teachings of the Old and New Testaments, producing the discipline known as Scholasticism. There were many steps in various directions along the way, but the ultimate direction was clear.

Before entering into efforts of this kind a little more closely we want to reflect on the first philosophers who began to reflect on first causes and the Creator. This is really a digression, presented as a brief background for those who like to speculate on beginnings. I believe that these Milesian thinkers (around the city of Miletus) were tired of the creation myths spread by the Aryans, and the other local peoples who worshipped a Mother Goddess. The Milesians began thinking for themselves.

In the sixth century B.C., Thales, the earliest known philosopher, was saying, "Since our soul, being air, holds us together, so do breath and air surround the whole universe." Anaximander of Miletus wrote: "the source from which existing things derive their existence is also that to which they turn after their destruction, according to necessity; for they give justice and make reparation to one another for their injustice according to the arrangement of rhyme." Xenophanes of Colophon said: "there is one god among gods and men, the greatest, not at all like us mortals in mind and body."

Thales taught that the chief material in heaven and in earth had been water. Heraclitus of Ephesus said: "To God all things are beautiful, good, and just; but men have assumed that certain things are just and others are unjust."

No date can be postulated as to when this new way of looking at things spread to Attica and to Athens, but it certainly had reached there by early in the fifth century. The men of the Age of Pericles were ravenous for new ideas and new explanations, defined often by man as heresy. The comic poet of Athens, Aristophanes, made it clear that many of his fellow citizens did not approve of the "new gods" and the new efforts to explain the phenomena of nature. The *Clouds* is a masterly bit of satire in which accusations were made against Socrates, chiefly for the corruption of youth in religious matters. The old man Strepsiades who is plagued by "horsing" debts incurred by his high-living son Pheidippides, has joined Socrates's "thinkery" to learn how to avoid his troubles. Socrates begins by praying over him to the new divinities.

> The old man must keep silent and listen attentively to the prayers. O Lord master, measureless Air, who occupy the upper spaces, shining Ether, where the revered goddesses the Clouds send forth thunder, lightning — rise up and appear, O goddesses, to this thinker... Come, o most honored Clouds, and show this fellow that these things alone are goddesses, that all other things are rubbish. (Strepsiades speaks up:) "Then Zeus, for land's sake, the Olympian one is he not a god?" (Socrates replies,) "What Zeus? Don't talk foolishness. There is no Zeus. What are you saying?"
> "But who is the one who rains?"
> "I will teach you by great signs. Did you ever see any rain without clouds? Zeus would be raining in clear

weather with them gone away. When the Clouds are full of water they are obliged to move about, heavy by necessity, being suspended full of rain — bursting, they collide and shatter."

"But who forces them to move about if it is not Zeus?"

"It is Whirligig in the upper air."

"I did not know about Whirligig. Zeus does not exist then. Instead of him Whirligig now rules?"

This conversation between the comic Socrates and his stupid pupil was intended to be farcical, but in it is given the new definition of rain which was then being held by Anaxagoras, Democritus, the Stoics, and others. The new Greek sophists of the sixth and fifth centuries were on a collision course with the old mythology.

I own a small piece of electrum (part gold, part silver) which was considered a coin at Phocaea in about 600 B.C. This was a city opposite the Isle of Lesbos. For me this bit of metal is a reminder of the new creative activity which took place at that time on the Ionian coast, as far south as Rhodes, Miletus, Ephesus, Colophon, Glazomenas, and then migrating to Abdera in Thrace. The chief pagan divinities of this area had been Artemis of Ephesus, perhaps a mother goddess, Athena of Priene, and Apollo of Didyma, located twenty miles south of Miletus.

At this time geometry and astronomy were coming to the fore. The chief philosopher who was concerned with order in heaven and earth was Plato, the greatest philosopher of all. Plato, writing in the *Timaeus*, saw the world, and man, as an ordered product of a single Creator (the Demiurgos). Plato's wonderful discussion of this hierarchy, couched in marvellous language, one of the great beauties of this world, struck chords which echoed throughout all antiquity, and thereafter deep into the Middle Ages, the Renaissance, and deeper, until our present century.

This Plato Aristides was born in 427 B.C., a scion of one of the best families of Athens. After preliminary studies in grammar and music he spent much of his time with Socrates, and became one of his chief intimates. About 390 B.C. (Socrates died in 399) Plato began to teach in the Academy, a grove of trees outside the walls of Athens. His extant compositions, of which we have twenty-five, took the form of dialogues in which the master Socrates is almost always the chief speaker. I believe that the ideas of Socrates were fundamental in these lectures, but it must be equally true that these notions represent Plato's own ideas.

Of these writings the Middle Ages knew directly only the *Timaeus*, and then only the first half of it (37 pages out of 75), which deals with the origins of the world. This was translated by a Christian deacon Chalcidius in the fourth century A.D. Further knowledge of Plato's writings came from Apuleius (second century, A.D.), Cicero, Macrobius, Boethius, Martianus Capella, and St. Augustine.

Plato was much concerned with his concept of an ideal state, and he went to Syracuse to study this further in 388, 367, and 361 B.C. He might have pursued this goal profitably if he had limited himself to the practical examination of the establishment of Dionysius, and his relative Dion, — a benign autocracy. But he insisted upon basic mathematical concepts as a preparation for rule, and this fatigued the Syracusan monarch. Plato claimed that a woman named Diotima of Mantinia had taught him the philosophy of Love, but I am led to think that Plato actually was not very fond of women. Abstract thoughts pleased him more.

When Plato returned to his Academy in 366 B.C., he found a new pupil, Aristotle, son of the physician Nicomachus of Stagira in Chalcidia. This boy, born in 384, had a deep interest in biology. He went first to Athens in 367 where he studied with Isocrates before joining the Academy. He remained with Plato until 347, the year of the master's death. He absorbed much from him, but his own ideas were not a mere rubber stamp.

Plato saw everything in the world as a reflection of the Divine mind; Aristotle was much concerned with the five senses. He felt that experience gained through the senses gives one knowledge. *Nihil est in intellectu quod non prius fuerit in sensu.* He developed his basic principles of thought in his *Logic*. Just as Plato had done before him, he conceived of an Ideal City; but his was not like Plato's. His ideal state was not on the sea coast, only near it, where trade could flow in and out. His young men were soldiers, the middle aged men were politicians, and the elders were priests. They had also artisans and merchants who had no vote. Private property was essential, but he recommended the existence of public lands for producing state revenue.

Aristotle said that, except in the case of God, all form was inherent in matter. Matter with its seeds of form planted within would grow. It could always change and assume a new form. God, of course, was pure Actuality, distinct from the potentiality of the physical order.

From 347 till 343 Aristotle moved about in the Assos-Mytelene area; then in 343 to 336 he was the tutor of Alexander the Great, at Pella. Probably he was not called to this duty because he was known as a great teacher; it was probably, rather, because of the influence of his father Nicomachus. Aristotle had no false ideas about his great pupil Alexander. He was too keen a thinker for that. In 335 Aristotle began to teach in Athens at the Lyceum grove and was there for thirteen years. When anti-Macedonian feeling arose in 333, he retired to Chalcis and died the following year.

We have spoken of Aristotle's creation of Logic in the six treatises of his *Organon*. This was all of his writing that was known in the West until later in the twelfth century when, through Arabic, translations of his New Logic appeared. *Physics, Metaphysics, De Anima, Ethics* and *Naturalia* were then read. These works form the New Logic. Remember that Plato thought of knowledge as a pale reflection of the eternal ideas, which Christian Platonists later considered the Divine Mind. For Aristotle knowledge was a revelation from sensual experience, God being the ultimate knowledge, which is revealed by progressive stages. High on the list in Aristotle's treatment of Logic are these Categories: substance, quality, quantity, relation, time and space, action, passion, passivity, and condition. The Causes are classified as material, design, the maker, and purpose. Purpose is chief among these.

We have already repeated that the philosophy of the Middle Ages was a reconciliation of the teaching of the Bible with Plato and Aristotle. It would be well to bear in mind the reference works recommended by Thierry of Chartres (d. 1155), who summarized the teaching of the Liberal Arts in his *Heptateuchon*. The teaching of Latin grammar should come from Donatus and Priscian; Cicero and Martianus Capella were the masters of Rhetoric; Boethius and the *Organon* of Aristotle taught Dialectic or argument. The quadrivium, the Sciences, were to be derived from fragments of Boethius, Martianus Capella, Isidore of Seville, Columella, Gerbert, de Garlande, Hyginus, and Ptolemy.

In the third, fourth, and fifth centuries, Neo-Platonism was the prevailing form of Platonic thought. Plotinus (c. 205-70), the chief master of this doctrine, wrote treatises which are called the six *Enneads* (books of nine chapters). He never revised them in any way. Plotinus was a native of Egypt, although he may have been of Roman descent. He settled in A. D. 244 in Rome, where he directed a school of his own. He had studied in Alexandria, beginning at the age of twenty-eight, and then he journeyed to the East in the train of Emperor Gordian III, who fought the Persians in Mesopotamia in 242-44. After that Plotinus settled in Rome. It is obvious that Plotinus was considerably influenced by the Quietistic or "Emanatian" slant of Eastern philosophy, but he never taught extreme asceticism. His doctrine, of course, was basically that of Plato.

Plotinus was concerned with the ontology of moral, intellectual, and aesthetic values. God is the One, boundless and infinite. The One emanated without lessening; and the Divine Mind, or Logos, was the result. In this Logos are all the Realities, reflected in our World. The Divine Mind emanated, in turn, without lessening, and its result was the active member of the Divine Essence, the World Soul. The most active division of this World Soul we call Nature. The One created this World in matter because it was a necessity for His expression to be revealed. Human souls, like ideas or forms, were within the Divine Mind. Ideas emanated from the Idea of Good. They were sent to the World, probably, to improve it, to make it good. In the World these ideas did not unite with matter; their new bodies existed alongside their matter. The highest categories, Truth, Beauty, and Goodness are supreme in Heaven (which is identical with the Logos). Creation is Contemplation of this spiritual World. Our World below is but a blurred and confused picture of what is above — yet it is beautiful. The individual soul understands itself only when it contemplates these ideal forms. Individual souls are not parts of the World Soul; they are active principles (or logoi) which correspond to forms or ideas within the Logos. The individual soul is an original cause which can perceive only that which is akin to it. Unification with the Highest cannot be achieved by thought; it is only by losing the restraint of the body that the soul can *realize* itself in union with the One — "The flight of the alone to the Alone." Time is a measure of finite activity. It is a qualitative change; eternal life survives time. Thus reliance on the future is a disease. The World of change, in which we live, was created by the World Soul after the patterns of heavenly ideas.

We are a golden chain around the feet of God. The earthly soul does not sin when it wishes to create. The World must continue to exist; but our souls should be stronger. The strongest souls understand Evil but do not experience it. Pleasure and pain are states of consciousness, not diseases of the soul. Memory and Imagination are related, but memory is less worthy because animals have it. Knowledge is sensation, then imagination, then mind. Discursive reasoning is a proper function of the soul. There are three phases to life: an external phase, discursive reasoning, and the life of the spirit. Our individual souls are always in correspondence with the World Soul; but in heaven (the Divine Mind) there are only pure souls and spirits. After death, opinion, reason and memory are superfluous. The soul of the body can be lost because of evil, but one never loses the soul that should have been here.

Plotinus opposed Christianity in a gentle way, but Christians made considerable use of his arguments, as we shall see. One of his immediate disciples was Porphyry (Malchus) who died in 304. He was the student who arranged and edited the *Enneads*. [He sought to combine the teachings of Plato and Aristotle, although, because of his strong religious bent Aristotle seems to have been lost in his piety.] He taught among other things that human souls do not remain permanently in the Divine Mind or Heaven. They descend and mount up in constant movement throughout the ages. Yet he did not teach transmigration, even though in the *Enneads* he refers to possible transmigration. [He did, however, introduce a strong ascetical note into Neo-Platonism which had a decided influence on Christianity.]

Proclus (410-85) was another significant Neo-Platonist, with a strong mystical orientation. He saw gods and visions and prayed to the Sun three times a day. [He wrote a great deal about the nature of the soul which strongly influenced Christian thought.]

Proclus, as well as another Neo-Platonist, Iamblichus (d. 330), defended the value of poetry against a sort of criticism that had stemmed from Plato's *Republic* and thus influenced the medieval mind. Plotinus followed Aristotle in teaching the Saros — the belief that everything in the World will be repeated in detail at great set intervals. A vast multitude of myths, symbols, and emblems were introduced by the Neo-Platonists (as well as by the earlier Platonists), resulting in multiple Allegory. Normal language was inadequate and symbols were needed, including poetic images. These produce a veil which only the initiated (or knowledgeable ones) can penetrate. The equation of Light with Truth was most influential.

Not to be confused with the Neo-Platonists and yet influential both on them and on medieval theology were the Gnostics, a group of sects which held that the force of Evil and the force of Good (represented by Light) are in eternal conflict. The world or Kenoma is ruled by the twelve archons of Evil, which include the Lord of the Old Testament. Secret formulas existed which at death would free Man from this Evil and restore him to the heaven of light.

Valentinus (135) at Alexandria taught that there was a succession of Emanations, or *aeons* as he called them. They generated pairs in the spiritual world from the Divine (spiritual powers). The thirtieth aeon was Sophia, who caused much trouble; the last three were Christ, the Holy Spirit, and Jesus the Savior. These last three were created to undo the harm of Sophia, who was banished from the Spiritual Universe or Pleroma. The Ruler of our world is the Demiurge who is the God of the Old Testament. The first aeons were abyss and silence, then mind and truth, and then Word and life. Jesus came to teach a Gnosis which will restore Man to the Divine order.

Basilides, also of Alexandria, said that he had a secret Gnosis handed down from Saint Peter. In this system there are three classes of Man; the corporeal (hylic), which will never be saved; Man which has soul (psychic); and Man which has already the Divine Spark (the pneumatics). Among the psychics are the Christians who can be saved by faith into a lesser salvation. Of course the main goal for Mankind is to throw off the evil of the world and achieve salvation within the pleroma. There is a sect within modern Iraq, called the Mandaeans, who are perhaps descended from the Gnostics.

Mani (276) was a Persian who taught another dualistic faith which contains many elements of Gnosticism, mixed with Zoroastrianism and Marcionism (an early form of Gnosticism). Marcion (b. 85) went to Rome about the same time as Valentinus (135) — and he too saw the God of the Old Testament as cruel and therefore in conflict with the merciful Lord of the New Testament. This presupposed that the old creating god was inferior. Marcion said that Jesus was a manifestation of the Father, and did not believe in salvation by Gnosis (knowledge), but by faith alone. Neo-Platonism, Gnosticism, Marcionism, and Manichaeanism all insisted upon the Neo-Platonic concept of Emanation rather than upon Divine Creation. God's substance flowed outward and produced new forms.

For Mani the realm of God is represented by Light and the realm of Satan by Darkness. Man is of matter (Dark) with a small amount of Light. Christ is all-Light and Christ wishes to redeem this Light, but women can not be redeemed. There is no sin — only misery — through contact with matter. The auditors were the ordinary people who could hope to be reborn as the *perfects* or elect, but are doomed to Hell. Sexual relations were also considered very evil. In the Middle Ages all these dualistic systems were thought of as one called Manicheanism (Albigensianism).

## *Augustine*

I have tried to make the origins of Medieval philosophy comprehensible to the modern reader. It all boils down to this: what is Reality in this world? Is it just a reflection of God in the Divine Mind, the Logos? If this is so, how much free will does an individual have to make a choice between good and evil? St. Augustine of Hippo was the seminal thinker who helped medieval man deal with this issue.

I have discussed dualistic systems evolving into Manichaeanism because St. Augustine, the greatest Christian teacher of the Middle Ages, always carried with him the influence of the Manichaean period. Evidently the confusion which brought about dualism, in opposition to Christianity and other great monotheistic faiths, was the inability to understand the relationship of evil to good, and the belief that the wrathful Old Testament God of the Jews was somehow incompatible with the New Testament's conception of the God of Mercy. All the philosophical systems which I have discussed have seen in Light the great personification of God. This belief was also strongly held by Augustine. From this vision of God as Light came the Franciscans' study of the rainbow and the discovery of lenses (c. 1200). Thus modern optics is the result of theological speculation!

Aurelius Augustinus (354-430) was born at Tagaste (40 miles south of Hippo in northern Africa). His mother, Saint Monica, brought him up as a Christian (although his father was a pagan until just before his death) but during his youth in Carthage he was persuaded to profess Manichaeanism because of his schooling and the gross immorality professed by Christians in that port city. At this time he developed a magnificent style and clarity in rhetoric; and he taught rhetoric in Rome, beginning in 383, having lost faith in Manichaeanism. Attracted to academic scepticism, he went to Milan in 384 to teach rhetoric there. While in Milan he steeped himself in Platonism as well as the Sceptics, and his reading of the *Enneads* strengthened his ultimate rejection of the materialism of the Sceptics in favor of the immaterial reality of the Neo-Platonists. A great influence upon him at this time was the preaching of St. Ambrose, who was bishop of Milan until 397. This combination of the influences of Neo-Platonism and the Christian community of Milan lead to his conversion in 386.

Not long after, in 388, Augustine returned home to Tagaste to lead a sort of monastic life with some of his friends. He was in Hippo in 391 when he was urged, practically by force, to become the priest of the Christian community there. He lived in Hippo for the rest of his life: he was the auxiliary bishop in 395 and became the diocesan shortly thereafter. He was engaged in defence of the faith against the Manichaeans, the Donatists, and the Pelagians, who denied Original Sin and the Fall of Man. Some of his lesser works were arguments against these heresies: *On Baptism, On the Correction of the Donatists*, and *Against Faustus the Manichaean*. However, his three great masterpieces were his *Confessions, The City of God*, and a magnificent system of Christian doctrine known as *On the Trinity*. Augustine was a significant source of Western monasticism, and for this purpose he wrote his manual *On the Work of the Monks*. Toward the end of his life he composed his *Retractions* in which he reviewed many of his writings and made some changes.

Two doctrines that he defended that strike us as especially important are evident in his belief in the authority of the Church as the principal protector of the Faith, and in his insistence that man can be whole only through the experience of grace, as he testified for himself. His view of grace led him to insist that the successors of the Apostles, the bishops, who receive their consecration in an unbroken line from the early Apostles, have the power of those

Apostles. This power includes valid administration of the Sacraments, and the transmission of this grace to those who receive their laying on of hands.

Saint Augustine was truly the preeminent theologian of the first thousand years of Christianity. It is necessary to understand that he was revered for this by the Catholic churchmen who followed him throughout all the Middle Ages. Of course, in his use of terminology and in his handling of concepts he used the tools and the modes of expression which had come to him from the masters that he originally followed: the Neo-Platonists, and, to a much lesser extent, the Manichaens. His *City of God* is concerned with the defense of Christian doctrine, but the idea of the Two Cities — one of Darkness and one of Light — and of Man's need to turn eventually purely to the City of God for salvation, reflect a division which is basic in Manichaeanism.

The *Confessions* is a beautiful account of the Saint's conversion, and of the thoughts that led him to it. This is the first book that a student of Saint Augustine should study. The *City of God* is the next; but it is so vast (being a defense of Christianity against the pagans) that I advise students to begin reading books eleven, fourteen, and nineteen in that order.

The purpose of this book is to examine medieval man's concept of mankind. The views held by the clerical class on Man, his nature, and his duties, were governed very much by their understanding of the ideas of St. Augustine.

The later Descartes' basic belief is close to that of St. Augustine. We shall assume, therefore, that Descartes was somewhat dependent on St. Augustine. [Reinhold Niebuhr has said that Descartes simply reviewed the Neo-Platonism of Augustine. Niebuhr did not intend this as a compliment.] He who can think must exist; if we seem to err, the Truth also from which we err must exist. All reasoning is an orderly succession of intellectual visions. That we have intellectual vision is proof of our existence. Reason alone cannot solve fundamental problems. There must be an Authority in the World which was set up by Providence. The Catholic Church is that authority. God would not have allowed Christianity to continue as it has if this were not real. When one examines the beautiful and wonderful Earth on which we live it is evident that this beauty could not come from within Earth itself — there must have been a Creator. Over everything — over our Intellect — there is also Truth.

All Good is in God. Evil, therefore, is the effect of Man's resistance to Divine Impulse. [This is an idea that Descartes got from the Neo-Platonists.] The World began within an instant. "Deus creavit omnia simul." But when our World was created, some of it came into being in perfect form — other parts were only *rationes seminales*. [This notion is originally Stoic in origin, but was adopted by Middle Platonism (first and second century A.D.) and then was inherited by Neo-Platonism.] These "seeds" were to germinate according to God's will at later times. Man is a combination of body and soul joined in a way that we cannot understand. The Resurrection of the body is therefore inevitable. Adam was created immortal in perfect felicity. His great sins of pride and disobedience produced the Fall.

The Highest Good is a vision of the divine essence. All education should be toward acquiring knowledge of this highest good. Salvation must come to us through illumination and education, searching for the Truth within ourselves. Heaven is the fatherland of the angels and of the Just Souls; it is the Celestial City — the Vision of God. There *videbimus, amabimus, et laudabimus*. Our minds can see the divine essence; the Intellect sees beyond that which is perceptible to the senses. Grace is the route that the soul takes to reach the perfection of celestial felicity. Grace is the moral aid emanating from Christ which we must have. Grace is most necessary for us to conquer sin. To be able to have charity is natural to man — charity is the intuitive vision of God. The Bible is indispensable as a light to Christian faith.

St. Augustine's definition of the Holy Trinity is too major for us to discuss here. In brief, unity is within the divine nature; but there is some distinction of relation. He begins with the Trinity as a whole. The Father is the generator; the Son is the generated, and the Holy Spirit proceeds from both. [St. Augustine used an intellectual analogy in discussing the Trinity which led to a weak distinction of the Three Persons called "modalism." Adolph Harnack makes the point that it was Augustine's *On the Trinity* that made Scholasticism possible.]

St. Augustine's teaching remained as the unique source of orthodox Christian thought until the era of St. Thomas Aquinas, in the latter part of the thirteenth century — and even after that date many held it in the special veneration, especially the Franciscans.

Note the importance which St. Augustine attaches to illumination (light), and to the fact that God created everything at once — and that subsequent differences are the result of his Divine Will for special reasons. His stress on charity as the "intuitive vision of God" also is most important. The interest in optics (c. 1200), the belief that monsters were not usually evil but portents of God's purpose, the emphasis upon possession of grace within the perfect knight — these are all part of the prevailing Augustinian concept. [One cannot understand the medieval *Weltanschauung*, unless he grasps the popularized Augustinian notions of "illumination" and "light" given as grace to man's mind and reflected in his life patterns.]

To summarize more fully, St. Augustine codified an understanding of the Certainty of God, the concept of the Trinity, definitions of Creation, of Illumination, of Original Sin, of the Word Incarnate, of Grace, of the Church, of the Sacraments, of Christian life, and of eschatology (the Ultimates).

It must be borne in mind that St. Augustine never read any of Plato's writings in the original. His background was Neo-Platonism rather than genuine Platonism. This meant that he was not aware of Plato's myth of the creation of men's soul by the Demiurge. He used the *Enneads* of Plotinus in the translation of Marius Victorinus, but the writings of Cicero and Macrobius's commentary on the *Dream of Scipio* furnished him with much food for thought. The introductions prefaced to Aristotle's *De Bestiis* and the first book of *Nicomachean Ethics*, as also the *Metaphysics* and the *De Animis*, contributed a considerable amount of Platonic doctrine to St. Augustine's thinking.

Something of the honor in which the medieval church held St. Augustine can be seen in the tradition that Liutprand of Lombardy bought the reputed body of St. Augustine from the Saracens for a vast sum in 710, and it now lies at Pavia in the Church of St. Peter Cielo di Oro on the floor directly over the altar where the bones of Boethius rest.

St. Augustine was also too much of a rationalist to succumb to some of the Neo-Platonic piety and superstition revived in the West by another Neo-Platonist, an Irishman, John Scotus Erigena

(d. 877), who came to France from Ireland. He knew Greek, so his greatest contribution was a translation into Latin of the works of pseudo-Dionysius the Areopagite: his mystical theology, *On the Divine Names*, and the heavenly hierarchy. These treatises were filled with a less original kind of Neo-Platonism, especially the thoughts of Proclus. It was believed that they had been composed by the same Dionysius who is mentioned in Acts 17:34, who was converted by St. Paul on the Areopagus hill at Athens. Much of the Neo-Platonic symbolism to which we have already referred occurred in the pseudo-Dionysius and came into the symbolism of medieval literature, particularly influencing Dante.

[Although the translation of the pseudo-Dionysius made available to the medieval world a whole array of images that gave expression to a rather fanciful piety, one should not presume from this that John Scotus Erigena was some kind of simpleton. He was, perhaps, a more deeply committed Neo-Platonist than St. Augustine, and therefore his attempts to reconcile this philosophy of the Christian Gospel were more tenuous. Nonetheless, he was the one profound theological mind that marked the somewhat bleak intellectual world of the Heroic Age of the medieval world. It is perhaps unfortunate that we remember him for his influence through the translation of the pseudo-Dionysius rather than through his own highly original works.]

*Later Developments*

The system of St. Augustine that I have discussed, with later accretions, remained the doctrine of the Church and wielded immense influence until the latter part of the twelfth century. Then the doctrinal system of St. Thomas Aquinas (1225-March 7, 1274) slowly began to take precedence. [Aquinas, however, only considered his work as an "expansion" of Augustine, and sometimes the logic of his system had to give way to the pressure of Augustinian piety (e.g., concerning the existence of the soul apart from the body).]

[It is important, however, that the reader understand that whereas St. Thomas was not aware of the radical methodological difference that existed between himself and St. Augustine, this in fact was there and inevitably meant that St. Thomas' system was in truth that (i.e., a "system") and consequently departed from St. Augustine's work in a fundamental manner. Bernard Lonergan has made the point that the *Academic discipline of theology* became a possibility, apart from religion, only in the twelfth century, because of the influence of Aristotle's *Posterior Analytics*. This work led scholasticism to distinguish between understanding and judgement, opening up religious experience to a systematic analysis on the basis of a cognitional theory. In St. Augustine philosophy and theology are confused, but in St. Thomas Aquinas they are carefully distinguished in a hierarchical structure. While this is to take nothing away from the genius of the former, it does remind us that he lived more than eight hundred years before the latter in a different culture. This leads to an inevitable difference in their interpretation of the Christian experience, and marks our period as a time when a subtle shift was beginning to take place in man's understanding of himself before God.]

St. Thomas, the future official Doctor of the Church, was born at Roccasecca near Naples in 1224 or 1225. He started his Church affiliations as an oblate at the famous Benedictine abbey of Montecassino, which was destroyed by Frederick II in 1239. Thomas then studied in Naples with Martin of Dacia and Peter of Ireland, and learned Greek while there. He was admitted to the Dominican order in 1243 or 1244 and was called to Paris, but encountered problems with Guillaume de Saint-Amant and others concerning the mendicant teachers of Paris. Thomas then went to Italy in 1259, remaining there until 1269. He prepared the *Ratio Studiorum* of the Dominican Order with Albertus Magnus and Peter of Tarantasia. He met William of Moerbeke whose fine translation of Aristotle into Latin was finished in 1266. In 1270-71 Thomas was once more in Paris and participated in more struggles with the Augustinians. He went to Naples on the invitation of Charles of Anjou, and was invited to attend the Council at Lyons, but died on route at the Cistercian Abbey of Fossanova in 1274. He was canonized by Pope John XXII in 1323.

As a writer and thinker St. Thomas Aquinas was indefatigable. His great *Summa Theologica* was composed between 1266 and 1273. After his death he was pronounced by Albertus Magnus to be "the splendor and the flower of all the World." He was designated as *Doctor Angelicus* and *Doctor Communis* of the Church [but not until his works were first condemned as heretical because of their deviation from Augustinian teaching].

The great passion of St. Thomas was to have texts as perfect as possible at his disposal. He used the Aristotle of Moerbeke in 1266. He was greately influenced also by the *De Causis* of Boethius, the Pseudo-Dionysius, and the commentary on Aristotle of the Arabian physician Avicenna (Ibn Sina, 980-1037) through the translation of Gerard of Cremona. He had something which St. Augustine did not have — the complete works of Plato — and he used particularly Plato's *Timaeus* in full, the *Phaedo,* and the *Meno.* [He saw himself as a synthesizer, which is to be expected from a medieval mind.]

St. Thomas accepted without quibbling St. Augustine's ideas on the Trinity, Sin, and Grace, or so he thought. [Aquinas did share with St. Augustine a modalist interpretation of the Trinity, rooted in the intellectual analogy of the relationship of the Three Persons. His notion of Original Sin did suggest that not only had man *lost* original righteousness, but there was a positive defect communicated by generation. This "defect," however, was not as likely in Aquinas to inhibit man's good intentions as in the Bishop of Hippo, and some would consider St. Thomas bordering on semi-Pelagianism. This meant, of course, that the depth of man's utter dependence on the grace of God was something less in Aquinas than in St. Augustine, which was perhaps a source of rational approval for prevalent opinions of superabundant merit and the value of good works.

What is important for the difference between St. Augustine and St. Thomas, aside from the clarification of method already noted, was that the latter thought of God not as St. Augustine did (i.e., the *essence* of "immutable being" — a very Neo-Platonic notion), but as pure *existential* act (an Aristotelian concept). The essence of God is his existence. Creation is not the institution at the beginning of time of *rationes seminales,* essential, immutable substances which are joined to man's body; but creation is an on-going process, perhaps eternal, in which the divine act of being is mediated to the created order.] Possibly St. Thomas is influenced here by reading Plato, as well as Aristotle — an opportunity which St. Augustine did not have. [The distinctions in man become, therefore, between soul (form) and body (matter), between existence (act) and essence (potentiality).]

This brings us to the point that for Aquinas there are the two great forces in the Universe: act and potentiality. Pure Act is, as we have said, God only. Act is an affirmation of being (*esse*); potential is a capacity to receive (*essentia*). There is some of both of these elements in everything in the world in ascending proportions — but the potential cannot move or change without something coming to it from act, which promotes motion. The potential is essence. The human body is a substantive form with prime motion derived from act. St. Thomas believed in the unity of substantive form. In man there is no substantial form other than the rational soul which covers many parts just as the square contains triangles — the superior figure contains the inferior. The intellect and the will are the first acts that set the soul in motion: the second act is awareness of understanding. The rational soul is a potentiality which gives all the other attributes. Grace is an act which moves the soul potential. This is *gracia efficax*. Man has two kinds of reasoning: *ratio superior* which comes from divine illumination; and *ratio inferior* which makes use of experience and empiricism. The form cannot be separate from the *esse*.

The Averroïsts, led by Siger of Brabant, separated Faith and Truth completely; the Augustinians thought of Truth as a question of Faith; St. Thomas taught that the Truths of Faith were complemented by those of Reason. [Because God does not, however, participate in the life of man in terms of any essential *rationes seminales*, but by the gift of existence, there are no innate ideas in man, no direct illumination of the human intellectual. Aquinas taught that knowledge is concrete and rooted entirely in experience, and that where natural knowledge leaves off (i.e., reason) faith in revelatory experience of the Church, found in its Scriptures and tradition, completes our knowledge. The power of this difference between the Thomistic intellectualism and the Augustinian essentialism was never felt among the average man of the twelfth and thirteenth century. The removal of God to the end of a syllogism did make possible, however, the gloomy outlook of the fourteenth and fifteenth centuries born of the "Black Death." It did provide a "whipping boy" for the Protestant Reformation, and yet it also enabled a Christian intellectualism to survive the radical critique of Immanuel Kant in the form of a "transcendental Thomism."]

*Medieval Gnosticism*

[Any comment on God and man in the twelfth and thirteenth centuries would not be complete without some passing reference to the movements counter to Christian orthodoxy and the Augustinian-Thomistic tradition.] Beginning slowly in the eleventh century and coming to a peak after 1200, the Catholic faith was faced with a strong rival which we know as Catharism or Albigensianism. We have already touched on the ancestral form of this, Manicheanism, and an even more remote influence, Gnosticism.

We do not know a great deal about the tenets of Catharism except what is found in the registers of the Inquisition and in certain of their religious texts: the *Great Supper*, the *Ritual*, the *Book of the Two Principles*, and others. They rejected most of the Old Testament, except Isaiah and a few other prophets. Christ, they said, had never been in this world, except spiritually in the body of St. Paul. Beneath the great God there are two cosmic principles: the one of Good and the other of Evil.

The members of the sect consisted of about a thousand *perfects* and a great body of *believers*. The *perfects* abstained from all carnal relations and ate only oil, fish, and vegetables. The *perfects* served as priests: they brought to the dying a *consolamentum*, a laying on of hands. The waiting for death was known as the *endura*, which relates to their concept of the human body as a prison for the soul. They believed in psychosomatic cures, which related to their notion that they should aid *sophia* (wisdom) to go up above out of the "shadows." When the *perfects* assembled the believers they had a public confession, called an *apparellamentum*. These *perfects*, known as the "good men," did not fear the punishment of burning (afflicted upon them by the orthodox), but considered it the most beautiful of deaths.

The fact that the Cathars took to its logical conclusion the Neo-Platonic piety, which had been shaped by so many cults of the past fifteen hundred years and which was in many ways implicit in much "orthodoxy," can be seen in their belief in the transmigration of souls among the lesser believers. Indeed, they thought that the soul might move back and forth from the body [which is a notion that is not uncommon at any time in the history of man including our own (e.g., as in the concept of out-of-the-body experiences)].

Converts to Catharism were usually eighteen, but they would take someone as young as twelve. They abrogated all oaths, which would create a social difficulty for any medieval man, but reminds us of the early Christians. To them the world was an illusion, and what they sought was the blessed existence of union with the God above good and evil. [This is, in passing, a notion of God that occurs in the analysis of the analytical psychologist, Carl Jung.]

[The Cathars, who are not to be confused with the more traditionally Christian Waldensians, were a reform movement like all "enthusiasts." Their protest was against theological sterility, empty religious practice, and the immorality of the ecclesiastical bureaucracy. They taught and practiced the immediate, direct experience of God, which, as we have seen, was suggested as possible by St. Augustine, but lost intellectual support in St. Thomas. Catharism was a direct invasion of a basically non-Christian Eastern religion, which drew upon the common imagery of the times of "light" and "darkness," which we have argued was also present in medieval Christianity.

The amazingly quick spread of Catharism throughout Europe testifies to the fact that it both spoke to a need of medieval man that his Christian faith was less and less successfully meeting and drew upon a stock of images that were very much a part of his thinking. Like the Franciscan movement, which found a home in the Church, it was a Puritan reform movement, seeking the assurance of the absolute and a sense of salvation. We have our contemporary counterparts for it — since "enthusiasm" is always a part of the religious scene in one form or another — in the charismatic or Neo-Pentecostal movement within the Christian Church and the Jesus movement that lies on its periphery. The revival of the interest in the occult has a more explicit identity with much of the Cathar imagery.

The *form* which Catharism took is, of course, the commentary that is peculiar to medieval man. The asceticism, dualism, rejection of the sacraments and sacred articles, gnostic divisions of the sons of light and sons of darkness, all depend heavily upon the symbolic world and *Weltanschauung* of the twelfth and thirteenth centuries. It is one possible religious derivation from Neo-Platonism and syncretism of pagan mystery cults. It lies, therefore, in a continuum with other medieval expressions of religious faith, with Scholasticism perhaps at the extreme opposite end of the spectrum.

*Summary*

The purpose of this postscript has not been, obviously, to give a comprehensive summary of the religion or theology of medieval man. Our desire has been to end our analysis of his self-concept where it inevitably ended for him: in the beatific vision. We have emphasized again and again the notion of the illumination of this world by the God who is light, and indicated how in reasoned thought and popular piety this all-pervasive ideal inspired philosophy (e.g., Augustine, John Scotus, Aquinas), science (e.g., optics), war (e.g., the Crusades), and the death of the Cathar martyr. Medieval man lived in an "enchanted world," not as the result of some logical deduction (as in early modern religious thought) but because of his intuitive, conditioned reflex to life. Max Weber speaks of our times as "disenchanted," and Dietrich Bonhoeffer described our century as one "come of age," for whom religion is meaningless. We will not debate whether or not that is true, but hope to have shown that from the greatest mind to the humblest peasant the world of medieval man was easily and without reservation considered the only slightly opaque reflection of God's presence. Unless the reader understands this he cannot comprehend the all-encompassing presupposition that undergirds all that we have previously described in these pages, and he cannot enter into that mode of thought to grasp the innate logic of the medieval life-style.]

Appendix

## THE ELIDUC OF MARIE DE FRANCE

Perhaps the twelfth-century observer whom we have been quoting the most in these pages has been Marie de France. She was most probably a lady living from 1150-1190. Marie herself says that she was born in the Ile de France (which she called simply *France*), but it is very probable also that she was married to an Anglo-Norman who had a residence in the west country bordering on Wales. Today this is Monmouthshire. Since this border country was where Welsh, Anglo-Normans, and English lived side by side we should expect it to be teeming with literary interests. Marie was a keen observer of the life around her, of the minor nobility, and in her days she may have acquired some fame as an expert on affairs of the heart. (This is largely an assumption on my part and must not be considered proven.) In her *Lais* and animal fables she gives much advice about love. One of her lais, *Eliduc,* is most remarkable in many ways. It is much the longest, and it discusses a most common problem — a knight of integrity, his wife, and another girl. This seems to depict most seriously the predicament, and the resulting decisions, which any young people in this class might have had to face. We can do no better than give a more or less literal translation, with carefully chosen words, so that our modern reader can reflect carefully on the attitudes and the decisions made. This is a real slice of late twelfth-century life, for it is God's will which makes the final decision in the story, and he does this with a portent, mentioned also early in this book.

\* \* \*

All the narrative and the account of a very old tale will I recite to you, just as I understand the truth to the best of my knowledge.

There was a knight in Brittany, valiant and courteous, bold and courageous in bearing. I believe he was called Eliduc, and there was not another so valiant man in the country. He had a wife, noble and prudent, of fine family. They had been together for a long time and loved each other very loyally. But finally because of a conflict he was obliged to find employment elsewhere. While away he fell in love with a girl, the daughter of a king and queen; her name was Guilliadun and there was no one fairer in the kingdom. His wife was named Guildeluec in her own country. From these two this *lai* has been called "Guildeluec and Guilliadun." Formerly it was entitled "Eliduc," but now this name is changed, because the adventure of the *lai* which I am telling happened from these two ladies. I will tell you the truth about it.

Eliduc's lord was king of Lesser Britanny, whom he served and cherished faithfully. Whenever the king was obliged to travel about Eliduc was given the land to guard. He kept it safe by his prowess. He had his reward for this, for he could hunt through all the forests; no forester was so bold as to wish to say him nay, or grumble once. But because of his virtue, as often is the case, he became embroiled with his overlord and slandered and accused. The lord sent him from the court without explanation. Eliduc did not know why. He often asked the king to take a denial from him and not believe slander, for he had served him with all his heart. The king answered nothing. Since he could not get a hearing, he felt obliged to leave.

Eliduc went to his own house and sent for all his friends. He told them about the king, his lord, and about the wrath which he showed. He had served him as best he could and the lord should not be ungrateful. A peasant says to his ploughboy, in a proverb when he disputes, that the affection of a master cannot be guaranteed. He is wise and skillful who can keep his lord's good will and the affection of good neighbors. He did not wish to remain in the country; he will cross the Channel and will go into England. He will stay there a while and will leave his wife in his land. He will order his men to keep her loyally and all his friends likewise. He decided upon this plan and made rich preparations. His friends were grieved that he was about to leave them. He took ten knights with him and his wife escorted him (to the ship). She showed great grief over her husband's departure; but he gave her strong assurance that he would be faithful to her; and then he left. He passed over the sea and came to Totnes (in Devon).

There were several kings in that region who had strife and war among them. Towards Exeter in that country there was a very powerful man. He was an old man; he had no male heir. He had only a daughter ready for marriage. Because he did not wish to give her to his neighboring king, the latter was warring against him and laying waste his land. He had shut him up within a castle. There was not in that castle any man so brave as to go out against him, to hold a skirmish or a battle. Eliduc heard tell of this. He did not wish to go any further when he could find combat there. He wished to stay in that country. The king was much tormented, damaged, and harassed. He will wish to aid him if he can and remain in his pay. He sent messengers to him and told him in letters how he had left his own land to come help him, provided he would tell him in return what he wanted done. If he did not need his services he should give him a safe-conduct through his land — he would then go further to seek employment. When the king saw the messengers he showed affection to them. He sent for his constable and bade him prepare a conduct speedily and bring the baron to him. Lodgings should be prepared where they could stay. They should be given as much as they could consume in a month. The conduct was made ready and Eliduc was sent for. He was received with great honor: he was made most welcome by the king. He was lodged in the house of a burgher, who was wise and courteous. The host turned over to him his fine private chamber, well curtained. Eliduc had himself well served. He brought to his table knights who were lodged uncomfortably within the town. He forbade all his men to be so bold as to accept any hand-out or amount of money for forty days.

On the third day of his stay a cry was raised in the city that their enemies had come and were spread over the countryside. They wanted to attack the town and got as far as the gates. Eliduc heard the noise from the stunned people and put on his arms without delay. His companions did the same. There were fourteen knights dwelling in the town who could still ride; they had also some wounded and quite a number of prisoners. They went arming themselves throughout the lodgings and they followed him through the gate without further invitation. "Sire," they said, "we will go with you and do what you will do." He thanked them and inquired whether anyone might know a narrow pass or a difficult passage where the attackers could be overwhelmed. "If we wait for them here perhaps we will come to close quarters; and that does not bring any advantage." They replied, "Sire, by our faith, there is, near the wood, in a reedy spot a narrow cart-road. They go back by there, when they have taken their booty. They will return that way, unarmed on their palfreys (palfreys were for leisurely riding, not fighting). In this way they will take a big risk. On this occasion we could worst them and do them damage." Eliduc said, "I pledge you my faith in this. If one does not go often to a spot where he might well lose he will never gain much nor will he rise in reputation. Come with me where I go and do what I will do! I promise you loyally that you will have no trouble as long as I can help you. If we can win something it will be worth our while to hurt the enemy."

They accepted his surety and they led him to the wood. They made an ambush near the road until the invaders returned. Eliduc showed them and demonstrated how they should spur towards them, crying out. When the enemy reached the narrow pass Eliduc yelled at them and called on his companions, bidding them to do their best. They struck hard and did not spare at all. The adversaries were stunned, completely broken and separated — conquered very shortly. Their constable was captured and many of the other knights. Eliduc's squires were loaded with these prisoners. Our people were only twenty-five in number (the fourteen knights and the eleven including Eliduc). They captured thirty of the others and much equipment. They won a lot.

Eliduc and his men were happy: they had performed well. The king was on the summit of a tower, where he was much afraid that he had abandoned his knights in treason. They were coming along in broken order, loaded up. They were more when they returned than they had been when they went out. The king did not recognize his own and was in considerable suspense and fear. He ordered the gates to be shut and his people to mount on the walls to shoot and hurl at them. But they had no need of that.

They had sent a squire, spurring forward, who told them about the new mercenary leader, how he had defeated the others and how he had behaved. There never was such a knight. He had captured the enemy's constable and twenty-nine of their knights, and wounded and slain others. When the king heard the news he was most joyful. He came down from the tower and went to meet Eliduc. He thanked him for his good work and turned over to him the prisoners [for ransom]. He divided the captured equipment among the others. He kept for himself only three horses which had been praised to him. He divided up everything and gave it away, to the prisoners as well as to the other people.

After this performance which I have described the king loved and cherished Eliduc very much. He gave him a year's employment and the same for those who came with him. He took a pledge of fealty from him and made him custodian of his land.

Eliduc was genteel and wise, a fine knight, valiant and generous. The king's daughter heard him spoken about and his good qualities listed. She besought him by her chamberlain to come and relax with her, to talk and get acquainted. She was very surprised that he had not already done so. Eliduc said he would come and make her acquaintance. He mounted on his war horse and took a knight with him, to speak to the girl. When he was about to enter her room he sent the chamberlain in first and delayed until the chamberlain returned. He spoke to the lady very frankly, simply, and gently, and thanked the lovely Guilliadun because she had wanted to summon him to speak to her. She took him by the hand and they sat together on a bed. They talked of many things. She looked at him very closely, at his face, his body, and his appearance, and she agreed that in him there was nothing that was not attractive. She esteemed him very much in her heart. Love sent forth a messenger who bade her love him; this caused her to grow pale and sigh. But she did not want to tell him of this, lest he mock her. He stayed there quite a while before he asked for leave to go. She gave it to him much against her will; but he did go finally. He returned to his lodging, sad and thoughtful; he is disturbed by the girl, the daughter of his lord, the king, who summoned him so sweetly, because of the fact that she had sighed. He considered himself remiss that he had been there so long without seeing her. When he said this he was sorry. He remembered his wife and how he had promised her that he would keep good faith with her and behave loyally.

The girl, after she had seen him, wanted to make him her lover. Never before had she esteemed any one so much. If she can she will get him. She kept awake all night — she did not rest nor sleep. The next day she rose early and went to a window. She summoned her chamberlain [who was probably a boy of thirteen or fourteen]. She showed him her trouble. "By my faith," she said, "I am not well. I have fallen into an unpleasant situation. I am in love with the new mercenary knight Eliduc! I did not rest at all last night, nor could I close my eyes to sleep. If he wants to love me with true love and assure me of his person I will do anything he wants — and he could gain much from this. He will be king of this land. He is so very, very wise and gentle; if he does not really love me I shall surely die in great sorrow." When she had said what she wished the chamberlain, whom she had summoned, gave her loyal advice; he should not be blamed for it. "Lady," says he, "since you love him, send him something and bid him come. Send him a belt, a lace, or a ring, and he will like it. If he receives this nicely and is joyful because of your invitation, you can be sure of his love. There is no emperor under heaven who should not be very happy if you want to love him." The lady answered when she heard this counsel, "How will I know by means of this present if he wants to care for me? I have never yet seen a knight who was besought in this way, whether he hated or loved, who was not glad to keep the gift that he received. It would be dreadful if he should mock me. However, from the outward appearances one can know some things. Get ready and go." "I am quite ready," he said. "You will take him a gold ring and you will give him my belt. Greet him for me a thousand times!"

The young chamberlain turned away and she remained so distraught that she almost called him back — but she let him go and began to torment herself: "Poor me, how my heart is involved with a man from another country! I do not know the kind of people he comes from, whether he will be leaving soon, leaving me alone in sorrow. I have set my mind on him foolishly. I never spoke to him before yesterday and now I am making him an offer of love. I think he will blame me; but if he is a gentleman he will be grateful. It is all a matter of chance now. If he does not want my love I shall feel very bad — I will never again have any joy."

While she was troubled in this way the chamberlain moved quickly. He came to Eliduc and greeted him advisedly with the many salutations that the lady had sent; he gave him the belt and the ring. The knight thanked him; he put the ring on his finger and girded the belt around him. The boy did not say anything more to him, nor did Eliduc ask anything, except that he offered him something. The boy took nothing, and left.

He went back to the girl and found her in her chamber. He greeted her on behalf of the knight and conveyed thanks for the present. "Please, speak! Do not hide it from me. Does he want to really love me?" He answered, "I am sure the knight is not faithless; I think he is gentle and prudent, knowing well how to hide his heart. I greeted him for you and gave him your gifts. He put your ring on his finger, and put on your belt. Each of us said nothing more." "Did he not receive these as tokens of love? Perhaps I am betrayed!" He replied: "I really do not know, but listen to this. If he did not respect you he would want nothing of yours." "This is silly what you are saying. I am sure he does not hate me, for I never did him any wrong, except that I love him so much. If he should wish to hate me he deserves to die. Never through you or through any one else will I ask him anything further, until I have spoken to him personally. I want to show him myself how I am tormented by love of him. I do not even know whether he will stay." The chamberlain answered, "Lady, the king has retained him for a year under oath to serve loyally. You will have leisure to show him what you feel."

When she learned that the knight was staying she was filled with joy. But she did not know anything about the trouble which he had since he saw her. He had no delight in anything except when he thought of her. He considered himself most unfortunate because he had promised his wife, before he left home, that he would love no one but her. Now his heart is in great agitation. He wished to keep his loyalty — he cannot keep from seeing her, speaking to her, kissing her, embracing her — but he will never seek her love to the extent of being dishonorable, in order to keep faith with his wife, and because of the fact that he must be honorable towards the king her father.

Eliduc was in deep trouble. He got on his horse without delay and called his companions to him. He went to the castle to speak to the king. He will see the girl if he can. That is why he was starting out. The king had got up from his meal and had gone into the chambers of his daughter.

There he began to play chess with a knight from across the sea. His daughter was to give advice to this opponent across the board. Eliduc went forward and the king was very agreeable to him, asking him to sit beside him. He spoke to his daughter and said, "Girl, you should know this knight better and treat him very honorably; among five hundred knights there is not a better man."

When the girl heard what her father commanded she was very happy. She got up from the others and invited the knight to sit with her far from them. They were now in love. She did not dare say anything to him and he was afraid to speak to her — except that he did thank her for the presents she had sent to him. He had never had such rich ones before. She said she was happy about that. She had sent him both the ring and the belt because she had given herself to him. She loved him with such love that she wished to make him her husband. If she cannot have him he should know that she will never have any other living man. He must tell her now what he wants to do.

"Lady," he said, "I am very grateful for your love — to be so esteemed by you I should be very happy. It will not grow less with me. But I have been a year with the king and he has a promise from me; I cannot break that promise in any way until his war has been ended. Then I will go back to my own country because I do not wish to stay here, if you will give me permission." The lady answered, "Dear love, thank you very much. You are wise and genteel, you will certainly have determined beforehand what you will wish to do with me. I love and trust you above everything."

At this point they felt reassured and said nothing more. Eliduc returned to his lodging; he was very happy because he had managed so well. He can speak to his lady frequently and their relationship is very close. He set about the war so vigorously that he captured the fellow who was warring against the king, and he freed all the land. He was greatly esteemed for his prowess, for his good sense, and for his generosity. He had been fortunate.

About this time his former overlord sent to him three messengers from home. This lord was much hurt and damaged and in trouble. He was losing all his castles and his land was being laid waste. He had often repented that Eliduc had gone away. He had had bad advice when he became displeased with him. The traitors who had caused all the trouble had been thrown out of his land and had been exiled for good. He sent for him in his great need and begged him in obedience to his feudal oath, which he made when he pledged homage, that he should come back to his aid. He had great need of him.

Eliduc heard the news and he was very sorry, because of the girl, for he loved her with all his heart and she could not have loved him more. But there had not been any misbehavior between them, any toying, anything low; their liaison had consisted only of conversation, coy exchanges, and giving each other pretty gifts when they were together. That was how he had wanted to keep it. But she intended to get him for good, if she could. She did not know about his wife.

"Helas," said he to himself, "I have behaved very poorly. I have been in this place too long. I am sorry I ever saw this land! I have been in love with Guilladun, a girl, the king's daughter, and she with me. When I am obliged to go home one of us will surely die, or both, perhaps. I must go because my lord has sent for me by letter and invoked my feudal oath, and my wife has sent for me also. Now I must take care. I cannot stay, I am obliged to go away. If I should marry my new love, Christianity would not permit it. It is turning out ill in every direction. God, I am so afraid of this departure! But no matter whom it may hurt I will always do the right thing by her. I will do what she wants and I will act according to her wish. Her father the king now has a good peace and I do not believe anyone will attack him again. Because of my other lord's need I will now have to depart before the date that was set for me to leave this country. I will go speak to this girl and will bare the whole business to her. She will tell me what she wants me to do and I will do this as best I can.

The knight did not delay any longer; he went to speak to the king and took his leave. He told him what had happened, reading him the letter from his lord in Brittany who had sent for him in distress. The king heard the decision that he will not remain any longer, which grieved him very much. He offered him an inducement — the third part of his own estates and promised him what he might wish of his treasures. If he will only stay he will never have cause to be sorry. "By God," said the knight. "Since my lord at home is in such trouble and has sent for me from so far I will go help him and will not remain under any conditions. But if you have need of my services again I will come back willingly with many knights."

The king thanked him for this and gave him leave to go. But first he offered him all his treasures: gold, silver, dogs, horses, and silken clothes fine and beautiful. He took a reasonable amount of these, and then he said nicely that he would like to speak to her.

When she saw him she called to him and greeted him six thousand times over. He asked her advice about his plans and showed her briefly his itinerary. Before he could show it or ask for leave to go she fainted from grief and turned very white. When Eliduc saw this he lost control of himself. He kissed her mouth again and again and wept very sorrowfully. He took her in his arms until she came out of her faint. "My dear love," he said, "let me tell you ... you are my life, my death, and all my joy. For this I must get your advice, for there is a trust between us two. I must go back to my country, and your father has given me leave. But I will do what you wish, however it may turn out." She replied, "Take me with you since you cannot stay. If you do not I will kill myself; I can never have joy again."

Eliduc answered her gently, because he loved her very much. "Dear girl, I am under oath to your father; if I should take you away I would break my faith before the day that my pledge is ended. I swear to you loyally, if you give me leave to go now and name a future date, when you wish me to come back nothing will keep me away, provided that I am alive and well. My life is in your hands." When she heard this great love expressed by him, she named for him a date to come and take her away. They were in great grief as they separated, they exchanged their gold rings, and they kissed each other very gently.

He came to the sea; he had a good wind and soon passed over. His lord was very happy indeed, also his friends and his relations, and every one else — his wife especially, who was very beautiful, prudent, and worthy. But he was always shut up within himself because of the new love which he now had. Never did he have any pleasure in anything that he could see until he might see again his new love. He kept to himself.

His wife was grieved in her heart and did not know what this could be. She frequently asked him if he had heard from some of his people that she had misbehaved while he was out of the country. She would be glad to suffer a test for this by ordeal before all his people whenever he wished. "Lady," said he, "I do not accuse you of misbehavior or of error. But in the country where I was I pledged to the king that I would return to him, for he needs me very much. If my lord the king here had peace I could not stay with him another week. I shall have to endure great travail before I can return here again. But until I can be back there is nothing that I see here which can give me joy." For the time being the wife said no more.

Eliduc was with his lord, helped him and was very useful. The king followed his counsel and he guarded all the land. When the time drew near which the girl had named, he set about making peace and accorded all his enemies. Then he prepared to set out with such people as he would name. Two nephews whom he loved well and a chamberlain he took along. The chamberlain had been in their counsel and was the one who had carried the message between them. Then he kept his own squires. There were no other people. He made these companions swear to keep his secret.

He set out on the sea without more ado. He reached the land where he was much awaited. He was cunning; he lodged far from the harbors. He did not wish to be recognized. He prepared his chamberlain and sent him to the girl, to say that he had come, following her command. At night when all was dark she must leave the city, with the chamberlain. He will meet them somewhere. The boy changed his clothes and went along on foot, straight to the city where the king's daughter was. He made such efforts that he got into her chamber. He greeted the girl and said that her lover had come. When she heard this news she was somewhat sad and dismayed! But she wept from joy and kissed the boy frequently. He said that at nightfall she must go with him. During the day they planned their trip. At night they left the town, the girl and the chamberlain — just those two. She was afraid they would be seen. She was clothed in silk finely embroidered with gold; she wore a short mantle. A bow shot from the gate there was a wood surrounded by a park. Her lover was waiting for them under the paling. When she came to him he dismounted and kissed her. They were so happy to be together.

He made her mount on a horse and he led her by the rein, from his horse. He came to the harbor at Totnes and they were soon in the ship. There was no one in the ship except his followers, and Guilladun. They had a good wind and calm weather. But when they were about to land a storm rose on the sea. A wind came up which brought them far from their harbor; it shattered their yard arm and shredded the sail. They called upon God devoutly, St. Nicholas, St. Clement, and the Blessed Virgin, that she might seek aid for them from her Son, that he might save them from peril and bring them to harbor. Now forward, now backwards, did they coast along. They were very near perdition. One of the sailors cried loudly, "What are we doing? Sire, you have with you the reason that we perish. We will not get to land. You have a loyal married wife and on top of this you are carrying off this other woman, contrary to God and the Faith. Let's throw her into the sea; then we shall land." Eliduc heard what he said and he almost burned with rage. "You evil s—— o b——, you bad traitor, if I should have to leave her I would sell her to you dear!" In his arms he held her and comforted her as well as he could from her seasickness and from the fact that she had heard that her lover had a married wife, in his own land. She fell into a faint, on her face — pale, discolored. She remained this way — did not recover or sigh.

He who was carrying her off thought that surely she was dead. He grieved mightily. He got up, went to the sailor, struck him with an oar so that he fell flat. He cast him out by a foot. The waves carried away the body. Then he grabbed the steering oar and brought the ship to land. When they arrived they put down the landing plank and cast anchor. She was still in her faint and seemed to be dead. Eliduc grieved and wished also to be dead. He asked his friends where the girl could be taken, for he would never separate from her until she could be buried, and placed with great honor and a fine service into holy ground; she was a king's daughter and had a right to it. They were all confused and gave him no advice. Eliduc began to ponder where he could carry her. His dwelling house was near the sea, he could be there for his dinner. There was a forest around it, thirty leagues in length. A holy hermit had his chapel there; he had been there for forty years. Many times Eliduc had spoken with him. He said he would carry her there and bury her in the chapel. He would give sufficiently of his land and would found an abbey there. He will put a monastery of monks there, or of nuns, or of canons; they will pray constantly for her. May God have mercy upon her soul. He sent for his horses and they mounted. He got a pledge from each of them that all this would not be revealed. He carried his lady on his palfrey in his arms.

They did not go astray; they went into the wood and came to the chapel. They called and beat upon the door. They could find no one to answer and unlock the portal. The holy hermit had died eight days before; he found the fresh tomb. Much was Eliduc troubled and dismayed. The others wished to make a grave in which to place the lady; he made them all draw back. He said, "None of that before I will have counseled with the wise men of this region as to how I can favor this spot with either an abbey or monastery. We shall place her before the altar and we will commend her to God." He had her clothes brought and made a couch at once. They left her for dead. When he was about to leave he thought he would die of grief; he kissed her eyes and her face. "Sweet girl," said he, "may it not please God that ever again I should bear arms or live or endure this world! Dear love, evil the hour that you first saw me. Dear sweet, woe that you ever followed me. Sweet one, you might have been a queen, were it not for that pure and loyal love with which you loved me. My heart is grieved for you. The day I lay you to rest I will become a monk, and on your grave each day my grief shall break forth." Then he left her and closed the door of the chapel.

He sent a messenger to his house and told his wife that he was coming, but that he was tired and worn out. When she heard this she was very glad. She prepared to go meet him. She received her husband joyfully, but little of joy did she find, for he never gave her a soft glance nor spoke to her a pleasant word. No one dared to speak a word to him. Two days he remained in the house; he each day heard Mass very early, and then set out alone on his way. He went into the wood, to the chapel where the girl was lying. He found her in her fainting spell, she did not wake nor sigh. This seemed so strange to him for he saw her always pink and white;

she never lost her color except that she was a little pale. He wept from the bottom of his heart and prayed for her soul. When he had made his prayer he returned to the house.

One day when he came out the church his wife had him watched by a young man. She had promised him much if he would follow at a distance and see which direction his lord would turn. She would give him a horse and arms (she would make him a knight). The boy followed her command. His master went into a wood, the young man followed him and saw how he entered into the chapel. He heard the grieving which was made. Before Eliduc had left the chapel the boy returned to his lady and told her what he had heard, the sorrow, the wailing and the cry which her husband made in the hermitage. Her heart missed a beat. She said: "Let us go at once! We will search the hermitage. My husband will soon go abroad; he goes to speak to the king. The hermit has been long dead. I know that he loved him, but never would he do this for him, nor would he show such grief." Then she said no more.

That very same day, in the afternoon, Eliduc went to speak with the king. She took the young man with her and he brought her to the hermitage. When she entered the chapel and saw the bed with the girl, who looked like a new rose, she pulled back the coverlet and saw her slender body — her long arms and white hands, her slender fingers, long and full. Now she knew the truth why her husband made such grief. She called to the boy and showed the unexpected sight. "You see," she said, "this woman who resembles a precious gem? That is the love of my husband, for whom he makes this sorrow. Truly I do not marvel when so lovely a woman has perished. As much out of pity as for love never more will I have any pleasure." She too began to weep and regret the girl. Before the bed she sat crying.

A vicious stoat came running — he had come out from under the altar. The boy struck it for fear that it would pass over the body. He killed it with a stick that he held and cast the body up in the air. It had fallen only for an instant when its mate came running and saw the spot where the other was lying. It walked around the head and touched the mate with a paw. When it could not revive the other it showed semblance of grief. It went forth from the chapel towards the herbs in the wood. It brought a flower in its teeth all of a red color. Quickly it returned and placed this in the mouth of its mate in such a way that immediately the other revived.

The lady saw this; she cried to the boy, "Stop it, throw at it, young gentleman, and do not let it get away." He threw and struck the stoat and the flower fell. The lady went for it and placed this in the mouth of the girl. In the instant it was there the lady came awake and sighed; then she spoke and opened her eyes. "God," said she, "I have slept so long." When the lady heard her speak, she began to thank God and asked her who she was.

The girl said to her, "Lady, I was born in England, the daughter of a king of that land. I loved a knight very, very much, Eliduc, the good mercenary. He took me away and committed a sin, because he tricked me. He had a wife, but he did not tell me, nor did he hint this in any way. When I heard tell of his wife I had to fall unconscious because of the grief which I experienced. Cruelly deceived he left me in another land. He betrayed me and I do not know what I should do. A woman is bereft of her senses who trusts a man!" "Dear girl," the lady answered, "nothing alive in this world could cause him to be happy; this you can be told for true. He thinks that you are dead, and he is in dreadful distress. He goes to look at you every day. He found you in this state. I am his wife, truly, and my heart is sore for him. Because of the sorrow which he was showing I wanted to know where he went. I followed him — and found you; I am so happy that you are alive. I shall take you with me and I will let you have your lover. I wish to give him his freedom and intend to take the veil." The wife comforted her very well and they went away together.

She prepared her boy and sent him for her husband. He rode until he found him and told him all. Eliduc mounted at once and asked for no company. He reached home by midnight, and when he found his love alive he thanked his wife gently. He was very, very happy. He kissed the girl often and she returned it; they were filled with joy. When the wife saw how they were she spoke to her husband and asked him for leave to go away. She wished to become a nun and serve God. Let him give her some of his land where she may found an abbey. He must marry the girl he loves so much, for it is not fitting to have two wives, and religion does not permit this. Eliduc gave her leave and agreed to do what she wished in the matter of land. Near his castle in the wood beside the chapel of the hermitage did she construct her monastery and establish its buildings. He bestowed much land and much money: she will have all she needs. When all was prepared the lady took the veil and with thirty nuns whom she had she established her life and her order.

Eliduc took his lady with great honor and a fine service the day that he married her. They lived together for many a day. They made great gifts and alms and their love was ideal. When they too were converted to God, near the castle, on the other side, Eliduc built a church very advisedly, and endowed it with much of his land and gold and silver. Men he put there and other people of strong religious faith, to maintain the order and the house. When all was ready he did not hesitate for long. He placed his dear wife with his first wife to serve almighty God. The first wife received her as a sister, showed her much honor and taught her to serve God according to her order. They prayed God for their former love and he in turn prayed for them. He often sent them messengers to learn how they were, and how they were comforted. Each one made great effort to love God in good faith and they all three had a worthy end, thanks be to God, the true divinity.

From this adventure of the three, the gentle Bretons made a *lai* as a remembrance, which should not be forgotten.

# BIBLIOGRAPHY

Adenet le Roi. *Bueves de Commarchis.* Ed. August Scheler. Brussels: Closson, 1874.
*Amis et Amiles und Jourdains de Blaivies. Zwei altfranzösische Heldengedichte des kerlingischen Sagenkreises nach der Pariser Handschrift.* Ed. Konrad Hofmann. 2nd. ed. Erlangen: Deichert, 1882.
*Aucassin et Nicolette, chantefable du XIII$^e$ siècle.* Ed. Mario Roques. 2nd. ed. rev. CFMA 41. Paris: Champion, 1929.
Baldwin, John W. "The Medieval Theories of the Just Price; Romanists, Canonists and Theologians in the Twelfth and Thirteenth Centuries." *Transactions of the American Philosophical Society.* New Series 49, pt. 4, 1959.
*Blancandin et l'orgueilleuse d'amour, roman d'aventure du XIII$^e$ siècle.* Ed. Franklin P. Sweetser. Genève: Droz, 1964.
Bodel, Jean. *Jeu de Saint-Nicolas.* Ed. A. Jeanroy. Paris: CFMA, 1925.
Boutière, Jean and A.-H. Schutz. *Biographies des troubadours: Textes provençaux des XIII$^e$ et XIV$^e$ siècles.* Toulouse: E. Privat, 1950.
Burns, Robert. *Poems and Songs.* Ed. James Kingsley. London: Oxford University Press, 1969.
*Carmina Burana.* Ed. Johann Andreas Schmeller. 4th ed. Breslau: M. & H. Marcus, 1904.
Chrétien de Troyes. *Christian von Troyes, sämtliche erhaltene Werke nach allen bekannten Handschriften herausgegeben.* 4 vols. Halle: Niemeyer, 1884-99.
―――. *Yvain.* Ed. R. W. Linker. Chapel Hill: University of North Carolina Press, 1940.
Cloetta, Wilhelm, ed. *Les Deux Rédactions en vers du Moniage Guillaume.* 2 vols. SATF. Paris: Didot, 1906-11.
Daude de Pradas. *The Romance of Daude de Pradas called "Dels Auzels Cassadors."* Ed. A. H. Schutz. Columbus: Ohio State University Press, 1945.
Dickinson, John. "The Medieval Conception of Kingship... as Developed in the *Policratus* of John of Salisbury." *Speculum,* 1 (1926), 308-37.
Dronke, Peter. *Medieval Latin and the Rise of the European Love-Lyric.* 2 vols. Oxford: Clarendon Press, 1965.
Eales, Samuel J., and Dom John Mabillon. *Life and Works of Saint Bernard, Abbot of Clairvaux.* 3 vols. London: John Hodges, 1889.

Faral, Edmond. *Les Arts poétiques du XII*ᵉ *et du XIII*ᵉ *siècle. Recherches et documents sur la technique littéraire du moyen âge.* BEHE 238. Paris: Mellotteé, 1924.
Franklin, Alfred L. A. *La Mesure du temps.* Vol. 2 of *La Vie privée d'autrefois; arts et métiers, modes, moeurs, usage des Parisiens du XII*ᵉ *au XVIII*ᵉ *siècle.* Paris: E. Plon, Nourrit et Cⁱᵉ, 1887-1901.
Friedrich II. *The Art of Falconry, Being the De Arte Venandi cum Avibus of Frederick II of Hohenstaufen.* Trans. & ed. Casey A. Wood and F. Marjorie Fife. Stanford: Stanford University Press, 1943, 1961.
Galbert de Bruges. *The Murder of Charles the Good, Count of Flanders.* Trans. James Bruce Ross. New York: Columbia University Press, 1960.
Garin de Monglane. "Les Enfances Garin: A Critical Edition." Ed. Jack David Brown. Diss. University of North Carolina, 1971.
Gautier de Tournoi. *L'Histoire de Gille de Chyn.* Ed. E. B. Place. NSH 7. Evanston & Chicago, 1941.
Gérold, Théodore. *La Musique au moyen âge.* Paris: H. Champion, 1932.
Giraldus Cambrensis. *Giraldi Cambrensis Opera.* Ed. J. S. Brewer. Rolls Series no. 21. 8 vols. London: Longman & Co., 1861-91.
Gregory of Tours. *The History of the Franks.* Trans. with an introduction by O. M. Dalton. Oxford: The Clarendon Press, 1927.
Guernes de Pont-Sainte-Maxence. *La Vie de Saint Thomas.* Paris, 1936.
Guillaume de Lorris and Jean de Meun. *Le Roman de la Rose par Guillaume de Lorris et Jean de Meun.* Ed. Ernest Langlois. SATF. 5 vols. Paris: Firmin-Didot; Champion, 1914-24.
Holler, William McFall. "Le livre de Sydrac: Fontaine de toutes sciences, Folios 57-112." Diss. University of North Carolina, 1972.
Holmes, Urban T. *Daily Living in the Twelth Century, Based on the Observations of Alexander Neckam in London and Paris.* Madison: The University of Wisconsin Press, 1952.
———. "The *Kambriae Descriptio* of Gerald the Welshman." *Medievalia et Humanistica,* NS I (1970), 217-31.
———, ed. *The Mediaeval Period.* Vol. 1 of *A Critical Bibliography of French Literature.* Ed. D. C. Cabeen. Syracuse: Syracuse University Press, 1947.
*Huon de Bordeaux, chanson de geste.* Ed. François Guessard and Charles Grandmaison. APF 5. Paris: F. Vieweg, 1890.
Jacobus de Vitriaco, Cardinal. *Lettres de Jacques de Vitry, évêque de Saint-Jean d'Acre.* Edition critique par R. B. C. Huygens. Leiden: E. J. Brill, 1960.
John of Salisbury. *The Metalogicon, a Twelth Century Defense of the Verbal and Logical Arts of the Trivium.* Trans. Daniel D. McGarry. Berkeley: University of California Press, 1955.
Joinville, Jean, sire de. *Histoire de Saint Louis.* Ed. Natalis de Wailly. SHF 144. Paris: Mᵐᵉ Vᵉ J. Renouard, 1868.
*Joufrois.* Ed. W. O. Streng-Renkonen. *AnnUA,* ser. B, 12. Turku, 1930.
Knudsen, Charles A. "'Hasard' et les autres jeux de dés dans le *Jeu de Saint Nicolas.*" *Rom.,* 63 (1937), 248-53.
"La Naissance du Chevalier au Cygne." Ed. Henry Alfred Todd. *PMLA,* 4, Nos. 3 & 4 (1888-89), i-xv; 1-120; 1-18.

Lecoy de la Marche, Albert. *Anecdotes historiques, légendes et apologues, tirées du recueil inédit d'Etienne de Bourbon, Dominicain du XIII*$^e$ *siècle*. Paris: Librairie Renouard, 1877.

――――. *La Chaire française au moyen âge, spécialement au 13*$^e$ *siècle*. 2$^e$ éd. Paris: Laurens, 1886.

*Le Roman de Flamenca*. Ed. Paul Meyer. BFMA 8. Paris: Bouillon, 1901.

*Li Romans de Claris et Laris*. Ed. Johann Alton. BLVS 169. Tübingen, 1884.

*Li Romans de Durmant le Galois*. Ed. Edmund Stengel. BLVS 116. Tübingen: Laupp, 1873.

*Li Romans de Garin le Loherain*. Ed. Paulin Paris. 2 vols. Paris: Techener, 1833-35.

Lot, Ferdinand and Robert Fawtier. *Histoire des institutions françaises au moyen âge*. Vol. 1. Paris: Presses Universitaires de France, 1957.

Lulle, Raymond. *Livre d'Evast et de Blaquerne*. Ed. Armand Llinarès. Paris: Presses Universitaires de France, 1970.

Marcabru. *Poésies complètes du troubadour Marcabru*. Trans. J. M. L. Dejeanne et A. Jeanroy. Toulouse: E. Privat, 1909.

Marie de France. *Les Lais*. Ed. Ernest Hoepffner. Strasbourg: Heitz, 1921.

Martin, Ernest, ed. *Le Roman de Renart*. 3 vols. Strasbourg: Trübner, 1882-87.

Michaëlsson, Karl. *Le livre de la Taille de Paris l'an 1296*. Göteborg: Almquist & Wiksell, 1958.

Migne, J. P., ed. *Patrologia Latina*. 221 vols. Paris: 1879-90.

Montaiglon, Antoine de, and Gaston Raynaud, eds. *Recueil général et complet des fabliaux du XIII*$^e$ *et du XIV*$^e$ *siècle*. 6 vols. Paris: Librairie des Bibliophiles, 1872-90.

Morawski, Joseph de, ed. *Proverbes français antérieurs au XV*$^e$ *siècle*. Paris: E. Champion, 1925.

Neckam, Alexander. *Alexandri Neckam De Naturis Rerum Libri Duo. With the poem of the same author, De Laudibus Divinae Sapientiae*. (Rolls Series.) London: Longman, Green, Longman, Roberts, and Green, 1863.

Nyström, Urban. "L'Oustillement au villain" in *Soumalaisen Tiedeakatemian Toimituksia: Annales Academiae Scientiarum Fennicae*. Series B, XLVI (1940), 51-71.

Oakeshott, Walter Fraser. *The Artists of the Winchester Bible*. London: Faber and Faber Ltd., 1945.

Raby, F. J. E., ed. *The Oxford Book of Medieval Latin Verse*. Oxford: The Clarendon Press, 1959.

Randall, Lilian M. C. *Images in the Margins of Gothic Manuscripts*. Berkeley: University of California Press, 1966.

Raoul de Cambrai. *Li romans de Raoul de Cambrai et de Bernier*. Ed. E. le Glay. rprt. of 1832-48 ed. Genève: Slatkine Reprints, 1969.

Raoul de Houdenc. *La Vengeance Raguidel. Altfranzösischer Abenteuerroman*. Ed. Mathies Friedwagner. In *Raoul von Houdenc. Sämtliche Werke*. Vol. 2. Halle: Niemeyer, 1909.

Reese, Gustave. *Music in the Middle Ages, with an Introduction on the Music of Ancient Times*. New York: W. W. Norton & Company, 1940.

Renart, Jean. *L'Escoufle*. Ed. H. Michelant and Paul Meyer. SATF. Paris: Didot, 1894.

Roberts, Kimberly S. *An Anthology of Old Portuguese*. Lisbon: Livraria Portugal, n.d.

Ross, James Bruce and Mary Martin McLaughlin, eds. *The Portable Medieval Reader.* Viking Portable Library, 46. New York: Viking Press, 1949.
Rothschild, Baron James de, ed. *Le Mistère du Viel Testament.* 6 vols. SATF. Paris: Didot, 1878-91.
Rutebeuf. *Miracle de Théophile. Miracle du XIII⁰ siècle.* Ed. Grace Frank. CFMA 49. Paris: Champion, 1925.
Stow, John. *Survey of London.* Introduction by H. B. Wheatley. Rev. ed. Everyman's Library 589. New York: E. P. Dutton, 1960.
Taralon, Jean. *Treasures of the Churches of France.* Trans. Mira Intrator. New York: George Braziller, 1966.
Treanor, Sapelo. "Le Roman de Sydrac, fontaine de toutes sciences." Diss. University of North Carolina, 1939.
*Tristan.* Ed. Bartina H. Wind. Genève: Droz, 1960.
Turner, Thomas Hudson. *Some Account of Domestic Architecture in England, from Richard II to Henry VII...* Oxford: J. Henry and J. Parker, 1859.
Uc Faidit. *The Donatz Proensals of Uc Faidit.* Ed. J. H. Marshall. London: Oxford University Press, 1969.
Wace. *Le Roman de Brut de Wace.* Ed. Ivor Arnold. SATF. 2 vols. Paris: Droz, 1938-40.
———. *Le Roman de Rou et des ducs de Normandie, par Robert Wace, poète normand du XII⁰ siècle.* Ed. Frédéric Pluquet. 2 vols. Rouen: Frère, 1827.
Waddell, Helen. *The Wandering Scholars.* 7th ed. London: Constable, 1934.

# NORTH CAROLINA STUDIES IN THE ROMANCE LANGUAGES AND LITERATURES

*I.S.B.N. Prefix 0-8078-*

## Recent Titles

UN TRÍPTICO DEL PERÚ VIRREINAL: "EL VIRREY AMAT, EL MARQUÉS DE SOTO FLORIDO Y LA PERRICHOLI". EL "DRAMA DE DOS PALANGANAS" Y SU CIRCUNSTANCIA, estudio preliminar, reedición y notas por Guillermo Lohmann Villena. 1976. (Texts, Textual Studies, and Translation, No. 15). *-415-2.*

LOS NARRADORES HISPANOAMERICANOS DE HOY, edited by Juan Bautista Avalle-Arce. 1973. (Symposia, No. 1). *-951-0.*

ESTUDIOS DE LITERATURA HISPANOAMERICANA EN HONOR A JOSÉ J. ARROM, edited by Andrew P. Debicki and Enrique Pupo-Walker. 1975. (Symposia, No. 2). *-952-9.*

MEDIEVAL MANUSCRIPTS AND TEXTUAL CRITICISM, edited by Christopher Kleinhenz. 1976. (Symposia, No. 4). *-954-5.*

SAMUEL BECKETT. THE ART OF RHETORIC, edited by Edouard Morot-Sir, Howard Harper, and Dougald McMillan III. 1976. (Symposia, No. 5). *-955-3.*

DELIE. CONCORDANCE, by Jerry Nash. 1976. 2 Volumes. (No. 174).

FIGURES OF REPETITION IN THE OLD PROVENÇAL LYRIC: A STUDY IN THE STYLE OF THE TROUBADOURS, by Nathaniel B. Smith. 1976. (No. 176). *-9176-2.*

A CRITICAL EDITION OF LE REGIME TRESUTILE ET TRESPROUFITABLE POUR CONSERVER ET GARDER LA SANTE DU CORPS HUMAIN, by Patricia Willett Cummins. 1977. (No. 177).

THE DRAMA OF SELF IN GUILLAUME APOLLINAIRE'S "ALCOOLS", by Richard Howard Stamelman. 1976. (No. 178). *-9178-9.*

A CRITICAL EDITION OF "LA PASSION NOSTRE SEIGNEUR" FROM MANUSCRIPT 1131 FROM THE BIBLIOTHEQUE SAINTE-GENEVIEVE, PARIS, by Edward J. Gallagher. 1976. (No. 179). *-9179-7.*

A QUANTITATIVE AND COMPARATIVE STUDY OF THE VOCALISM OF THE LATIN INSCRIPTIONS OF NORTH AFRICA, BRITAIN, DALMATIA, AND THE BALKANS, by Stephen William Omeltchenko. 1977. (No. 180). *-9180-0.*

OCTAVIEN DE SAINT-GELAIS "LE SEJOUR D'HONNEUR", edited by Joseph A. James. 1977. (No. 181). *-9181-9.*

A STUDY OF NOMINAL INFLECTION IN LATIN INSCRIPTIONS, by Paul A. Gaeng. 1977. (No. 182). *-9182-7.*

THE LIFE AND WORKS OF LUIS CARLOS LÓPEZ, by Martha S. Bazik. 1977. (No. 183). *-9183-5.*

"THE CORT D'AMOR". A THIRTEENTH-CENTURY ALLEGORICAL ART OF LOVE, by Lowanne E. Jones. 1977. (No. 185). *-9185-1.*

PHYTONYMIC DERIVATIONAL SYSTEMS IN THE ROMANCE LANGUAGES: STUDIES IN THEIR ORIGIN AND DEVELOPMENT, by Walter E. Geiger. 1978. (No. 187). *-9187-8.*

LANGUAGE IN GIOVANNI VERGA'S EARLY NOVELS, by Nicholas Patruno. 1977. (No. 188). *-9188-6.*

BLAS DE OTERO EN SU POESÍA, by Moraima de Semprún Donahue. 1977. (No. 189). *-9189-4.*

LA ANATOMÍA DE "EL DIABLO COJUELO": DESLINDES DEL GÉNERO ANATOMÍSTICO, por C. George Peale. 1977. (No. 191). *-9191-6.*

RICHARD SANS PEUR, EDITED FROM "LE ROMANT DE RICHART" AND FROM GILLES CORROZET'S "RICHART SANS PAOUR", by Denis Joseph Conlon. 1977. (No. 192). *-9192-4.*

MARCEL PROUST'S GRASSET PROOFS. *Commentary and Variants*, by Douglas Alden. 1978. (No. 193). *-9193-2.*

---

When ordering please cite the *ISBN Prefix* plus the last four digits for each title.

Send orders to: University of North Carolina Press
Chapel Hill
North Carolina 27514
U. S. A.

# NORTH CAROLINA STUDIES IN THE ROMANCE LANGUAGES AND LITERATURES

I.S.B.N. Prefix 0-8078-

## Recent Titles

MONTAIGNE AND FEMINISM, by Cecile Insdorf. 1977. (No. 194). *-9194-0.*
SANTIAGO F. PUGLIA, AN EARLY PHILADELPHIA PROPAGANDIST FOR SPANISH AMERICAN INDEPENDENCE, by Merle S. Simmons. 1977. (No. 195). *-9195-9.*
BAROQUE FICTION-MAKING. A STUDY OF GOMBERVILLE'S "POLEXANDRE", by Edward Baron Turk. 1978. (No. 196). *-9196-7.*
THE TRAGIC FALL: DON ÁLVARO DE LUNA AND OTHER FAVORITES IN SPANISH GOLDEN AGE DRAMA, by Raymond R. MacCurdy. 1978. (No. 197). *-9197-5.*
A BAHIAN HERITAGE. An Ethnolinguistic Study of African Influences on Bahian Portuguese, by William W. Megenney. 1978. (No. 198). *-9198-3.*
"LA QUERELLE DE LA ROSE: Letters and Documents", by Joseph L. Baird and John R. Kane. 1978. (No. 199). *-9199-1.*
TWO AGAINST TIME. *A Study of the Very Present Worlds of Paul Claudel and Charles Péguy,* by Joy Nachod Humes. 1978. (No. 200). *-9200-9.*
TECHNIQUES OF IRONY IN ANATOLE FRANCE. Essay on *Les Sept Femmes de la Barbe-Bleue,* by Diane Wolfe Levy. 1978. (No. 201). *-9201-7.*
THE PERIPHRASTIC FUTURES FORMED BY THE ROMANCE REFLEXES OF "VADO (AD)" "PLUS INFINITIVE, by James Joseph Champion. 1978 (No. 202). *-9202-5.*
THE EVOLUTION OF THE LATIN /b/-/ṷ/ MERGER: A Quantitative and Comparative Analysis of the *B-V* Alternation in Latin Inscriptions, by Joseph Louis Barbarino. 1978 (No. 203). *-9203-3.*
METAPHORIC NARRATION: THE STRUCTURE AND FUNCTION OF METAPHORS IN "A LA RECHERCHE DU TEMPS PERDU", by Inge Karalus Crosman. 1978 (No. 204). *-9204-1.*
LE VAIN SIECLE GUERPIR. A Literary Approach to Sainthood through Old French Hagiography of the Twelfth Century, by Phyllis Johnson and Brigitte Cazelles. 1979. (No. 205). *-9205-X.*
THE POETRY OF CHANGE: A STUDY OF THE SURREALIST WORKS OF BENJAMIN PÉRET, by Julia Field Costich. 1979. (No. 206). *-9206-8.*
NARRATIVE PERSPECTIVE IN THE POST-CIVIL WAR NOVELS OF FRANCISCO AYALA "MUERTES DE PERRO" AND "EL FONDO DEL VASO", by Maryellen Bieder. 1979. (No. 207). *-9207-6.*
RABELAIS: HOMO LOGOS, by Alice Fiola Berry. 1979. (No. 208). *-9208-4.*
"DUEÑAS" AND "DONCELLAS": A STUDY OF THE "DOÑA RODRÍGUEZ" EPISODE IN "DON QUIJOTE", by Conchita Herdman Marianella. 1979. (No. 209). *-9209-2.*
PIERRE BOAISTUAU'S "HISTOIRES TRAGIQUES": A STUDY OF NARRATIVE FORM AND TRAGIC VISION, by Richard A. Carr. 1979. (No. 210). *-9210-6.*
REALITY AND EXPRESSION IN THE POETRY OF CARLOS PELLICER, by George Melnykovich. 1979. (No. 211). *-9211-4.*
MEDIEVAL MAN, HIS UNDERSTANDING OF HIMSELF, HIS SOCIETY, AND THE WORLD, by Urban T. Holmes, Jr. 1980. (No. 212). *-9212-2.*
MÉMOIRES SUR LA LIBRAIRIE ET SUR LA LIBERTÉ DE LA PRESSE, introduction and notes by Graham E. Rodmell. 1979. (No. 213). *-9213-0.*
THE FICTIONS OF THE SELF. THE EARLY WORKS OF MAURICE BARRES, by Gordon Shenton. 1979. (No. 214). *-9214-9.*
CECCO ANGIOLIERI. A STUDY, by Gifford P. Orwen. 1979. (No. 215). *-9215-7.*
THE INSTRUCTIONS OF SAINT LOUIS: A CRITICAL TEXT, by David O'Connell. 1979. (No. 216). *-9216-5.*

---

When ordering please cite the *ISBN Prefix* plus the last four digits for each title.

Send orders to: University of North Carolina Press
Chapel Hill
North Carolina 27514
U. S. A.

The Department of Romance Studies Digital Arts and Collaboration Lab at the University of North Carolina at Chapel Hill is proud to support the digitization of the North Carolina Studies in the Romance Languages and Literatures series.

www.ingramcontent.com/pod-product-compliance
Lightning Source LLC
Chambersburg PA
CBHW022011220426
43663CB00007B/1044